DAVENPORT

9421539

8/79

D1179615

8211

:E

Please renew/return this item by the last date shown.

So that your telephone call is charged at local rate, please call the numbers as set out below:

	From Area codes 01923 or 0208:	From the rest of Herts:
Renewals:	01923 471373	01438 737373
Enquiries:	01923 471333	01438 737333
Minicom:	01923 471599	01438 737599

Hertfordshire
COUNTY COUNCIL
Community Information

NOV 1992

N 1999

08 DEC 1992

09 Jan '92

14 JUN 200

N 1988

04 APR 1998

12 JUN 1999

18 J/ 9 JAN 1990

1 MAY 1992

-7 MAY 1998

The Art of the Gawain-Poet

The Art of the Gawain-Poet

W. A. DAVENPORT

UNIVERSITY OF LONDON
THE ATHLONE PRESS
1978

Published by
THE ATHLONE PRESS
UNIVERSITY OF LONDON
at 4 Gower Street London WC1

Distributed by Tiptree Book Services Ltd
Tiptree, Essex

USA and Canada
Humanities Press Inc
New Jersey

© *W. A. Davenport* 1978

ISBN 0 4851 1173 X

Printed in Great Britain by
WESTERN PRINTING SERVICES LTD
Bristol

To Hester,
Imogen and Olivia

Acknowledgements

I have to thank the then Principal and the Council of Royal Holloway College for granting me sabbatical leave during the session 1972–3, when most of the first draft of this book was written, and Professor Francis Berry and my colleagues in the English Department for putting up with the various inconveniences which this caused. I am grateful to Professor Barbara Hardy, formerly head of the English Department at Royal Holloway College, now head of the English Department at Birkbeck College, for her interest and encouragement during the ever-lengthening period of time which this book has taken to complete. To the anonymous academic adviser of the Athlone Press I am grateful for some unsparing criticism of my first draft, as a result of which this book is better than it was, though doubtless still imperfect in many ways. My greatest debt is to my wife for her constant encouragement, criticism, typing and everything.

Contents

6. The Poet and his Art

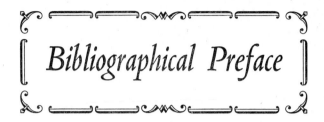

Bibliographical Preface

Abbreviations

The following abbreviations have been used in the notes.

Anderson	*Patience* ed. J. J. Anderson (Manchester, 1969).
Benson	L. D. Benson, *Art and Tradition in Sir Gawain and the Green Knight* (New Brunswick, NJ, 1965).
Bishop	Ian Bishop, *Pearl in its Setting* (Oxford, 1968).
Blanch	R. J. Blanch (ed.), *Sir Gawain and Pearl: Critical Essays* (Indiana, 1967).
Brewer, 'Courtesy'	D. S. Brewer, 'Courtesy and the Gawain‑Poet', in J. Lawlor (ed.), *Patterns of Love and Courtesy: Essays in Memory of C. S. Lewis* (London, 1966).
Brewer, 'The Gawain‑Poet'	D. S. Brewer, 'The Gawain‑Poet: A General Appreciation of the Four Poems', *Essays in Critiscim* 17, 1967, 130–42.
Burrow, Reading	J. A. Burrow, *A Reading of Sir Gawain and the Green Knight* (London, 1965).
Burrow, RP	J. A. Burrow, *Ricardian Poetry* (London, 1971).
Conley	J. Conley (ed.), *The Middle English Pearl: Critical Essays* (Notre Dame and London, 1970).
ESts	*English Studies.*
Everett	Dorothy Everett, *Essays on Middle English Literature* (Oxford, 1955).
FMLS	*Forum for Modern Language Studies.*
Gordon	*Pearl* ed. E. V. Gordon (Oxford, 1953).
Gradon	Pamela Gradon, *Form and Style in Early English Literature* (London, 1971).
Howard and Zacher	D. R. Howard and C. Zacher (ed.), *Critical Studies of Sir Gawain and the Green Knight* (Notre Dame and London, 1968).
JEGP	*Journal of English and Germanic Philology.*

Kean	P. M. Kean, *The Pearl: An Interpretation* (London, 1967).
MS	*Medieval Studies.*
Menner	*Purity* ed. R. J. Menner (New Haven, 1920, reprinted 1970).
MLN	*Modern Language Notes.*
MLQ	*Modern Language Quarterly.*
MLR	*Modern Language Review.*
MP	*Modern Philology.*
Moorman	Charles Moorman, *The Pearl-Poet,* Twayne English Author Series (New York, 1968).
N & Q	*Notes and Queries.*
PQ	*Philological Quarterly.*
PMLA	*Publications of the Modern Language Association of America.*
RES	*Review of English Studies.*
Spearing	A. C. Spearing, *The Gawain-Poet* (Cambridge, 1970).
TG/Davis	*Sir Gawain and the Green Knight* ed. J. R. R. Tolkien and E. V. Gordon. Second edition revised by N. Davis (Oxford, 1967).
Waldron	*Sir Gawain and the Green Knight* ed. R. A. Waldron, York Medieval Texts (London, 1970).

Texts

I have quoted from the editions of the works of the *Gawain*-poet listed above under Anderson, Gordon, Menner and TG/Davis, but I have re-punctuated when necessary, and I have modernised the spelling by eliminating obsolete letters (thorn and yogh) and by adopting modern practice in the use of i/j and u/v.

I have also made some use of *Patience* ed. H. Bateson (Manchester 1918), *Sir Gawain and the Green Knight* ed. I. Gollancz (London, E.E.T.S., 1940), and Waldron (listed above). For original manu-script readings, the reader is referred to *Pearl, Cleanness, Patience and Sir Gawain,* reproduced in facsimile from MS Cotton Nero A.x., with introduction by I. Gollancz (London, E.E.T.S., 1923).

The reader who finds the original language of these poems too daunting will find it easier to use Waldron's edition of *Sir Gawain* or *Pearl, Cleanness, Patience, Sir Gawain and the Green Knight,* ed. A. C. Cawley and J. J. Anderson (London, Everyman's Library, 1976), both of which are in slightly modernised English and provide glossaries and explanatory notes on the same page as the text. An edition of all four poems, edited by R. A. Waldron and M.

Andrew, is expected to appear in the York Medieval Texts series in 1978.

I have not discussed *St Erkenwald* because I am sure, on subjective grounds, that this is by a different author. See L. D. Benson, 'The Authorship of *St Erkenwald*', *JEGP* 64 (1965) 393–405, and *St Erkenwald* ed. Ruth Morse (Cambridge, 1975).

In quoting the Bible I have used the Vulgate text when the exact words of the Latin are necessary to the point, but have quoted the Authorised Version in some places where only the gist is required.

Bibliography

The books and essays listed above form a basic bibliography for study of the *Gawain*-poet. Other works on particular aspects of the poems are referred to in the notes. Among works which appeared too late to be adequately taken into account, the most important are A. C. Spearing, *Medieval Dream-Poetry* (Cambridge, 1976) and Edward Wilson, *The Gawain-Poet* (Leiden, 1976). Wilson's approach to the four poems is so different from mine that our accounts of them rarely coincide.

For fuller bibliographical detail the reader is referred to J. Burke Severs (General Editor), *A Manual of the Writings in Middle English 1050–1500*, Vol. I (New Haven, 1967), pp. 54–7 and 238–43 for *Sir Gawain* and Vol. II (New Haven, 1970), pp. 339–53 and 503–16 for 'The *Pearl*-Poet'; to G. Watson (ed.), *The New Cambridge Bibliography of English Literature* I 600–1660 (Cambridge, 1974), col. 401–6 and 547–54; and to the annual volumes of *The Year's Work in English Studies*.

1. Introduction

Though the *Gawain*-poet may not have existed, it has proved necessary to invent him. If evidence turned up that in Cheshire or Staffordshire in the late fourteenth century there were three medieval Brontës, working simultaneously on *Patience*, *Pearl* and *Sir Gawain and the Green Knight* after writing *Purity* as a collaborative effort, then the case would be altered, but with virtually no evidence but the unique manuscript, British Museum MS Cotton Nero A.x., in which the four poems survive, the simplest way of accounting for the similarities among them is to assume that they had a single author.[1] However, though most scholars now accept the idea of 'the *Gawain*-poet' (or 'the *Pearl*-poet', as some prefer), nearly all have been fittingly but disappointingly cautious about presuming on the idea. The poems have been mainly studied singly and the few critics who have discussed them jointly have been rather tentative in their approach, as if the fear of being proved wrong or the burden of demonstrating similarities weighed on their minds. The most thorough book to appear so far on the four poems is A. C. Spearing's *The Gawain-Poet* but, in spite of his title, Spearing offers 'a critical study of four great medieval poems' which 'would not, I think, be invalidated if it should eventually be proved by objective evidence that the poems were the work not of a single poet but of a school of poets'.[2] It is true. It would not be invalidated, and this is, in one way, to be regretted. A critical study of a poet's works ought to be invalidated by the discovery that those works were written by several different people. But here lies the weakness of the case. In writing of the *Gawain*-poet one is simply backing one's judgement that a single mind seems to be at work in four anonymous poems. Naturally enough, caution keeps creeping in.

Yet the case for the common authorship of the poems is a strong one which has stood the test of time and which is based on wide-ranging evidence. Though the evidence of common dialectal, linguistic and metrical features and of some shared characteristics of style has to be weighed against the similarities among poems of the alliterative tradition in general, there are enough features peculiar to the Cotton Nero poems to isolate them as a group. When this evidence is added to parallel structural devices, recurrent images and conceptions and shared themes and effects, the argument seems weighty.[3] It is solid enough, to my mind, for one to hope that critical study of the poems may now take a bolder and more probing turn. It seems time for one to be able to take as read all that part of the consideration of the Gawain-poet which feels it has to make a case for the man's existence. Therefore, in writing this book, I have assumed that the four poems were written by one man and I have ignored the need to demonstrate the idea. I want to treat the poems as if we knew them to form a body of work and, as one would with the works of an identified writer, to bring out the in-dividual quality of the separate works and to make comparisons not on the basis of trying to prove their similarity but with the in-tention of trying to understand the writer, how his mind worked and how his art developed.

Further, I intend to write about Pearl, Purity, Patience and Sir Gawain primarily in terms of their effectiveness as poetry and as fiction. The informed reader's response to poetry, rather than generic or historical criticism, seems to me a key which has not been tried often enough in this particular lock. It seems possible that what one can observe of the art with which each of these poems was com-posed may tell one more about the poet's individual cast of mind than has been thought, or than has been identified by other means.

I have ventured on this approach for a number of reasons. The basic reason for writing at all is, obviously, that I think the Gawain-poet was a great writer. The individual poems have, in themselves, qualities which are striking and enjoyable enough, but if the four were written by one man, as I believe they were, then he is a major poet whose works deserve exploration. He is the only English poet of the Middle Ages whose works have a range and quality com-parable to those of Chaucer. He, like Chaucer, used a variety of genres, was capable of writing poetry of widely varying mood, had a professional command of the craftmanship of verse, and showed freedom and a rich imagination in his handling of borrowed tales and themes. For a full appreciation of his skill as an artist, close examination of the poems seems necessary.

Secondly, I feel dissatisfied with what the tools of historical scholarship have so far managed to show about the poet. This is not to disparage the work of many good scholars whose investigations have cleared up obscurities in the poems. Indeed it will be obvious that I have benefited a great deal from the writings of many more scholarly than I am. But, when one turns from factual scholarship about the text, about the meanings of words or about allusions and source-material, to more speculative work of interpretation and criticism, then one feels less confident of the value of much of the work published about these poems. There are many different reasons for this, and it is not possible, in a limited space, to do more than make superficial reference to one or two of them. One is the fact that in the past the predominantly philological and anti-quarian interests of many experts on the Middle English period meant that such literary discussion as editors, for example, felt obliged to engage in was often very limited in nature. Another is the present state of things where there is much evidence of un-certainty about the most appropriate way of discussing Middle English poetry; many essays on Middle English poems have been more concerned to demonstrate a particular critical method (script-ural exegesis, literary anthropology, numerical symbolism and so on) or to assert a particular line of argument than to follow the logic of the poems themselves. *Sir Gawain*, in particular, has been the hive to which many a bee from a bonnet has come buzzing. But even if one ignores extreme, eccentric or inflexible views of these poems, one finds that more critics are concerned to relate the four anony-mous works to a historical, cultural or moral context than to try to define the effects they have on the reader and the way the reader responds to them. Though it is necessary to study the putative source-material of the poems, to attempt to relate them to contemporary thought and to identify common medieval literary traditions within them, the cumulative effect of seeing the works of the *Gawain*-poet so often studied in relationship to something else is the loss of a sharp sense of their individual qualities and a tendency to assimilate the poems into generalisations about the medieval period. The individual qualities have not yet, in my opinion, been fully identified. Before one dusts out the recesses of medieval Latin prose and poetry (many of which it seems doubtful that the *Gawain*-poet could ever have had the opportunity to look into), and even before one consults the more frequented shelves of medieval school texts or of contemporary vernacular work in order to explain the poems under review, it seems appropriate to look harder at the poems themselves, with no more preconceptions than those which are unavoidable with poetry written six hundred years ago. Because of this gap of time one does need some background knowledge, but I have tried to keep it in the background and have used only obvious contemporary English works and writers as sources of comparison, where possible.

A third reason for my particular approach is the product of the peculiar situation of the *Gawain*-poet, of which I spoke at the beginning. Much of the work on the *Gawain*-poet's works as a group, even when necessary and good in itself, has been distorted by the need to make a case for common authorship. Minor aspects of the poems have often occupied a disproportionate amount of space because they are features common to two or more poems. Similarities have often been over-stressed, as if the shared quality gave them pride of place in any critical assessment of the poet's art. Of course, resemblances are of interest and it is necessary to identify them since one may find clues to the single mind which may have imagined the poems, but to argue all the time from similarities tends to blur the individual quality of each poem and can lead, at worst, to forcing poems to fit into a mould devised from one of the others. So, for example, more emphasis than is appropriate has been put on the lines in *Sir Gawain*:

As perle bi the quite pese is of prys more,
So is Gawayn, in god fayth, bi other gay knyghtez. (2364-5)

because in the use of the pearl as an image of value and, by implication, of moral purity, is seen a parallel to the symbolism in *Pearl* and to the passage, itself different from *Pearl* in significance, about the round, pure pearl in *Purity* (1115-32). In *Sir Gawain* the reference is not developed or emphasised and in context acts as a vivid amplification of the preceding statement 'sothly me thynkkez/ On the fautlest freke that ever on fote yede', and is completely subordinate to the nature of the judgement being made by the Green Knight. The *sense* would not be significantly different if the comparison were between a beryl and a bean; what one would miss in that case would be the visual precision of the comparable roundness and whiteness of pearl and pea. One judges the comparison by its visual and notional appropriateness, not according to a sense of symbolism unique to pearls. The argument from similarity tends to inflate the importance of such things. A more distorting product of the desire to prove common authorship has been the degree of emphasis placed by many modern critics on the didactic or moral element in *Sir Gawain*. Because the romance has to be shown to be similar to the other three poems it has repeatedly been characterised as an exemplary narrative, a homily in praise of 'trawthe', a moral case-history, a punishment of pride and moral taint. In truth, most readers are more conscious of the differences between *Sir Gawain* and the other poems, particularly *Pearl*, than of the similarities; apart from the obvious differences of subject and genre, *Sir Gawain* is fun, full of lightness and laughter, action and movement, set in a precisely depicted, 'real' world of elegant society, its manners and trappings, and of natural sights and sounds, whereas *Pearl* is intense, static and serious, ornate, dominated by formal speech, set in a world of ideas and beliefs, literary allusions and images. It is more to the point to recognise such differences than to focus on, and risk distorting the importance of, aspects which seem to prove a common identity.

And so, for these various reasons, I have tried to look freshly at *Pearl*, *Purity*, *Patience* and *Sir Gawain and the Green Knight*. I have made fairly sparing references to scholarly articles and books, while doing this; this is both because I do not want to clutter the discussion, though I have indicated where further treatment of particular aspects of the poems may be found, and because much modern criticism is not centred on the aspects of the poems which seem to me of greatest interest, though I have tried to acknowledge debts wherever I am conscious of them.

I have chosen to discuss the poems in the order in which they occur in the manuscript, *Pearl*, *Purity*, *Patience*, *Sir Gawain*, because that order at least has some authority, even if only that of a scribe. We have no evidence of the order of composition other than what the poems say, and though there have been various theories about the order, none has achieved general acceptance. Some early critics tried to construct a biography for the poet from the four poems and produced pretty pictures such as that of a man who in younger and happier days composed an Arthurian romance, whose soul was humanised by the deep distress of bereavement recorded in *Pearl*, who turned to Christian asceticism (*Purity*) and who, in old age and poverty, cultivated the calm and philosophic mind (*Patience*).[4] This is a game that anyone can play. How about a serious young man, training for the clergy and producing didactic poetry (*Purity*), who decided not to take orders, married, lost his daughter (*Pearl*), was deserted and robbed by his wife (*Patience*), but who found consolation in good food, sport and laughter, with the occasional dash of sober reflection (*Sir Gawain*)? All that this type of invention makes clear is how little the poems really reveal about personal matters; since even the most 'personal' poem, *Pearl*, could be based on a fiction, the biographical basis for the order of the four poems is non-existent. Similarly, the attempt to establish an order by identification of echoes and derived phrases is useless, because one can always think of other explanations of how similarities came about than by dependence of a late poem on an earlier.[5] The only basis for an order other than that of the manuscript is one's critical assessment of the nature and achievement of each of the poems, and that sort of judgement is unlikely to be unanimous, and is certainly not a point from which to begin.

Because *Purity* and *Patience* are less well-known than the other two, and even when known, less well understood, I have given more attention in their cases to illustration and explanation; in the cases of *Pearl* and *Sir Gawain* I have assumed a greater degree of familiarity in the reader and have taken some aspects of the poems for granted.

2. Pearl

1. The main elements of subject-matter and presentation

In a hundred and one rhyming stanzas, arranged in an elaborate pattern, *Pearl* presents us with a first-person account of a man's grief at the loss of his precious pearl, and of the 'consolatory' (though not necessarily very consoling), educative experience of a heavenly vision, by means of which he comes to accept the inevitability of loss and the limitation of this mortal life. Once past the considerable linguistic difficulties, the reader is likely to have mixed impressions of the quality of the poem, but the strongest impression, and the one most often either taken for granted or even defensively pushed away by modern commentators is that it makes a very direct appeal to the reader's sympathies, largely because it is a first-person narrative about feelings and about the universal theme of coming to terms with mortality. Like Wordsworth's *Resolution and Independence* or Coleridge's *Dejection*, *Pearl* is a poem about the self, in which the speaker moves from initial depression through a process of moral development towards a more balanced frame of mind. Despite the differences between Romantic poems about life and a medieval poem about death, the process which culminates in the blessing and yielding up of the dead child in *Pearl* is essentially that growth from inward-turning obsession to out-going generosity, to resolution of mind, and to a recognition that the self does not exist alone, which leads to Wordsworth's 'God be my help and stay secure', or to Coleridge's final benediction. But, while the theme of *Pearl* is inherently capable of calling up a strong sense of involvement in the reader, it is the poet's handling of it that makes such involvement seem utterly necessary. The poetry is often lyrical, evocative and rich. The poet expresses emotion passionately and movingly. It seems to be the poet's main aim to communicate intense inner experience, rather than moral significance. This is most self-evident in the early sections of the poem, less obvious later, but still, I think, true; it is the voice of a man experiencing things which holds the parts of the poem together. This voice, however, strikes the reader's ear differently at different times and one's first task, in trying to grasp the nature of the poet's art, is to follow the course of its modulations through the poem.

The absence of an explanatory introduction gives the opening stanzas of *Pearl* an initial intensity which is closer to the manner of courtly love-lyric than that usual in a vision-poem. At first, the narrator speaks of his loss in disguise, like the anguished lover protecting the name of his sovereign lady, but the references to the lost pearl are soon coloured by human associations. Though the feminine possessives could refer to the literal gem, the sixth line, 'So smal, so smothe her sydez were' with its echoes of the praise of women in courtly poetry, identifies the pearl as having human qualities, and the statement of love-longing at the end of the stanza confirms this:

> I dewyne, fordolked of luf-daungere
> Of that pryvy perle wythouten spot.   (11-12)

It seems wrong to suggest, as some commentators have, that one begins to make moral criticisms of the speaker on the grounds that, by using the phrase *luf-daungere* ('love's power to hurt') of a pearl, he displays uncontrolled emotions and a wrong sense of values.[1] It is because he uses a phrase associated with courtly love-lyric that one knows that he is speaking of a human being, and that one recognises the pearl-image as an example of the metaphorical use of jewels to convey the qualities of a beloved woman.[2] Since 'thurgh gresse to grounde' indicates that the beloved is dead, the word 'daungere' has a peculiar poignancy.

The second stanza is a rhetorical elaboration of the anguish of deprivation, cast in the familiar medieval form of a contrast between past 'wele' and present 'wo', and it skilfully combines a number of poetic devices. The antithesis of past and present is characterised first by the contrast between the homely, conventional pairing of *happe* and *hele* and the succession of the harsh and striving *thrych . . . thrange,* and the insistence of *bale, bolne, bele;* then by the contrast between remembered past moments of peace, sweeter than song but as fleeting and transitory, and the hideous present reality.[3] Horror is mimed by the exclamation, placed in the tenth line where the *c*-rhyme brings a new sound into the line-endings.[4] The apostrophe to the defiling earth is intensely personalised by the derogatory 'thou' and the possessive phrase 'My pryvy perle', which replaces 'that pryvy perle' of the first stanza. The inter-play of sound and sense, the mixture of nostalgia and dismay, and the rhetorical double contrast of past and present, together leave no doubt that the poet is here concerned to com-municate passion as forcefully as his command of poetry will allow.

The third stanza is as poetic, as rhetorical and as intensely concerned with the evocative expression of grief. The parallel presence of the idea of the human corpse, associatively indicated by *clot, moul, rot,* and *moldez dunne,* and the lost jewel gives an extra level of meaning to 'richesse'; the pearl remains, in the speaker's mind, precious and spotless but is at the same time 'run to rot', rich only in its potentiality as the seed from which may grow the pro-gressively hopeful succession of spices and flowers, wheat and good. The stanza thus relates present and future as the second had related present and past. Again I think it wrong to suggest that here 'we are intended to adopt a critical attitude towards the narrator';[5] the allusion to John XII, 24-5 in lines 31-2 serves to make us *less* inclined to be critical, not more, because it implies that spiritual good may yet come and thus justify the death, and it also implies the beginning of a movement of thought from mortality to im-mortality, though this is, as yet, only a seed which may grow from the speaker's grief. I am continually astonished by the readiness with which interpreters of *Pearl* condemn the grief of mourning, and argue from the point of view of the learnt lesson rather than of the ignorant sufferer. Why should we assume that we are in any position to judge? It is inevitable that bereavement should cause an excess of feeling, which time and reason gradually diminish. Medieval Christian teaching may state that weeping for dead children is 'folly', but assertions that faith in the after-life supplies the corrective to the pain of loss presuppose that it is a folly which is

universal. When the Dreamer is later reproved by the Maiden, we
see the corrective process at work; reminders of the transience of
human life and of the need for moderation and self-control are part
of that application of traditional consolatory wisdom which every
bereaved person receives in one form or another, and which each man
absorbs as he best may. I do not believe that in the opening stanzas
of the poem we are in any way meant to distance ourselves from
the grieving speaker. The first three verses are a ceremony of mourning in which the evocative luxuriance of the poetry invites us to
take part. Why did the poet so richly endow his opening with
language and imagery which invites us to partake of the feeling
expressed, if 'our response to the narrator's grief should not be one
simply of surrender'?[6] A responsive giving of oneself to the poetry
seems just what the elegiac poeticism is designed to elicit, and though
one may not respond simply, there is nothing in the interplay of
reality and symbolism, of past, present and future, or of pictorial
images and direct expressions of feeling which leads us to judge the
narrator. Indeed the two stanzas which complete the first section
make any such judgement supererogatory. Before the reader has
thought of it, the narrator himself puts his feeling into perspective:

> A devely dele in my hert denned,
> Thagh Resoun sette myselven saght.
> I playned my perle that ther watz spenned
> Wyth fyrce skyllez that faste faght.
> Thagh Kynde of Kryst me comfort kenned,
> My wreched wylle in wo ay wraghte. (51–6)

Any inclination to judge is forestalled because he judges himself.
These lines are, in effect, what the reader expected at the opening of
the poem, a comment by the narrator's present self on his past self,
which acts as an identification to the reader of what the poem is
going to be about: grief will be controlled and mortality accepted
through Reason, and comfort will be found in the humanity of
Christ. The waking man cannot receive such counsels; the liberation of dream is necessary to free him from the here and now, the
grave, the grief, the moment, the limitation of earth and of the human
will. Only after such liberation may the feelings be explored, exposed and judged. Unless one is willing to share the Dreamer's

emotions, the exploration will have little effect; one must be with him as he experiences surprise and humiliation.

The first five stanzas of *Pearl* plant in one's mind the potentialities of the symbolic pearl, of the imagery of growth, and of the conflict between Reason and Will, but it is the moving intensity of expression that makes the strongest mark in the first three stanzas. In the fourth the narrative proper begins as the narrator enters the garden. The imagery now shows that the healing current of time is already flowing onward: it is August and the future wheat of stanza 3 is waiting to be cut; the spices and flowers, including pearlwort, which were prophesied as the product of rich decay, already cast their shadows on the grave.[7] The place of earthly loss is already a place where good grows and more good may come to be; the stanza promises healing and benefit. The speaker's assessment of his state of mind in the fifth stanza shows him ready to receive the benefit, if he can find a way to control the 'wreched wylle', to become open to the spiritual good promised by the place, and if he can learn that pain opens the door to divine truth. The closing lines hint that he can:

> Such odour to my hernez schot
> I slode upon a slepyng-slaghte,
> On that precios perle wythouten spot.[8] (58–60)

The pungency of healing spices pierces to the brain, excited to extra sensitivity by grief, and brings him into a 'slepyng-slaghte', a kind of death, gateway into the region beyond earth. Thus he is released from pain and passes through the barrier of mortal limitation into a kind of limbo where he is neither dead nor alive. The implied levels of meaning of the section lead us not towards moral disapproval, nor a sense of distance from the speaker; they allow the reader simply to recognise where he is. The punning refrain-word, *spot*, identifies the place where the narrator stands as a place of stain and mortality. The imagery of the senses, involving not only sight (lines 27–8), but also touch (line 6), sound (line 19), taste (line 29), and smell (line 46), enhances the impression of feeling and supports the allegorical suggestion in the last stanza, that the garden is a Garden of Will from which Reason is excluded.

When the Dreamer begins his adventure and moves into a transformed world, it is still through sensory imagery and on the

level of feeling that the poetry mainly works. The same eyes, ears
and nose report, though what they perceive is a fixed, gleaming
world other than the mutable one of Nature. As the Dreamer's
failing powers are refreshed by sights, sounds and flavours, the
poetry is repeatedly mimetic, inviting one to experience the wonder
of the new world. The onomatopoeic qualities of alliteration are
strongly in evidence, as in;

> Swangeande swete the water con swepe,
> Wyth a rownande rourde raykande aryght. (111–12)

Evocative comparisons are mainly visual and enhancing in effect,
as, for example,

> In the founce ther stonden stonez stepe,
> As glente thurgh gles that glowed and glyght,
> As stremande sternez, quen strothe-men slepe,
> Staren in welkyn in wynter nyght. (113–16)

and

> Her ble more blaght then whallez bon,
> As schorne golde schyr her fax thenne schon. (212–13)

The familiar medieval heightening devices are also frequent:

> More of wele watz in that wyse
> Then I cowthe telle thagh I tom hade. (133–4)

With these and other, similar, devices the poet presents the adornment of Section II, the increasing joy of Section III, and the fear
and awe brought by the sight of the Pearl-Maiden in Section IV.
The situation of the Dreamer by the river, across which he can
only look, makes a pictorial tableau out of these moments of
astonishment, satisfaction and trepidation. The massed details of
what he sees create a strong impression of the devouring appetite of
the innocent eye presented with a new, hitherto unknown world.
The identification of the child has a simplicity in tune with this
innocent receptivity:

> I knew hyr wel, I hade sen hyr ere. (164)

With recognition, the current of his feeling for her begins to flow
again, first with anxiety and disbelief, then with a recollection of the

opening stanza ('So smothe, so smal, so seme slyght'), and then with repeated images of whiteness and pearls.

With the beginning of the dialogue in Section V, the quality of the poem changes. We move from recollected personal experience to dramatised emotion, mainly in the present tense. The Dreamer becomes a dramatic character as monologue changes to dialogue. Only now does the poet encourage one to judge his words and it is only when the dialogue begins that there is a sense of separation between Dreamer and poet. This comes from the fact that there is a second voice, equally the poet's, to answer the Dreamer, but it is also produced by a different quality in the Dreamer's words. Though he has told us of his joy at being able to speak to the Maiden, his words at first return to the grief with which he began; we take a second look at his feelings, but it is a more complicated one, in that we are less inclined to surrender to his point of view because of the development of his situation. His grief is now marred by an unlovely though understandable reproachfulness:

'Pensyf, payred, I am forpayned,
And thou in a lyf of lykyng lyghte,
In Paradys erde, of stryf unstrayned.
What wyrde hatz hyder my juel vayned,
And don me in thys del and gret daunger?' (246-50)

The self-pity gives this reference to 'daunger' almost a note of parody, and enhances the sympathetic effect of the courteous first speech of the Maiden, which, though a reproof, is a gently sorrow-ing one, transforming the pearl-image into one of permanence opposed to transience. The pearl still is enclosed in the casket of a gracious garden, but free from loss and grief, and is, in fact, only now a pearl:

'For that thou lestez watz bot a rose
That flowred and fayled as kynde hyt gef.
Now thurgh kynde of the kyste that hyt con close
To a perle of prys hit is put in pref.' (269-72)

Because we have been encouraged to sympathise with the Dreamer's sorrow and his new experiences, we do not turn against him as soon as he displays his lack of reason, but the continuity of imagery makes

us see that his view of loss was not the only view that could be
taken. His second speech is more controlled but brings the startling response, placed strategically in the last stanza of the section,
of much stronger reproof:

> 'Wy borde ye men! So madde ye be!' (290)

The unexpectedness of the rebuff leads on to explanations and to
what one recognises as the beginning of education. The gentle
voice has become authoritative, instructive and adult, as his mis-
understanding, his failure to appreciate the difference between the
earth he has left and the world he has entered, and his presumption are exposed. Section VI, with the link word *deme*, calls his
judgement more and more into question, as he is reproached again
and again, particularly for believing only what his senses tell him.
The question of grief is now brought to a head by the Dreamer's
passionate and moving protest:

> 'Now haf I fonte that I forlete,
> Schal I efte forgo hit er ever I fyne?
> Why schal I hit bothe mysse and mete?
> My precios perle dotz me gret pyne.
> What servez tresor, bot garez men grete
> When he hit schal efte wyth tenez tyne?' (327–32)

Though this may display his worldliness, his lack of true Christian
faith, and his unreasoning passion, it draws on the earlier strength
of feeling and expresses with painful truth the sense of injustice
that all the bereaved, particularly bereaved parents, feel, turning it
into the general questions: 'What is the point of possession on earth
if it gives one only the pain of losing it? When the thing that matters
most is taken away, what is life but misery?' The answer, of course,
is dust and ashes. Possession on earth has no point and should be
recognised as the transitory, worldly thing it is; misery for 'trivial'
things is ridiculous excess which distracts men from the higher good.
All of which, the bereaved might feel, is easily *said*, but it is well said
in the Maiden's reply, with some forceful and deflating language:

> 'For anger gaynez the not a cresse.
> Who nedez schal thole, be not so thro.
> For thogh thou daunce as any do,
> Braundysch and bray thy brathez breme,

When thou no fyrre may, to ne fro,
Thou moste abyde that he schal deme.' (343–8)

The energetic style of such reproof seems an appropriate response to
the Dreamer's passion and creates a sense of true dramatic dialogue
at this stage of the poem, in spite of the role of moral instructress
into which it is clear that the figure of the Maiden is gradually
being absorbed; her advice takes force from the strength of the
Dreamer's feeling and a convincing conflict of attitudes is presented
in the alternating speeches. This first movement of the poem,
concentrating on feeling, is completed in the Dreamer's speech in
the first three stanzas of Section VII.

This is one of only two long speeches given to the Dreamer
during the dialogue; he has three stanzas here and at lines 901–36,
two at 469–92, but his eight other speeches are only one stanza
long. This one represents a modification in his attitude in that his
request for knowledge of the Maiden's life is an implicit acceptance
of the difference between past and present. The speech has a greater
humility than in his first addresses, a humility towards which mixed
feelings are aroused, for, though the humbling of pride may be
necessary for the Dreamer's good, the reader, involved in his feel-
lings, simultaneously sees the humility as humiliation and responds
to the sorrowful courage. The Dreamer impresses one here as having
learnt already from experience, having learnt how to reprove gently,
how to speak with a controlled recognition of his earlier indiscipline, and how to plead movingly that the natural feeling of
grief needs comfort and that the former love between the two should
eliminate 'debate'. In the first stanza (361–72) he both apologises for
and defends his wild raving; though he may go astray his heart
was afflicted by his loss, 'As wallande water gotz out of welle'.
This image combines allusion to the use of surging or troubled
water in courtly love poetry as a metaphor for the lover's yearning,
with allusion to Psalm xxi.[9] The secular and scriptural combination heightens the sense of desolation to a moving plea for sympathy
and help, which is further intensified by the controlled expression of
the reproach which earlier had seemed self-pity but now, fortified
by the psalm's support, seems simple truth:

'Of care and me ye made acorde
That er watz grounde of alle my blysse.' (371–2)

In the second stanza he shows again his acquisition of control and
a movement away from self-absorbed grief by a recognition that no
good will be achieved by going over the past; it is more important
that they should be in harmony with one another:

> 'I wyste never quere my perle watz gon.
> Now I hit se, now lethez my lothe.
> And quen we departed we wern at on:
> God forbede we be now wrothe,
> We meten so selden by stok other ston.' (376–80)

The simple colloquialism of the last two lines, where the stanza's
relaxed alliteration is satisfied by common idioms, communicates
a sad intimacy which is most moving. The third stanza restates and
moves on, again combining his lonely grief with acceptance that
it is better to leave contentious subjects, and an outward movement of thought as he expresses his pleasure in and curiosity about
her new estate. The dignity, feeling, and self-control of this speech
restore the Dreamer to one's respect. His adjustment to the situation makes it clear that in the process of the poem not only are the
Maiden's words offered as a 'correction' of his misunderstandings,
but also that the Dreamer's words are, here at any rate, being used to
put into the perspective of feeling the lessons which must be applied
to modify excessive grief and to come to terms with loss and death.
Sorrow does not cease to exist because Christian philosophy puts
mortality into the light of eternity, and we should think less of the
poet if he suggested that it did.

This speech, showing in the change of attitude the completion
of the first phase of the poem, simultaneously leads into the second
and central phase (Section VII, stanza 4 to Section XIII, stanza
3), where, in response to his words, the Dreamer receives two long
speeches from the Maiden (lines 493–588 and 601–744), in which
the poet presents the ideas which the Dreamer needs for an understanding of the nature of the heavenly kingdom and the relationship
between earthly and heavenly life. Any impression of dramatic
dialogue between equal participants now ceases. This brings up a
problem of which every reader is conscious in one way or another.
In the poet's presentation of the Maiden there is necessarily an
abstract, adamantine quality: the fact that she is a figure translated
into something other than the human child and that the world she

inhabits is one where human rules no longer apply have to be represented by an absence of human feeling and of a sense of earthly relationships. She is, therefore, allegorically incapable of offering comfort to the Dreamer, since the relationship which might make comfort appropriate no longer in her world exists. In the central part of the poem the dialogue is thus not only between two unequal characters but two unlike ones, one changing and vulnerable, the other rock-like and allegorical. The relationship between the two is a difficult one for the poet to sustain at a consistent level. If we judge by the human level of feeling from which the dialogue began, then the Maiden seems, at times, smug, unsympathetic and uncharitable; the Dreamer asks for bread and is given a stone. If we subdue the literal and judge by the allegorical level at which the poet has conceived the Maiden, then the Dreamer becomes simply a representative of worldly limitation. In fact, one perceives both levels at once and is conscious of their pulling against one another, but, because the poet began his poem by making us identify with the narrator's sorrow, and because he applies language of greatest colour to the realisation of the things the Dreamer sees and feels, we are emotionally attuned to thinking on his level and therefore living through his experience, his set-backs and humiliations, and his developing sense of things. He is our surrogate. As a result, the aspect of the dialogue which seems most important is not so much the actual lessons which the Maiden offers to the Dreamer, but the Dreamer's (and our) capacity for receiving them. That this is the emphasis intended by the poet is indicated not only by the stress on feeling and the modulation of doctrine through sorrow, but also by the superficiality of the level of the argument in the central part of the poem. This part has often been described as a 'debate', but there is no real inter-change, nor any attempt to probe any of the points made; there is, in the alternation of direct speech from two different mouths, the external appearance of discussion, but the material is cut and dried and, in reality, as the Dreamer speaks briefly and ignorantly and the Maiden with knowledge and at length, Dreamer and reader are simply presented with a series of carefully pre-packaged instruction parcels.

We are faced with the case for the child's heavenly reward first through narrative, in the exemplum illustrating the pointlessness of judging heavenly reward in terms of earthly payment;

this case the Dreamer rejects as 'unreasonable'. The Maiden then leaves questions of *quid pro quo* and presents the case through assertions of the plenitude of God's grace, the right of the innocent, and through the emotive image of the pearl, now transformed into a symbol of the heavenly kingdom. This case the Dreamer accepts, but without explicit signs of having absorbed the ideas or of taking notice of the Maiden's warnings that he himself should direct his life to earning his 'perle maskelles'; these signs do not appear until the closing stanzas of the poem. The process to be observed is the second stage in the rehabilitation of the Dreamer. He has accepted that he must put behind him thoughts of self, and that he will get no comfort for his grief in the form he desired it. Now he has to learn to understand the otherness of the Maiden and of the heavenly world. His protests and rejections are all attempts to keep the Maiden within the framework of reference which he understands and which give him a sort of claim over her. His acceptance of her second speech is in fact an acceptance of her otherness, and one made not through reason but through imagination; he recognises that she is no longer the pearl he knew but the creation of another greater power:

> 'Quo formed the thy fayre figure?
> That wroght thy wede, he watz ful wys.
> Thy beauté com never of Nature.'   (747–9)

The sense of awe and reverence he has acquired lead on to the latter stage of the vision, in which he has become worthy to look upon the heavenly city and the Lamb, and through which his humility is assured, but before he has reached that point, he has to suffer the full course of that humiliation which began with the quelling of his presumption. So in Sections VIII to X he is de-moted from the position he had acquired in our eyes at the beginning of Section VII; from the moving frailty of his balance between grief and loving desire to learn more he is reduced to the level of a petulant fool, and in the strategy of the poem he becomes merely the stooge who asks stupid questions so that authoritative answers may be given.

Though there is no difficulty in fitting this change into a sense of the Dreamer's moral progress, at the allegorical level, it is difficult for any reader who has felt responsive to the strength of feeling

communicated in the earlier part of the poem not to have a diminished interest in this part of *Pearl*. The blocks of solid didacticism in
lines 493–576 and lines 601–720 are unpalatable to most readers of
poetry, even those who share the beliefs expressed. The parable of
the workers in the vineyard is a particularly irritating narrative,
claiming to show similitude when what it reveals is difference, and
claiming to clarify the paradox of heavenly reward by explaining it
in story form, when what it actually does is to reveal, by reducing to
a concrete example, just how difficult the concepts of 'the last
shall be first and the first shall be last' and 'many are called but
few are chosen' really are. In terms of earthly justice the parable is
absurd, and the poet's treatment of the story, with added touches of
colloquialism and vigour, increases one's consciousness of this, by
making the workers more vividly representative of typical human
attitudes and more akin to the Dreamer's own comically indignant
protests about the Maiden's too great social elevation.[10] One's
sense of unease, however, stems mainly from the fact that the two
speakers cease to be interesting as the figures involved in a narrative,
and become mouth-pieces fulfilling roles determined by the didactic
matter. One can just about accommodate the stupid, protesting
Dreamer, if one assumes that his former signs of intelligence have
been numbed by his experiences and that he is now really facing up
to new knowledge for the first time, though one may resent the fact
that one's stand-in should be quite so literal-minded as he is shown
to be in Sections VIII and IX, but the Maiden's lengthy discourses
cannot be taken as anything but a body of matter put into a convenient mouth. Unease also arises because the style of the poetry has
changed. Whereas earlier the poetry was often sensory and evocative,
now it is, until Section XIII, mostly explanatory and notional.
Instead of musical verse with regular alliteration, now the alliteration is occasional and the verse is, as a result, colourless and seems
to have lost its bite. There is a reduction of the level of verbal
pleasure one has come to expect and even the refrain-words (*date,
more, innoghe, ryght*) are less rich in meaning than their counterparts
elsewhere. In spite of this it is possible to justify, in some ways, the
poet's proceedings.

First, his conception of the Dreamer's task is that he must learn
difficult things. The poet's strategy in relation to the reader has
been to make one sympathetic to the Dreamer and thus encourage

one to live through his experiences. It is, therefore, consistent with the strategy that the reader should be made to experience the same sense of struggle as the character. The prosaic and paradoxical pill of the parable presents ideas which the reader and the Dreamer are able to swallow only when they are converted into emotive terms as in the image of God's gifts as ever-flowing water, in references to the familiar subjects of Adam's Fall, redeeming blood and cleans-ing water, in emphasis on innocence, culminating in quotation ot the text most likely to touch a bereaved father's heart ('let chylder unto me tyght/To suche is hevenryche arayed.'), and, most power-fully, in the closing stanzas of the Maiden's second speech, in return-ing to the pearl symbol and in recalling earlier passages in the poem.

Secondly, the poet's sense of what is didactic was undoubtedly different from that of most modern readers. For the medieval poet, scriptural material in quotation, paraphrase or allusion, and reference to standard moral and ethical ideas and traditional wisdom function as imagery, rather than as substance; they reflect on, augment and vivify the poem's theme. So the parable is an exten-ded narrative image, providing a dramatised acting-out of the problematic point (and so demanding a plain, illustrative style), preparing the way for the less fully presented, but more powerful images of the Fall, the Crucifixion and the Pearl of Great Price. Critics who have placed emphasis on the doctrine of the Maiden's speeches and on the idea of debate between the two speakers and, indeed, on the whole theological aspect of the poem seem to me to have their priorities wrong. There is, in these two speeches of the Maiden, a discourse and a sequence of thought but no real argu-ment; rather one sees a series of pictures identifying ideas, arranged to fit into the poem's movement towards its second moment of revelation.

The question of the disruption one may feel in the 'characterisa-tion' is one which I wish to postpone for the moment, since it involves reviewing one's whole sense of what the Dreamer and the Maiden represent, but certainly, if one reads the dream assuming, as I have done so far, that the Dreamer is the same character as the 'I' of the first section, then there comes a point when the characterisa-tion no longer firmly holds, and one suspects the poet of adjusting his figures to become functions of his theme.

Section XIII is the second turning-point in the Dreamer's education: the course of the poem so far is gathered up into the concluding stanzas of the Maiden's central speech (lines 721–44), as daughter ironically instructs father that to earn the kingdom of heaven each man must become even as a little child. The image of the pearl returns, transformed into an explicit symbol – the endless round which is both token of peace and an emblem of the pure realm of heaven. Through the symbol, the Dreamer achieves recognition of the Maiden's otherness, and so we move into the last third of the poem and the apotheosis of the Maiden as one of a hundred and forty-four thousand redeemed virgins in the procession of followers of the Lamb. The Dreamer remains, for the moment, the naive questioner, but his questions have no element of protest about them, no attempt to assert human judgements; they are merely indicative of a contrived ignorance, unacceptable in strictly logical terms, since the Dreamer has expressed knowledge earlier which makes it impossible to believe in any 'realistic' sense that he had never heard of Brides of Christ or the New Jerusalem, but necessary as part of a process. The questions elicit the Maiden's third long speech (lines 781–900) which, even more than the earlier ones, is a mosaic of scriptural images and quotations. These first recall the association of Jerusalem, new and old, with Christ as Lamb, thus assembling pictures of sacrifice, redemption and apocalypse, and then move, by the connection of the whiteness of the wool of the Lamb, to pictures of the wives of the Lamb, a vast and jolly band of pearl-clad virgins, whose assembly and song is described by paraphrase of Revelations. This speech is the most emotional of the Maiden's discourses and it continues the gradually increasing use of figurative and poetic language, already present in Section XIII. Besides the assembling of scriptural pictures, images of spotlessness and joy make the contrast between heaven and earth, and the relationship between Maiden and Dreamer is transmuted into a general statement of the Brides' transcendence of mortality:

> 'Althagh our corses in clottez clynge,
> And ye remen for rauthe wythouten reste,
> We thurghoutly haven cnawyng;
> Of on dethe ful our hope is drest.
> The Lombe uus gladez, oure care is kest.' (857–61)

The Dreamer's response is to ask another 'stupid' question, since he muddles the earthly and heavenly Jerusalem, but one which is coloured by a revival of earlier imagery and by a return, in his language too, to poetic expression:

> 'I am bot mokke and mul among.
> And thou so ryche a reken rose.'   (905–6)

The heightening of style prepares the way for the Dreamer's sight of the City; the end of the dialogue and the departure of the Maiden pass unnoticed as the Dreamer's request to 'let me se thy blysful bor' is granted and he hurries off to see. His stupidity is forgotten; his role (gradually resumed with the return to poeticism) becomes the one we met in the first part of the dream, that of observer and re- porter, filled with marvel. What he sees brings the jewel images crowding back, as their brilliant beauty achieves apotheosis in the symbolism of the foundation of the heavenly city, with gates of pearl. The luxuriant catalogue of jewels develops into sublime poetry in Sections XVIII and XIX, where the poet conveys the Dreamer's awe and the complete subjection, not only of the Dreamer's self and of his earthly concerns, but of all things earthly, all things of this dim, spotted, sublunary world. At last the poetry satisfies the desire for mystery and powerful enchantment which the emotional opening of the poem had aroused and even as the spirit's quest is achieved, the poet subtly brings us back to the Dreamer's feelings and inner life:

> Anunder mone so great merwayle
> No fleschly hert ne myght endeure,
> As quen I blusched upon that bayle,
> So ferly therof watz the fasure.
> I stod as stylle as dased quayle
> For ferly of that frelich fygure,
> That felde I nawther reste ne travayle,
> So watz I ravyste wyth glymme pure.
> For I dar say wyth consciens sure,
> Hade bodyly burne abiden that bone,
> Thagh alle clerkez hym hade in cure,
> His lyf were loste anunder mone.   (1081–92)

In Section XIX, which follows this, the procession is presented

as the city itself was not, in terms not merely of his seeing it, but
of his experiencing it and reacting to it. Its distant appearance and
closer approach are conveyed by progression from the visual image
of the pearl-white company as a radiant light, rising like the moon,
to a more personalised sense of the individuals who make up the
company, all dressed similarly to 'my blysful anunder croun'. In
each stanza of the section one is reminded of the Dreamer's presence and this personal quality has at its climax his moved reaction
first to the wounded Christ:

> Alas, thoght I, who did that spyt?
> Ani brest for bale aght haf forbrent
> Er he therto hade had delyt.   (1138-40)

and then to the sight of his own 'lyttel quene' among the virgins.
The return to the waking world is thus preceded by a return to
personal feeling after poetry of heightened intensity; the effect is of a
selfless giving of the senses by the Dreamer to the scene he is allowed
to witness, but which he rashly, in an excess of emotion, tries to
enter.

We come back full circle at the end to the lonely narrator,
bereft now not only of his pearl but also of his visionary experience
and the glimpses it gave him of the immortal. The waking is
dramatically satisfying, as is the current of subsequent thought from
rueful acceptance of the Prince's right to cast him out, through
sadness, moderated by his satisfaction that his pearl is 'to that
Prynsez paye', to a recognition that he should have devoted himself in the past and should devote himself in the present and future
to becoming a delight and satisfaction to his Lord. So the process
of education is completed; he has learnt to accept his loss, to turn
his eyes away from self and the world, to recognise the other nature
of the eternal life. But, true to the personal feeling from which the
poem began, the poet leaves us in no doubt that his blessing of
and yielding of the child to God remains in a context of sadness and
'pyty of my perle'; the world remains a 'doel-doungoun' in which
we may at best be 'homly hyne', even if potentially we may be
precious pearls.

So, as one reads through the poem, one's initial impression of
Pearl as an evocative and emotional poem becomes qualified. There

is no doubt about the main lines of the poem, however. It describes an educational experience through which the narrator learns to accept what at first he found unacceptable, and learns to control the indiscipline of the human will. It falls into three acts or stages: first, the Emotional Phase, the narrator's grief, translation and humiliation, through which he painfully suffers the knowledge that the past is gone and that the will needs control; secondly, the Didactic Phase, through which the stubborn, earthly mind is opened to the nature of the other life and the meaning of the symbolic pearl; and, thirdly, the Sacramental Phase, the apotheosis in which the mortal world is placed in the perspective of eternity and revealed as a place of inevitable grief and a place of preparation.

But, within this clear outline, there are aspects of the poem about which the reader feels less certain. The absence of the commenting voice of the poet is a major element in the reader's sense that the poem is often enigmatic. At the beginning we are left to sort out for ourselves what the lost pearl actually means; we are never told exactly who the Pearl-Maiden was, though we are told clearly enough that we are to think in terms of a human child not an allegorical abstraction.[11] Such crypticness seems to connect with the shifts of perspective in the poem, for a second negative impression is that it is not very easy logically to account for the poem's changes of focus, nor fully to grasp that duality in unity which is implied in the combination in the Dreamer of a past and a present self.[12]

The Dreamer, ostensibly a consistent voice throughout the poem, really has two different voices. One voice speaks movingly of pain and loss, and has awareness and honesty, as in his summing-up of his situation in the fifth stanza as well as at the end; he can rise to serious eloquence in the closing sections of the poem and, even at much earlier stages, he can speak with aesthetic response and intelligent literary allusion. This is the voice that convinces one that *Pearl* is a serious poem about pain, a poem which displays the power of the imagination to explore and to contain the most terrible things of life and to give glimpses of the supernal. The other voice, if not quite that of an old, half-witted sheep, is insensitive and stupid, and sinks to bewildering depths of bathos in his questions to the Maiden. The ignorance of his questions and protests is a device designed to elicit particular expansive responses, which suggests that the poem, rather than being exploratory and open to the complexity of reality, is ponderously rigged; the Dreamer becomes the stooge who feeds the Sunday-school teacher with leading questions. Can one satisfactorily account for the shift from one voice to another simply by relating *Pearl* to the 'conven-tion' of dream-narrators, when the disparity is more extreme than in any other case?

Equally disconcerting is the varying quality of the poetry. For much of the time *Pearl* is written in heightened poetic language, with devices of sound and imagery used to elaborate the expres-sion of feeling. The combination of simple but evocative words, alliterative patterning and traditional lyrical rhetoric in the third stanza is a good example:

> That spot of spysez mot nedez sprede,
> Ther such rychez to rot is runne;
> Blomez blayke and blwe and rede
> Ther schynez ful schyr agayn the sunne.
> Flor and fryte may not[bot] fede[13]
> Ther hit doun drof in moldez dunne,
> For uch gresse mot grow of graynez dede –
> No whete were ellez to wonez wonne.
> Of goud uche goude is ay bygonne;
> So semly a sed moght fayly not,
> That spryngande spycez up ne sponne
> Of that precios perle wythouten spotte. (25–36)

The images of healing spices, brilliant flowers and restorative grain are called up to express the grieved man's instinctive hope that death is not the end, through the idea that natural growth goes on; the pictorial detail combines with rhythmic and alliterative height-ening of the sense to give a rich, allusive effect of mourning's being expressed and sublimated through the ritual of stylised poetry. The images of transience and continuity are traditional. The human corpse is seen simultaneously as decaying flesh, as precious pearl and as wholesome seed; the multiple layers again create an im-pression of resonant poeticism. If one attempts to relate *Pearl* to poetic tradition on the basis of this stanza, then one thinks primarily of the long lyrical association between death and flowers, found already in classical times and in the Bible, and leading on to other poets who have prayed that 'from her fair and unpolluted flesh/ May violets spring', have seen that 'In Flanders fields the poppies blow', have judged that 'Only the actions of the just/Smell sweet and blossom in their dust', or have prophesied that 'the dust shall sing like a bird/As the grains blow, as your death grows, through our heart'. That is the kind of poetry that *Pearl* is at its most emotional, and the poignancy of such poetry calls for the reader to respond with sensibility rather than moral judgement. It sorts ill with the very different tone found in the didactic sections of *Pearl*, as, for example:

> The court of the kyndom of God alyve
> Hatz a property in hytself beyng.
> Alle that may therinne aryve
> Of alle the reme is quen other kyng,
> And never other yet schal depryve,
> Bot uchon fayn of otherez hafyng,
> And wolde her corounez wern worthe tho fyve,
> If possyble were her mendyng.   (445–52)

By comparison this language is flat and assertive and the sense fits the rhythm awkwardly; it reads like versified prose. It is not possible to read the parts of the poem written in this style with the same sensibility that is required of the reader elsewhere, and so one has an uncomfortable sense of having to switch one's responses on and off. It is difficult to have a unified impression of a poem with such shifts of style, even though *Pearl* is a much more symmetrical and unified work than most medieval poems.

The enigmatic quality of *Pearl* and such shifts of perspective are the source of much of the controversy, past and present, about the interpretation of the poem. The debate used to be mainly as to whether one should read it as an autobiographical elegy for the poet's dead child or as an allegory.[14] Though that debate has become muted, the uncertainty that gave rise to it remains. *Pearl* is too personal and too specific about the dead child to be read as a purely allegorical or even as a purely didactic work, and yet there is too much didacticism and doctrine for one to read purely in emotional and dramatic terms. It does not solve the problem to identify the poem, as several recent critics have, as a Christian *consolatio* in a medieval Latin literary tradition, because it has always been clear that the Dreamer was being offered enlightenment on the subject of grief.[15] It is not that aspect of *Pearl* which creates problems for the reader, but the poem's internal logic. In an attempt to identify that logic I intend, in the sections that follow, to look at two aspects of the reader's sense of the kind of poem that *Pearl* is: the nature of the dream and the dreamer; and the poet's use of structural patterns and word-play.

2. The dream and the dreamer

The appeal of dream-poems is basically that of mental adventure. Dream releases the poet from the actual world and gives him opportunity to create a new world, which his dreamer, sometimes with the help of a guide, has to explore and to describe for the reader. Anything can happen in a dream, and though medieval dream-poems are apt to fall into one of a limited number of well-worn patterns, there remains a sense in the reader, as he begins an unfamiliar vision-poem, of readiness for the unexpected. The vision-journey may take one into a picturesque courtly masque, or an overheard allegorical debate, or an analysis of the workings of the human mind, or a prophetic revelation. Because of the differ-ent traditions, classical, scriptural and contemporary, on which medieval poets could draw, the vision-poem was potentially the freest of medieval narrative genres.[16] Because of this the author of a vision-poem had the reader much more at his disposal than the author of a more circumscribed form. The poet of *Pearl* seems to me to be aware of and to exploit this sense of adventure for dreamer and reader.

So the vision landscape of *Pearl* is another new, unknown world into which a disconcerted hero is thrust, and according to whose laws he has to learn to fulfil a role; the Dreamer is one in a long line from Odysseus to Henderson the Rain-King. The place is a Paradise belonging with other depictions of supposedly per-fected worlds, and so related to a long line of literary Utopias, lost Golden Worlds and hoped-for Promised Lands. Obviously it is in the context of scriptural teaching that *Pearl*'s pictures of the imagined world must be placed, and in the context of medieval Christian morality that the development of the Dreamer belongs, but there is a romantic strain in *Pearl*, both in the nature of its concern with feeling and identity and in the sense of adventure which is involved in the Dreamer's spiritual journey.

Moreover, the poet handles the basic elements of the genre with unusual seriousness and imaginative power. This is particularly striking in his treatment of the waking experience of his narrator, if one compares this with the treatment of the same idea by other medieval poets. At the beginning of *Piers Plowman* Langland is so casual about his narrator's waking moments as to be perfunctory; his narrator tells us that in summer he travelled about to hear of 'wonders', felt tired in the Malvern Hills, and fell asleep. The poet seems anxious to hasten as soon as possible into the vision world, and at later stages in the poem he takes little trouble to create a plausible relationship between the waking and dreaming exper-iences; for the most part, Will wakes and falls asleep again merely to separate one part of the vision from another; only at the end of Passus XVIII, when Will is awakened by Easter bells and takes his family to church, is there a meaningful continuity between action within the vision and action without. In Chaucer's dream-poems, on the other hand, the reader is asked to relate waking and sleeping experience, but the kind of relationship is significantly different from that in *Pearl*. Chaucer speaks in his waking moments in the voice of the artist, engaging us in informal chat about the nature of dreams, the writer's interests and his personal habits. Chaucer's dreams become aspects of his creative not of his emotional life; when his narrators wake, it is to resolve to write a poem (*The Book of the Duchess*) or to go on reading edifying books (*The Parlement of Foules*), not to express the powerful emotional impact which the vision-experience has had upon them. By contrast, the poet of *Pearl* takes it more seriously and creates a relationship between the waking and dreaming worlds which is much more highly charged. The narrator's sleep is no haphazard drowsing-off, but a swoon caused by the stress of feeling; there is greater cause supplied to the reader for the vision to occur. At the end of the poem, similarly, it is excess of ecstatic joy and desire which brings the dreamer's dramatic leap into the river, which brings him ironically back into the current of life. Not until Skelton's *The Bowge of Court* does a poet again so effectively exploit the possibility for dramatic climax in the return to the waking world. In the stanzas that follow the waking the narrator speaks as emotionally and intensely as in the opening stanzas; nowhere does he speak as the poet who creates the work, but only as the man who suffers, experiences and learns.

The actual entry into the dream in *Pearl* is presented as a leap too, a leap of the spirit from the earth and from the body into the world of adventure; the narrator, at once himself and yet only part of himself, is lost in an unknown place, where strange things happen:

> Fro spot my spyryt ther sprang in space;
> My body on balke ther bod in sweven.
> My goste is gon, in Godez grace,
> In aventure ther mervaylez meven.
> I ne wyste in this worlde quere that hit wace.   (61–5)

Pearl is one of the very few poems that really convey a sense of the difference between the place the Dreamer finds himself in and the one he has left. Cliffs, hills, rocks, woods and water, in themselves the components of a romantic and Gothic landscape, are made marvellous by gleaming brilliance, by blue and gold; the very gravel is precious pearls; rich luxuriance appeals to the senses, in the fruits, brilliant colours, birdsong, spices, the sound of running water, and all are distinguished from their earthly counter-parts by the light which shines through every stanza of the second section of the poem, and by the materials from which the light comes, silver, gold, pearl, beryl, 'emerad, saffer, other gemme gente'. Images crowd together, the dense richness emphasised by strong alliteration:

> The playn, the plonttez, the spyse, the perez,
> And rawez and randez and rych reverez,
> As fyldor fyn her bonkes brent.   (104–6)

The combination of a romantic landscape, as full of adventurous possibilities as the forests and fords of chivalrous romance, a crowd-ing of sensory images and repeated sounds, and the strange opulence of the jewels, brilliantly justifies the sense of wonder in the Dreamer and conveys the marvellous otherness of the place. That joy and desire replace grief in 'those floty vales' is again characteristic of the man on a quest in strange places, and the building-up of suspense in Section III, through the repetition of 'more and more' and the

Dreamer's search for a ford, enhances the arrival of the expected marvel, the unexpected sight of the child.

The appearance of the child and the progressive enrichment of our sense of her and of the Dreamer's reaction to her in the depiction of her pearly whiteness and his fearful astonishment and joy, all belong to the world of a romantic tale, wonderful and strange, the same world that contains the milk-white doe of Rylstone and the Woman in White. Until she speaks the Pearl-Maiden is imagina- tively conceived as a ghost. The Dreamer's sight of her across the water is held in a long, staring absorption of her appearance; one is startled when she rises and again when she silently comes down the bank to greet the man whom one now guesses to have been her father. In this early part of the dream the Dreamer's role is partly that of the traveller in strange lands whose innocent eye reports what it sees for the reader's wonder and delight. It is no surprise that among the medieval works of which echoes may be found here is not only *Le Roman de la Rose* but also the Alexander romances and Mandeville's *Travels*, works of exotic exploration and marvel.[17]

When the Dreamer returns to this observing and reporting function at the end of the vision, the sense of wonder is revived for the second great moment of revelation, the Dreamer's sight of the New Jerusalem and of the heavenly maidens. Just as he had stared at the Pearl-Maiden 'as hende as hawk in halle', so he stands looking at the bejewelled city 'as stylle as dased quayle' and sees 'merwayle'. The description of the city borrows its richness from the most exotic book of scripture, and masses together jewels, gleaming gold and glass, architectural detail, stronger alliteration than in the preceding sections, and rhetorical enhancing of the light. The sight and sound of the pearl-clad maidens, his view of the Lamb, horned with burnished gold, dressed as in pearl, wounded and joyful, and of the Dreamer's 'lyttel quene' play upon his receptive, awestruck emotions with that same effect of the jungle-dweller's first film-show as in his earlier revelation. The poet again engages the reader's attention in a dramatic tableau, in which the Dreamer's mind becomes a sort of Aeolian harp played upon by visual and sacramental symbols.

In the dialogue the sense of wonder is muted, but the Dreamer takes on the other 'adventure' role of the errant hero on a spiritual progress, though he remains a traveller, now in the realm of ideas rather than sights. The exchanges between Dreamer and Maiden reveal him as essentially of the earth, though he is released from the body into the spiritual world; he brings the preoccupations of his own world to the new, applying the wrong criteria and vainly protesting against the laws of the society whose ways he encounters. The Maiden speaks as a guide in more senses than one, a guide not only to his beliefs and feelings, but also to the society of which she is an habituée; she speaks of the place as 'thys countré', makes him conscious of the customs of the country:

> 'Maysterful mod and hyghe pryde,
> I hete the, arn heterly hated here.'   (401–2)

and lectures him on its laws and hierarchy (in 445–56, for example). Through the story of the workers in the vineyard and the consequent explanations and assertions, the Maiden presents the Dreamer with a social and political system in the paradoxical combination of the complete equality of all the inhabitants at the highest social level, and the hierarchy of the kingdom beneath the powerful sway of the Lord, Christ and the Virgin Mary. Though for the Christian reader the teaching has a truth and sanctity which the laws of Utopia, El Dorado or Erewhon cannot possess, yet, in terms of the literary handling of the material, the process in *Pearl* and the type of ideas presented to the Dreamer belong to the same area of imaginative experience as these later pictures of 'ideal' societies. As do other Utopian explorers, the Dreamer has to jettison his own standards, become open to new experience and the standards of another world.[18] Thus his adventure is a spiritual quest for self-knowledge and consciousness of the other world, framed and coloured by experiences of the marvellous which ravish the senses.

Even if one eventually classes *Pearl* as a didactic poem in which the poet's main aim was to offer a lesson, it seems clear that he wanted the reader to apprehend in terms of romantic narrative, wonder, journeying, seeking and finding, and of inner development seen as the result of hazardous experience. His conception of the poem was, at least in part, of the other-world journey as an adventure of the spirit and imagination. Whether he chose the vision-poem as the form most appropriate to the treatment of inner life, or developed the matter out of an interest in imaginative exploration of the genre, it is obvious both that the poet exploited

the freedom of the form to combine in the Dreamer different exploratory roles and to create a shifting perspective, and that he
devoted his poetic energies to evocation and mimesis in order to
invite the reader into the imagined world, to make him experience
the otherness of his picture of the heavenly kingdom, and alternately to identify with and to be surprised by the narrator's account
of his adventures.

The sense of adventure is conveyed to the reader in a variety of
ways: by the Dreamer's bewilderment and impressionability, by the
poetic rising to eloquence in the scenes of revelation and transformation, by the journey, both physical and spiritual, which the
Dreamer undertakes, and by the forward progress along the road to
understanding. It is also conveyed intermittently by the secular
connotations which the poet gives to the Dreamer's experience.
The opening stanza's suggestion that the Dreamer is the bereaved
or rejected lover is confirmed in some of his speeches, as, for instance,

> 'Art thou my perle that I haf playned,
> Regretted by myn one on nyghte?
> Much longeyng haf I for the layned.'   (242-4)

Such uses of the yearning language of the courtly love-lyric are
mainly in the early stages of the poem, but the 'luf-longyng' of line
1152 is obviously intended to recall earlier references. Courtly and
chivalrous qualities are present also in the language and imagery
used to describe the heavenly city, the court and the kingdom, the
'Queen of Courtesy' and the Pearl-bedecked Maiden; even the
use of a rose as an image of transience is coloured by its associations
with love. Further, as Spearing notes, the dream-world contains
ghosts of the personifications from Le Roman de la Rose in the shifting
feelings of the Dreamer.[19] These allusions support the reader's
sense of the Dreamer as 'hero', support the authority of the first-
person narrator and confirm that he is to be sympathised with.

The reader's sense of the Dreamer varies, and the variation comes
partly from the adventure element in the poem. The poet has
combined the adventures of two figures. the traveller in unknown
lands and the vulnerable hero on a spiritual quest. Within the
dream the Dreamer's function, therefore, shifts from that of observer and reporter, who speaks to the reader and whose words are

automatically 'true', as far as the reader can judge, to that of the central figure of the Everyman type, in a psychological process of education, who speaks to his guide and whose words are much of the time patently 'wrong'. Between the two is his function in the 'political' sphere, where his questions elicit explanations of the ways of the unknown society and where his own criteria come into conflict with them. The multiplicity makes it difficult to judge or place him, and this is the source of that fluctuation in the characterisation of which I spoke earlier. Is it possible, given the shifts of role, to have a consistent sense of the relationship of the dreamer-narrator and the poet?

Though it may be that in vision-poems there is something of the personal in the figure of the dreamer-narrator,[20] comparison of the vision-poems of Chaucer, *Pearl* and *Piers Plowman*, even if one goes no further afield, makes it plain that, unless by coincidence the three major poets of the late fourteenth century were remarkably similar in outlook and temperament, there is much in the characterisation of dreamers which is merely a function of the form. It was necessary for the strategy of the poem that the dreamer should be an ignorant being who wonders at marvels and asks stupid questions. If there is an autobiographical element in such poems, it is not in that sort of detail that it is to be found, but rather in the inessential information which is casually present in the dreamer's discourse. So, for example, one can safely believe that Langland spent some of his life in the poorer parts of London, because it is not necessary to the poem that he should have done, without believing that he was, as his narrator is, a stubborn and lazy man, 'unholy of werkes'. The distinction between the two kinds of information is more difficult in *Pearl*, because the narrator does not speak as poet, but simply tells us of his feelings and his dream and is, therefore, a less detached and more personal 'I' than either Langland or Chaucer.

The Dreamer's voice is a dramatic one in a situation. He takes no account of the reader except in the most general terms in the concluding lines, unless we see the narrator's comments on his own grief in the fifth stanza as an implicit declaration to the reader that the dream will explore the relation of reason and will.

The cryptic quality of such indication is evidence of how far the conception of *Pearl* is as a fiction. The narrator himself and the process of narration have become completely fictionalised: there is no sense of the experience of the poem and the composition of the poem as two separate events. The narrator's story, though still serving the function of the vision‑poem's necessary frame, is itself the plot. This produces a curious relationship between what one may call the 'story' (of the father and the dead child) and the 'argument' (the ideas which the Dreamer has to have explained). When, in a work of art, narrative is subordinated to argument, we see an illustra‑ tive tale as a particular example of a general truth; the argument is wider than the story and is open to the considerations which one may bring to bear upon it from one's own beliefs and experience of the world. But the reversed process, as in *Pearl*, where discourse is enclosed within a narrative, means that the argument is displaced from its expected function; the ideas cease to be open ideas, but become *ad hoc* ones which we judge not by their general validity but as they reflect on the story. Our understanding of *Pearl* thus seems to me to depend very little on the ideas used within it, because it is to their effect, to the experiencing of them, that our attention is directed; so, for instance, the reader is not asked to bring to the poem an understanding of the operation of grace, but is asked to bring a sympathetic confusion about it, and a recognition of how illogical Christian doctrine can seem. Our understanding of the poem depends on our understanding of the process through which the first‑person narrator is going.

The truly basic question which faces the reader of *Pearl* is, in fact, a variation of the question which lay behind the old debate between autobiographical elegy and allegory. How are we meant to understand the relationship of the poet, the narrator within the poem, and the Dreamer? The continuity of manner and tone be‑ tween the opening section and the early stages of the dream suggests that the 'I' of the waking moments is the same 'I' as in the vision, and the absence of any commenting voice encourages one to identify both with the supposed 'I' of the artist. On the other hand, the qualities displayed by the figure vary, and the 'I' of Sections VII–XVI is not the same man as the 'I' of I–VII or of XVII–XX; therefore one feels the need to distinguish between the different functions of the Dreamer, between the narrator and the Dreamer, and between both and the poet, since one recognises that he is manoeuvring the figures for particular fictional purposes. The two obvious answers to the question of the relationship are, that is, both difficult to maintain. To make the point clear I will spell out the possibilities again.

There are at least three distinct possible answers to the question of understanding these relationships.

First, the poem is autobiographical and the poet is writing of his own personal experience of bereavement and of a real vision in which either a supernatural or an hallucinatory force dictated the Maiden's words to him. *Pearl* would then be a work similar in nature to the *Revelations* of Julian of Norwich, except that it is composed in an elaborate verse form and that it does not make its personal truth explicit; one would thus understand poet, narrator and Dreamer to be one. Although there are elements in the poem similar to elements in works describing mystical visions, in the absence of any definite evidence that the poem is autobiographical, this answer is a non-starter.[21] Apart from the unfitness of the Dreamer for the role of mystic, no medieval Christian visionary wishing to communicate profound and rare religious experience would have chosen to be cryptic about it, nor have communicated in the way *Pearl* communicates. There are too many things in the poem extraneous to a genuine mystical experience for it to be a possibility.

Secondly, the poem is fictional (or partly autobiographical and partly fictional) and the poet imagines a bereaved man who has a real visionary experience. The narrator and the Dreamer are thus the same person and one follows the course of his educational progress. To effect this progress the poet invents a second character, the redeemed soul of the dead girl, and puts into her mouth the didactic matter which the Dreamer's confusion needs. This is the explanation that most readers, consciously or not, accept, but acceptance of it does involve acceptance also that the poet allowed his fiction to be warped by his didactic intent, that the characterisation of the Dreamer breaks down, that the Maiden is merely a mouth-piece, and that the poem is really a confidence trick, whereby the reader is persuaded that he is being drawn into an exploration of deep human feeling, while in actual fact at the centre of the poem his surrogate in the poem's world becomes a trivialised buffoon, and the exploration turns out to be no probing of troubled areas of human experience, but a juxtaposition of human stupidity and standard images and asseverations of Christian faith. If one reads in this way, one is left with a sense that some parts of the poem satisfy less than others, and that the form of the poem implies a consistency which the course of the work does not actually demonstrate.

There is a third possible answer. This is to accept *Pearl* as a work of the creative imagination in which the poet has invented a figure with whom we are meant to identify and sympathise (the waking narrator) in the opening and closing passages of the poem, but that we are meant to understand the vision, or at least the dialogue portion of it, as a projection of the conflict in the narrator's mind. To the narrator, the vision is a real experience of the supernatural, a revelation, a 'gostly dreme', a 'very avysyoun', but to the reader it is a fictional piece of schizophrenia whereby the poet divides his narrator into the half that obstinately is ignorant and the half that serenely knows, and follows the interchange between them.[22] In other words, the Dreamer and the Maiden are figures representing elements within the narrator's mind, but simultaneously they are the bereaved father and the redeemed child. We would thus under-stand, at the representative or allegorical level, that the Dreamer in the early stages of the vision represents the 'wreched wylle in wo', obstinately refusing to accept mortality, perceiving only through the senses; in Section VII, Will accepts the counsels of Reason, in so far as he tempers his grief and accepts the law of Kind in recognis-ing that the Maiden now belongs to another life. In the middle sections of the poem, he represents Will modified by Reason, but Reason only at a limited, human, earthly level; the limitations of human reason are exposed by his unwillingness to accept, and his exaggerated inability to understand, anything beyond earthly law and earthly nature. He attempts himself to use reason to come to terms with the otherness of the Maiden and the heavenly kingdom (that is, to come to terms with divine kind, reason and law) but is able to begin to do it (in Section XIII) only through a response of the imagination. This aesthetic response, elicited first by the spotless beauty of the symbolic pearl, continues to be called up by pictorial representations and emotional images of the Lamb, the New Jerusalem and the procession of Brides. So an aesthetic element involving imagination and beauty is added to Reason and Nature; this element is identifiable with the third thing the narrator at the beginning had lost, his joy. The beauty of the pearl and the heavenly kingdom, in both pictorial and moral terms, bring a rebirth of joy (the 'delyt' of Section XIX). Thus the 'wreched wylle' gradually adds to itself through the course of the vision, and we return to the whole man.

If one reads in this way, then the Maiden is the Dreamer's *alter ego*, combining a number of different aspects of the narrator's own nature. She is a restoration of that part of himself which he had lost and which he mourns, and so she begins as the child, recreated in imagination as an image of pearl-adorned innocence. When the dialogue begins, she represents those aspects of himself which he is unable to accept in his waking state, and so becomes the spokesman of reason and natural law, opposing his stricken passion with the counsels of moderation, and his refusal to accept death with reminders of the inevitable course of nature. Subsequently she partakes of divine reason and law, in representing the Christian faith and doctrine which the narrator cannot bring to bear on his grief, though he knows he ought to. So she becomes an instructress in both belief and beliefs, representing that better part of himself which can see beyond limits and terms, which has an imaginative response to the joy brought by knowledge of the nature of Christ, and so on.

The poem, seen thus, combines the course of moral education, by means of which the narrator's initial passionate sorrow is controlled, by means of which the transience of earth is accepted, and by means of which the inevitable otherness of life beyond death is imaginatively realised, with a *psychomachia,* which divides the speaker into the component parts of his nature, and by means of which the poet argues out the inner conflict of feeling and reason, reaching a reconciliation of the warring elements when the Dreamer becomes one whole being again as he awakes.

It is through accepting this combination that we can best, I believe, understand the shifts in our sense of what the Dreamer and Maiden stand for. They both are and are not allegorical; the experience in the poem is both real and unreal. It is a combination present in other dream-poems. James I of Scotland shows a simple example of the combination in *The Kingis Quair,* when he says:

> suich a fantasye
> Fell to my mynd, that ay me thoght the bell
> Said to me, 'Tell on, man, quat the befell'.

Thoght I tho to myself: 'Quhat may this be?
This is myn awin ymagynacioune.
It is no lyf that spekis unto me.
It is a bell, or that impressioune
Off my thought causith this illusioune . . . '23

The moment is both natural and supernatural, seemingly a divine
command but realistically explained as the product of the mind.
A more complex example is the process in *Piers Plowman*, where
the dreamer is both a real William and an allegorical Will, and
where the narrating figure finds himself, in the *Vita*, in a world
which represents the mind of man, peopled by personified human
qualities, which are simultaneously the component parts of his
own nature and general forces in the world at large. It is a mixture
of modes, neither purely allegorical nor purely literal, working at
one level for the fictional narrator and at another level for the reader.

The clues to this response to *Pearl* are, first, the poet's indications
that his subject may be thought of as an allegorical contest;
secondly, the simplification of language and verse-form at those
stages of the poem tending most to the allegorical; and, thirdly, some
indication that the experience of the narrator may be viewed in
more than one way, when he says:

'O perle', quod I, 'of rych renoun,
So watz hit me dere that thou con deme,
In this veray avysyoun,
(If hit be veray and soth sermoun
That thou so stykez in garlande gay)
So wel is me in thys doel-doungoun
That thou art to that Prynsez paye,'24   (1182–8)

The fact remains, however, though this double reading may account
for the variations within the poem, that the relationship of poet,
narrator and dreamer is not clearly or logically indicated to the
reader. Such a combination of literal and allegorical, of an internal
and an external sense to the poem, supposes a poet of sophisticated
mind who demanded a sophistication in his readers greater than
most of them feel obliged to supply.

3. Formal devices in *Pearl*

When one turns from the substance of the poem to its form, one finds further evidence of the poet's interest in complexity. The three-rhymed scheme of each stanza, the grouping of stanzas in fives (six in Section XV) by the use of a refrain and rhyme, the linking of the stanzas and groups by concatenation, create three layers of patterning. The poem's over-all structure provides a fourth layer by the symmetrical arrangement of the material. The narrator's waking moments, which frame the dream, are described in the first and last groups of five stanzas. Approximately the first four groups and the last four groups are devoted to the Dreamer's account of his experiences and these eight groups enclose the twelve groups of dialogue.[25] Within these twelve groups, the centre is formed by three long speeches from the Maiden with brief inter-polations from the Dreamer, and these speeches are in turn enclosed by passages of more equal dialogue. The entry into the dream land-scape leads to the first view of the transformed child, radiant in the distance, and the last view of her, as radiant and distant in the procession of the Brides, leads to the exit from the vision world. The middle one of the Maiden's long speeches begins at the poem's central stanza, deals with the poem's main concepts and its dominant symbol. The division into twenty sections creates a patterned se-quence of disparate but linked parts, each having its focal point and yet leading on; the effect is somewhat like that of a sonnet-sequence. This combination of completeness and continuity is implied also by the hundred and one stanzas.

The patterning suggests two contrasting things about the poet's sense of his art. First, *Pearl* is an intellectual poem, in the sense that the symmetry shows a pleasure in formal design and in the idea that a poem's shape may be emblematic. This confirms the reader's sense that the poem is, in parts, written in the manner of an enigma; this is most obviously so in the earlier sections which have antithetical ideas as their base (pearl was joy, pearl was sorrow; pearl was lost and now is found, etc.), and which present the subject of the poem in disguise. The poet begins by 'using a technique of care-fully calculated ambiguity', as Pamela Gradon puts it;[26] this

enigmatic approach is expressed later in patterning and word-play
such as

> 'O maskelez perle in perlez pure,
> That berez,' quod I, 'the perle of prys . . .'   (745-6)

where the use of *perle* in three different senses belongs to that type
of academic rhetoric of which Shakespeare's 'Light seeking
light doth light of light beguile' is an extreme example.

Secondly, however, the poem's structure is inherent in the genre,
and the symmetry, therefore, not only symbolic and decorative,
but also a formal indication of the basic narrative pattern of journey
and return which all vision-poems use. The symmetry marks out
the stages of story and feeling; the poem can be read as a movement
of flow and ebb, which augments the sense of the Dreamer's journey
as an adventure, out of space and out of time, returning to the here
and now, and conveys to us that

> the end of all our exploring
> Will be to arrive where we started
> And know the place for the first time.
> *(Little Gidding)*

The end of the poem is a return to the Dreamer's own feelings and
reflections from the dramatised, detached presentation of the middle
sections. It is a return to earth, waking and living after a journey
through a country which is simultaneously a country of the mind
and a potentially 'real' other-world. It is, therefore, a return to the
problem from which the poem started, the Dreamer's attitude to the
difficulty of living with loss and mortality.

The symmetry of the poem is, thus, at once imitative of the
waking-sleeping-waking design of the genre, and emblematic, in
that its hundred and one stanzas form a symbolic chain, whose end
is looped back to fashion the links into a circle. At both mimetic
and emblematic levels the structure has the effect of making the
subject-matter as tightly constrained as the material of a geometrical
theorem. Although the poem presents a process of education, the
Dreamer learns only what he has known from the beginning; the
only difference is that he has come to accept it instead of fighting
against it. The poem presents us with a justification of the *status
quo*, in spite of the impression given within the vision of new

experience, of revelation and transformation. The return to earth is an anti-climax, but also a withdrawal into a circumscribed area of thought, less adventurous than the vision's powerful imagery seemed to promise. The end of the poem completes a pattern by providing the refrain which the first line has, in a sense, been seeking, and this refrain-word, *pay*, 'satisfaction', itself emphasises the idea of completion. To begin a poem with a line which fits into an elaborate pattern visible only at the end inevitably gives to the poem a sense of limitation; the meaning is not simply given form, but fixed in a mould, trapped within a circle of emblems and sounds.

On the other hand, it is quite clear as one reads that the poem is to be understood as a developing sequence. It describes an experience which is progressive and through which the narrator at the end is *not* what he was at the beginning.

As with the question of the poet and the Dreamer, it seems that more than one structural principle is at work in the poem. Again we have to resort to a complex, double view of it, if we are to accommodate both. The internal structure of the story is something like a road or a ladder, where the Dreamer cannot see beyond the next step; he progresses until he looks differently upon the world. The external structure of the symmetry and metrical patterning is detached from involvement in experience; it is the shared intellectual pleasure of poet and reader from which the Dreamer is excluded. So one perceives the psychological circle which the poem has described, and sees how the contending elements in the narrator's nature have been separated and reunified. Whether the reader finds it possible to keep the two systems running concurrently is open to question.

Support for the idea of a double structural principle is found in the relationship between the stanza groupings and the course of the poem's narrative and argument. The refrains and link-words make one see each of the twenty sections as a unit. The poem consists of a number of circles, somewhat in the manner of Henry James's *The Awkward Age*, each one centred on an idea or an image or an ambiguity. The patterning establishes in the reader's mind the idea that as one moves from one section to another, one enters a new aspect of the poem. But if we look at the *content* of the stanza-groups and follow its sequence, we find that different groupings suggest themselves in places. While at the beginning of the poem the subject-matter is fitted into the stanza-groups (I, waking; II, the vision landscape; III, the Dreamer's exploration; IV, description of the Maiden), once the dialogue begins the poet tends to work across rather than within them. Each of the Maiden's long speeches ends in the middle of a group, so that the changeover of voices does not happen, as one might expect, at a new section. Several times the fifth stanza of a group contains a reproach or protest or question which, rather than completing the sense of the group, makes it very obviously incomplete and leads on to the next group. Examples of this are Section V with the Maiden's unexpectedly brusque re-proach on three counts which are identified in VI, stanzas 1 and 2; the Dreamer's protest in VIII, stanza 5 and IX, stanza 1; the Dreamer's rejection of the parable as unreasonable in X, stanza 5; the Dreamer's questions in XIII, stanza 5 and in XV, stanza 6, XVI, stanzas 1 and 2. This device occurs often enough to establish an alternative to the metrical pattern in the middle parts of the poem, whereby the first stanzas of a group continue or respond, while the last stanza introduces new material. The patterning according to repeated sound and repeated concept does not, therefore, always cor-respond to the development of the sense, but runs counter to it. While the poet may well have thought that such counter-pointing provided a necessary variety (and it is dramatically very effective in places, especially in V, stanza 5 and X, stanza 5), it does tend to undermine the poet's obvious desire for order and form, and to give the reader the sense that the patterned form of the poem is running at a different aesthetic and conceptual level from the actual events of the poem. The speeches are, after all, very formally shaped in other re-spects; only in one instance at the very end of the dialogue does a speech begin and end in the middle of a stanza. The poet seems to be working for effects of classical shaping with one hand, while his other is devising romantic effects of strong feeling breaking into patterns.

A somewhat similar double effect seems to be created by the use of refrains to group the stanzas together.[27] Repetition of the word or phrase which brings the stanza to a close and which is echoed in the first line of the next stanza makes the particular con-cept or image very dominant. Each of the twenty groups has its characteristic leading motif and hence a separable identity. This is most obviously so when the refrain is a fixed one. So *John* (Section

XVII) focuses attention on the scriptural authority on which the description of the New Jerusalem is based, while *Jerusalem* (Section XIV) puts emphasis on the place of sacrifice and redemption which is linked by sound-echo to the idea of the sacrificial Lamb and of Christ as the beloved *lemman*. These refrains have the effect not of giving expression to an emphasis which is inherent in the subject-matter but rather of clamping an arbitrary shape upon it. This is true also, though less obviously, of some links which are based upon a word of varying senses; the punning quality adds colour to *dubbed* (Section II) since the heavenly kingdom's adornment of earthly landscape is thereby characterised as an access of honour, as if the rocks and plains had been knighted; similarly *pyght* (Section IV) characterises the embellishment of the lost child as also a dehuman-ising, since she is 'fixed' as well as 'adorned', and the fact that one sense undermines the other gives the repetition a certain piquancy. But the effect of both is one of local isolation, of giving obsessive attention to an aspect of the subject which does not eventually seem centrally important in the scheme of the poem as a whole.

More effective is the treatment in some parts of the dialogue, where the refrain-words apply differently to the Dreamer and to the Maiden, or where new meanings seem to grow out of old ones. At times the two points of view meet and separate through the prism of the repeated phrase and the play of shifting senses creates effects of dramatic antithesis and of irony. The senses in which the Dreamer proclaims himself a *jueler* (Section V), crafstman, con-noisseur and owner, are each given an ironic twist by the Maiden's responses. Through *deme* (Section VI) the Dreamer's want of judgement is contrasted with the decreeing power of God, and through *blysse* (Section VII) the poet explores the antithesis between earthly and heavenly joy, and between the Dreamer's sense of what he has lost, what he now experiences and what he hopes for in the future, and the Maiden's own superior sense of the nature of true bliss. Through the idea of *cortaysye* (Section VIII) religious and secular ideas are brought into conflict.[28] These refrains contribute to the dramatic texture of the early part of the dialogue; the continual reference to key concepts gives a precise basis to the antithesis of attitudes. But the effect is of a spotlight illuminating one thing at a time, then switching to another area of attention.

It is only when one perceives some development and continuity in the use of refrains that one becomes convinced of the necessity for this metrical arrangement of the material. This happens in the poem's main defining sections and enriches what otherwise can seem a rather arid portion of the poem. The word-play seems at home here because the defining is itself paradoxical, and one of the most elaborate Middle English examples of that traditional piece of rhetoric whereby a poet does something by saying how impossible it is to do it. The technique here is to focus attention on words which indicate limits and quantities – *date* (Section IX), *more* (Section X) and *innoghe* (Section XI) – while saying essentially that quantities are irrelevant and cannot be judged anyway:

> 'Of more and lasse in Godez ryche',
> That gentyl sayde, 'lys no joparde.' (601–2)

The idea is expressed in terms of conflict between the Dreamer's insistence on quantities and the Maiden's brushing them aside:

> 'Bot a quene! Hit is to dere a date.'
> 'Ther is no date of hys godnesse.' (492–3)

The workers in the vineyard and the Dreamer combine in an all too recognisable human insistence on fair play and union rules, while the Maiden responds with an all too recognisable human delight in making nonsense of measuring principles, by blurring the attempt to define in a cloud of paradox and equivocation. The sections with 'quantity' refrains do not, therefore, depend so much on a play of the senses of individual words as on a play between the attempt to define and the indefinable. They also act to characterise the attitudes represented in the Dreamer and the Maiden and, in this, the concentration on quantity is part of a continuous thread running through the poem's refrains.[29] This thread begins with the *more* of Section III where the Dreamer's growing excitement as he explores the visionary world becomes a pursuing appetite for experience:

> And ever me longed ay more and more.
> More and more, and yet wel mare,
> Me lyste to se the broke byyonde. (144–6)

The thread is taken up again with the refrain *never the les* (Section XV) where the Maiden expresses the mutual desire of the wives of the Lamb that their honour shall be available to all and the fact that their love and joy may never be reduced in quantity. It surely cannot be coincidence, either, that this section with 'less' in its refrain actually has more stanzas than any other section; this suggests that the poet derived some sort of pleasure from ingenious playing with quantities.[30]

Such concern with quantity is part of an undercurrent of meaning whereby the Dreamer is simultaneously characterised as greedy and mean. He wants more than he has a right to and more than he has earned, but, at the same time, wishes to limit the Maiden's reward and the generosity of God. The twin failings are part of his lack of reason and self-control; he is continually trying to impose measures but has no actual power to judge them; he gives what he ought to withhold and withholds what he ought to give. His grasping for more (with which the grumbling labourers are identified) and his desire for limits are opposed by the Maiden's association with words implying amplitude and undefined quantity, especially the refrain of Section XI, 'The grace of God is gret innoghe', and by the sense that she speaks with Measure, a sense of moderation and controlled judgement. His greed is opposed by moderation, his niggling tendency to limit by generosity. The quantity references lie behind the choice of *pay* as the final refrain-word of the poem. This combines a sense of delight with satisfaction and the settling of debts, and brings together the Dreamer's acceptance of God's terms and dealings, his yielding of the pearl to the Prince's pleasure, and his own sense of the debt he owes to God.

Another set of refrains is formed by the opening *spot, maskellez/makelez* (Section XIII), *mote(les)* (Section XVI) and *mone* (Section XVIII), though all of these are richer in meaning and association than the words of quantity. Section XIII is unique in basing the refrain and linking on two similar words; some editors[31] have emended *makelez* in lines 733 and 757 to *maskellez* in order to regularise the links, but Gordon's comment seems to me to hit the nail on the head: 'the poet may well have deliberately utilized the similarity in sound of the two epithets to make play on the two aspects of the pearl symbolism – the purity of innocence and the peerlessness of the heavenly state . . . the final union of them both in the last line of the stanza group . . . gives the impression of conscious stylistic purpose in the alternation'.[32] The combination of uniqueness and spotlessness reminds the reader of the same

pairing in the opening stanza of the poem, as well as of the references to the Virgin Mary in Section VIII. The pearl of great price,
as a symbol of the heavenly kingdom, is as 'wemlez' as the jeweller's
lost pearl but unique in a sense she was not, though the Dreamer
has as yet to understand this fact. Dreamer and Maiden are therefore at one in their use of *maskellez*, but the Maiden applies *makelez*
to the symbolic pearl and to the Lamb of God, rejecting the
Dreamer's attribution of the epithet to herself. The word-play here
thus leads to an explicit distinction between the two parallel words
and so introduces the final phase of the vision with the subject of the
144,000 Brides:

> 'Maskelles', quod that myry quene,
> 'Unblemyst I am, wythouten blot,
> And that I may wyth mensk menteene;
> Bot "makelez quene" thenne sade I not.
> The Lambez wyvez in blysse we bene,
> A hondred and forty (fowre) thowsande flot.' (781-6)

The precision of this distinction is itself a strong indication of the
poet's interest in verbal analysis and of a fascination with the coming
together of varying senses in similar sounds.

The same fascination is at work again, in Section XVI, on the
same area of meaning. The refrain *mote* brings together two,
possibly three, different words: *mote* means 'stronghold' or 'city'
(OFr *mote*) in lines 936, 937, 949 and 973, 'spot' or 'stain' (OE
mot) in 924, 960, 972 and, in the form *motelez*, in 925 and 961.
The two senses occur together in 948;

> The Lompe ther wythouten spottez blake
> Hatz feryed thyder hys fayre flote;
> And as hys flok is wythouten flake,
> So is hys mote wythouten moote.   (945-8)

The third sense 'quarrel', 'dispute' (OE *mōt*) may possibly be
present in the fourth stanza, where attention is again focused on the
distinction between two related things and on verbal analysis by
the etymological interpretation of 'Jerusalem', and where the discussion of peace suggests that the city and its company are 'wythouten
mote' in the sense of 'without dispute' as well as being spotless.

The combination of place and stain in *mote* echoes the two senses of
spot; it is spotlessness which distinguishes the inhabitants of the
New Jerusalem from those of the cities of the earth, and the Dreamer
may see the heavenly city but not enter unless he were 'clene
wythouten mote'. The distinction remains the subject after the
Maiden has ceased speaking and we return to the Dreamer's report
of his experiences. The transcendent brilliance of the bejewelled
city is described in terms of distinction between heavenly and earthly
worlds in the superb poetry of Section XVIII, with its refrain *mone*.
The dazzling light's superiority to the light of sun and moon leads
to the limits of the sublunary world and to the same ambiguity of
spot from which the poem began:

> Ther entrez non to take reset
> That berez any spot an-under mone.   (1067–8)

The ambiguity of line 1068 (meaning both 'that bears any earthly
spot' and 'that any earthly spot holds') and the spottedness of the
moon itself ('To spotty ho is, of body to grym') serve both to en-
hance the pure splendour of the heavenly city and to convey the
humbling and diminishing of the Dreamer and the complete
extinction of all his earthly claims. So the stain of earth and the
contrasting purity of what is other and greater than earth pick up
the earlier references to spots and blemishes and turn into apocalyptic form the sense of division from which the poem started.

Thus, when refrains link up to form nets of cross-reference
through the poem, form and meaning come together. But at other
times one suspects that it is simply a love of intellectual play and
formal ingenuity on the poet's part which determines the expression.

Section XIII of *Pearl* is the place where one is most conscious of
the complex demands made by the poet on one's attention and
where one is most aware of the multiplicity of the poet's art. Here, in
a section whose refrain itself plays on words and on the parallel
of uniqueness and spotlessness, there is a concentration of ingenious
devices. First the link between the section and the preceding stanza
is irregular. Gordon goes as far as to say: 'This group of stanzas is
not linked with the preceding group; only here does the system
of linking fail.'[33] Though one knows what Gordon meant, the
statement is untrue, and in fact the link is more binding than

anywhere else in the poem, though not made in the regular form. It occurs over eight lines and uses not only the expected link-word *ryght* but also *Jesus, chylde(r)* and *ryche*:

> Jesus thenne hem swetely sayde:
> 'Do way, let chylder unto me tyght.
> To suche is hevenryche arayed.'
> The innocent is ay saf by ryght.
>
> Jesus con calle to hym hys mylde,
> And sayde hys ryche no wyy myght wynne
> Bot he com thyder ryght as a chylde,
> Other ellez nevermore com therinne. (717–24)

One can be in no doubt that these two stanzas are linked together; they virtually merge into one another. The result is to give a sense of continuity and to stress the phrase 'ryght as a chylde', since the ear is waiting for the syllable *ryght*, and to alert one for the unusual because the pattern has been broken. The poet then, in the sub-sequent stanzas of the section, gathers together as many of the pre-ceding refrain-words as fit into the current of meaning: *spot* (Section I) in line 764; *pyght* (Section IV) in 742 and 768; *jueler* (Section V) in 730 and 734; *blys* (Section VII) in 729; *cortez* (Section VIII) in 754. There is also reference to the principle of the earlier parable in 739 and emphasis on the key idea of spot-lessness. All these internal allusions and verbal patterns are gathered round the poem's central symbol, the pearl of great price, and serve to make one review the course of the poem so far, to measure the distance one has moved from the first appearance of the pearl, and to relate the Maiden's teaching and the Dreamer's reaction to the feelings and judgements from which the poem started.

Nor is this the only evidence of a deliberate ingenuity and delight in patterned play involving Section XIII. The speech of the Maiden which has its climax in the pearl symbol begins at stanza 51 (line 601), the central stanza of the poem; the speech is a hundred and fourty-four lines long and the speech has as its own centre the twelfth section of the poem. Taken in conjunction with other evidence that numbers are used symbolically in *Pearl*, the concen-tration in this speech seems significant.[34]

It is possible to interpret the density of Section XIII in more than one way. One could suggest that the unusual link and the recalling of earlier ideas are emphatic devices designed to stress the importance of the passage thematically and the centrality of the symbol. Certainly the passage does this, but the very complexity and number of the devices, as well as the inorganic nature of some of them, inclines me to believe that it is design rather than theme which is the prime motive. What the section does in terms of the patterning of the poem is to show that the 'circle' of *Pearl* is not created simply by the closing lines' return to the opening line. In the Maiden's speech the poem begins, at its central stanza, to turn back on itself. The *more* of Section X is checked by the *innoghe* of Section XI, and Section XIII, by recalling earlier refrains, by returning to the pearl, and describing it as an 'endelez rounde' gives us the sense of acting as a climax or centre, and simultaneously taking us back in an arc to the earlier stages of the poem. The process continues in the sections that follow in a number of related ways. Reference backwards is made both by the recurrence of central ideas, such as I have mentioned in the *mote* and *mone* sections, and by the simpler echoing of earlier phrases and images such as Section XV's 'I am bot mokke and mul among/And thou so ryche a reken rose'. There is a sense too of travelling back by the same road we came along, as lengthy scriptural quotations and allusion in Sections XIV to XVII balance the earlier parable; the jewel imagery of Revelations balances the earlier jewelled description; and we return to earth and the waking life. After the checking of *more* by *innoghe* comes the receding refrain *less*. Even at the level of the sounds of the poem there is a backwards sequence as the alliterative base of the refrain lines of the first three sections, *pryvy/precious/ perle, dubbed, more* is repeated in reverse in the last three with *mone, delyt* and *precious/perlez/ pay*.

Study of the formal devices and the wordplay in *Pearl* can lead one in several different directions, and suggest various ways of harmonising the poem's multiple effects.

Emphasis on the poem's symbolism is one way. The pearlsymbol is embedded in all the aspects of the poem's inner patterning. The idea of the pearl as an 'endless round' can be linked to the poem's 'circular' form. The poet's use of wordplay could have grown from the concept of a central emblem whose various aspects were to be gradually revealed and added to one another in the course of the poem. As a pictorial and notional symbol it is involved in all the main emblematic moments of the poem.[35]

Another way is to think of *Pearl* as a circling meditation on inter-laced themes: the translation from 'muck and mould' to the spotless roundness of the pearl, whose purity and beauty are trans-figured into the Apocalyptic symbolism of the City of God, built on a rock of gems; the moral states needed and desired by the human being, and the qualities possessed and displayed by the divine for the translation to be effected; and the way the translation operates according to right, justice and grace.

A third way is to accept the dominance of formal patterning. On the basis of the puns, repetitions, numbers and so on, it would be possible to make out a case for *Pearl*'s being regarded as a different type of meditation, a meditation on the words *margery* and *perle*, whereby the poem was generated from the letters of the words, the associations of the words by means of alliteration, sound echoes (e.g. *perles* – peerless and *marjorys* – Jerusalem), synonyms, con-nected ideas, scriptural allusions, and some personal feeling con-nected with the name.[36] Equally it is not surprising that some readers have suspected that the composition of *Pearl* conceals acrostics or other clues to the author's name.[37]

One is eventually left with the fact that *Pearl* is a very elaborate poem whose elaboration seems to be based on more than one intention on the poet's part. The shaping and texture of the poem are too variously suggestive for us to have any simple view of it.

4. Conclusion: feeling versus form

Though at first reading *Pearl* impresses as a poem which is in-tensely moving, subsequent analysis reveals it to be a work which may be read in a variety of ways and which contains conflicting and ambiguous elements. The poem begins and ends with high poetry and strong feeling; between the two peaks lies a tract of stony ground, the enclosed, 'intellectual' portion of the poem, which is, in parts, prosaically presented and rigid in effect. The poem's power to move the reader and to induce his imaginative apprehension of mortality, learned through experience of loss and pain, is, to my mind, *Pearl*'s real strength. Though the poet's purpose may be, in one sense, to offer 'a simple song for thinking hearts', the means by which he works are designed to make the reader respond to 'the moving accident'; these means include a command of emotional and evocative poeticism and the subtle use and combination of layers of suggestion. The poet uses traditions, images and echoes not only belonging to vision poetry but also taken from courtly love-lyric, elegy and Grail romances, to charac-terise his story as a romantic adventure of the spirit, where the reader feels the satisfaction of following, through danger, doubt and obscurity, the quest of the 'hero', to the revelation and the muted satisfaction of the end. Though the symmetry and concatenation suggest that all the elements of the poem are links in one continuous chain, this is poetic illusion. If one reads according to what affects and moves, then the links and patterns are eventually seen to be on he surface. Connections between the various aspects of the matter are not made explicit through the formal design; the true connec-tions are made obliquely, through imagery and association. Experience and change are acted out for us by the poetry. As a result of the curious combinations in the poem, it is difficult to identify with certainty the individual qualities of the poet who created it.

If one ignores the irrelevancies of autobiographical readings, then it seems clear that the fiction which the poet has invented is a moral fable involving the facing of difficult things. He presents to us a man faced with the most difficult human problem, that of accepting mortality, and faced with it in its most extreme and poignant form, the death of a beloved child; emotional intensity and pull is added by the child's having been a baby and a girl, whose early death could well seem the most unjust blow of provi-dence. Beyond the death itself is the most extreme test of faith in the after-life, since a baby's translation into a serene, blessed maiden represents a supreme test of the imagination. One could say, there-for, that *Pearl* is a poem dealing with a problem subject, initially conceived in intensely emotional terms.

The poet's answer to the question of how one comes to terms with grief and loss is by leaving the bonds of self, by believing in an existence other than the earthly, and by recognising that the child's fate is the common lot of man. The means by which the course of development is effected is a complex process, conceived in terms of

Christian teaching, involving different layers and aspects. The best thing that the bereaved man can hope for is that the child still exists in some other state, and so hope may be said to be the foundation of the vision of the beautiful, adorned Maiden, whose earthly innocence is transformed into the symbolism of whiteness and pearls. The imagery in the vision world is a recompense for the transience of the world of nature; the jewels console for the loss of the one who was 'but a rose'. From the satisfaction of hope, the poet moves on to the necessary corollary of the child's existence in another life, that the life is other, and that union is possible only across the river of death. Though she may exist she can no longer be what the Dreamer lost. The poet represents this through the Dreamer's struggle to retain the child within the terms he under-stands, but, for the process of acceptance to be accomplished, he has to be brought to think of the relationship according to justice and the nature and operation of grace. In Section XIII the poem turns the focus from the child back to the Dreamer's state by recalling the jeweller and the symbolic pearl; the Dreamer's own imagery is turned against him, and it is in terms of imagery and symbols that the process of enlightenment is completed, with a gradual poetic crescendo from acceptance of the otherness of the world beyond nature and response to the scriptural emblems with which he is presented, to the heights of poetic eloquence in Sections XVIII and XIX. The symbols of innocence, purity and sacrifice, the glory and permanence of the heavenly kingdom, the salvation and beatification of the virgins, are all emblematic transformations of the hope from which the vision began. The ceremony is built up to enhance the effect of reversal at the end, when the narrator grasps the otherness of the heavenly world in a different, more down-to-earth and painful way, as the thing he has yet to attain and from which he is cut off. He can live in such a way as to attempt to earn the other state; his knowledge of it can not, because of his separation from it, cancel out grief and loss, but instead generalises the pain so that grief is no longer the sense of self, but the sense of mortality.

Though initially conceived in emotional terms, the problem subject is thus developed in a combination of terms, emotional, analytical (particularly in the elements of psychological allegory), and generalising, so that the poem shows the individual case as also a typical human instance, which, through symbolism and pattern, we recognise as an inevitable circle of feeling and thought. From this combination come the poem's different levels of meaning, and the sense that *Pearl* includes contradictory or antithetical qualities. The different levels may be said to grow from contrasting elements in the poet's mind, and his sense of feeling and form. To the concept of the poem as an imaginative exploration of a difficult subject belong the emphasis on feeling, the sense of spiritual adventure and marvel, the course of the Dreamer's moral and aesthetic development, the mimetic qualities of the poetry (implying that poet and reader are to enter into the hero's feelings and ex-periences), the sense of change as the poem progresses, and the impression that the poem is a genuine attempt to take account of the painful contingencies of man's real condition. From these things comes the sense that *Pearl* is open to the world, serious and not predetermined, inviting the reader to live through experience.

In contrast to these related aspects are the intellectual shaping of the poem, its word-play, riddles and numbers, its symbols and emblems, its use of elements of the allegorical contest between aspects of the human mind. These represent an impulse not to enter in, to imagine and to evoke, but to control, to codify, to simplify, and to abstract. From these things comes the impression of *Pearl* as a determinist poem, not looking beyond a fixed circle of meaning, justifying conventional thought, offering the reader the closed and distanced world of doctrine and of the understanding of moral ideas through classification.

The rich appeal of *Pearl* may be said to depend on the tension between the two aspects it presents, but the tension can also seem to leave the poem troubled and unclear. The conclusion may be seen as a triumph of the spirit over grief and undisciplined wildness, a triumph of measure and faith. But in opposition is a sense that involved in measure, reason and perspective is a diminution of the sense of human sorrow, human dignity and of the truth of exper-ience; knowing and feeling are constrained by doctrine and belief. Hence the tragic and elegiac character of the poem: acceptance involves contempt for the world, which, to the modern reader at any rate, is an idea shot through with a poignant humiliation of human independence and individuality. Form and symbolism work at the level of the reader's perception of a complete movement round a moral circle; narrative and feeling work at the level of the Dreamer's confusions. One level operates within the poem's world, the other without.

The two elements of the combination are found, of course, in other medieval poems, but the particular quality of *Pearl*'s treat‑ment emerges clearly if one makes a comparison with such another work. In *Orpheus and Eurydice*, for example, Henryson tells, vividly and evocatively enough, the story of a lover seeking his lost love, and then adds his moral significance later, transforming the moving story into an allegory of reason's conflict with desire. The poet of *Pearl* attempts to make emotional narrative and allegory work together by fusion, rather than by dealing separately with the two aspects, producing what one reader may see as subtlety and another as a lack of explicitness and clarity. The lack of express directives to the reader in the detached, mediating voice of the poet leaves the relationship unresolved. However, only if one reads in a complex way, finding means by which the poem may simultaneously be experienced as a story of grief, adventure and discovery and as a patterned, allegorical meditation on linked themes does *Pearl* work If one rejects the double standards as too complex, then one has to accept that the poem is inconsistent and the work of a poet too ingenious and too complicated in outlook to reconcile the different impulses of his mind.

3. Purity

1. Introduction

It is easier to make up one's mind about the second of the four poems, *Purity* or *Cleanness*. It is an unsuccessful poem which contains some of the most powerful poetry composed by a Middle English poet. The power comes mainly from the poet's imaginative response to the three Old Testament narratives, the stories of the Flood, the destruction of the Cities of the Plain and Belshazzar's Feast, which he retells and expands. In the best parts of the poem is poetry of high seriousness, capable of involving, moving and surprising the reader. The elaboration of the Biblical stories shows an imagination which not only brings them to life, but also extends their range of feeling and meaning. The failure of *Purity* is a failure satisfactorily to integrate these vivid tales with one another and with the poem's framework, which consists of intermittent assertions of God's hatred of human impurity.

Since *Purity* is the least familiar of the four poems, I propose to begin with its positive qualities. Separating the tales from their contexts, as I intend to do, is no proper way of reading a poem and is, in a sense, prejudging the issue, but I find it impossible to view *Purity* as other than a composite work; its parts are linked consecutively, in the manner of a train whose compartments are hitched on to one another and given an over-all identity and purpose by having an engine on one end (the opening definition of the theme) and a guard's van at the other (the summary repetition of the theme at the close). My purpose in uncoupling the parts is to try to show what the poet actually does, rather than what he says he is doing. The few critics who have discussed the unity of *Purity* have been too ready to trust the teller rather than the tale and to assume that the poet's declared intention does actually define the poem's meaning and effect.[1] If we ignore that intention, for the moment, we are, I suggest, more likely accurately to perceive the character of the poet's art.

The basic facts about the text of *Purity* are as follows. It consists of 1812 unrhymed, alliterative long lines, possibly, unless the four-line marks in the manuscript are simply the copyist's way of keeping tally, meant to be read in groups of four lines at a time, though this division does not make much difference to the impression of the verse. The large initial capitals in the manuscript indicate only the broad division into three parts of roughly equal weight, each containing one of the Old Testament tales: 1–556, 557–1156, and 1157–812. Smaller capitals (three lines in depth as opposed to the eight at line 1 and the four at 557 and 1157) sub-divide the parts, showing the beginning of new phases within each section, at lines 125, 193, 249, 345, 485, 601, 689, 781, 893 and 1357. This sub-division is not consistently done, the sections getting longer as the poems proceeds, and editors have divided the text further; Menner divides the poem into eighteen sections. A division into parts according to the sense can be made in several ways, but the simplest way of understanding the structure is to recognise five homiletic and four narrative parts, as follows:

1. an introductory passage about the virtue of purity (1–48);
2. the parable of the Man without a Wedding Garment (49–160);
3. homiletic passage, including a brief presentation of God's punishment of Lucifer and Adam (161–248);
4. the Flood (249–540);
5. homiletic passage (541–600);
6. the destruction of Sodom and Gomorrah (601–1048);
7. homiletic passage, moving from one conception of impurity to another (1049–156);
8. Belshazzar's Feast (1157–804);
9. homiletic epilogue (1805–12).

2. The poet as teller of tales

The most striking instance of the poet's imaginative treatment of Biblical matter comes in the story of the Flood, where the anger of

God against the whole race of man is shown in terms which concentrate not on the just punishment of sin, but on the fear and resigned sorrow of man and the hapless terror of beasts, innocent victims of God's vengeance:

> The moste mountaynez on mor thenne watz no more dryye,
> And theron flokked the folke, for ferde of the wrake.
> Sythen the wylde of the wode on the water flette;
> Summe swymmed theron that save hemself trawed,
> Summe styye to a stud and stared to the heven,
> Rwly wyth a loud rurd rored for drede.
> Harez, herttez also, to the hyghe runnen,
> Bukkez, bausenez, and bulez to the bonkkez hyyed;
> And alle cryed for care to the Kyng of heven;
> Recoverer of the Creator thay cryed uch one.
>   That amounted the mase, his mercy watz passed,
> And alle his pyté departed fro peple that he hated.[2]
>   Bi that the flod to her fete flowed and waxed,
> Then uche a segge sey wel that synk hym byhoved.
> Frendez fellen in fere and fathmed togeder,
> To dryy her delful deystyne and dyyen alle samen.
> Luf lokez to luf and his leve takez,
> For to ende alle at onez and for ever twynne.   (385–402)

The dramatic irony of the contrast between a God activated by hatred and characterised as the one who 'amounted the mase' ('created the chaos'), and the plea of the desperate, who, too late, think of him as Creator and source of rescue, shows a bold imaginative grasp of emotional effect on the poet's part, a grasp evident too in the heart-wringing modulation into the present tense of 'Love looks to love'. The poet succeeds in arousing in the reader a common feeling with the damned, and so involves him in moral conflict, rather than offering him a simple illustration of a moral point. The sense of tragedy conveyed by these lines gives a bitter and satisfying irony to God's later words:

> 'For I se wel that hit is sothe, that alle mannez wyttez
> To unthryfte arn alle thrawen wyth thoght of her herttez,
> And ay hatz ben, and wyl be yet, fro her barnage:
> Al is the mynde of the man to malyce enclyned.'   (515–18)

Since in God's own acts there is 'malys mercyles', the distinction between man and God becomes a distinction between weakness and strength, rather than between evil and good. The undercurrent adds significance to God's promise to Noah, a promise which it has come to seem he owes, as repayment for the sorrow he has caused:

'Sesounez schal yow never sese of sede ne of hervest,
Ne hete, ne no harde frost, umbre ne droghthe,
Ne the swetnesse of somer, ne the sadde wynter,
Ne the nyght, ne the day, ne the newe yerez,
Bot ever renne restlez. Rengnez ye therinne!' (523–7)

The subtle combination in these lines of varied alliterative patterning, echoing of vowels, antithesis and balance of words and phrases, and a simple, timeless diction memorably intensifies the pledge that man shall know for ever the rhythmic succession of the seasons of time in their due order. In this epic narrative of the punishment of man's sin, it is God who learns, softens, forgives, recognising that the descendants of the man he has preserved will repeat the sins of the men he has destroyed. The medieval poet at every point intensifies the course of the working out of God's anger at man's impurity, from the condensed expression of the growth of sin, through the very simple characterisation of Noah, to the violence of the punishing tempest, in which the plight of the saved, tossing helplessly in the Ark, is realised as vividly as that of the doomed. Here the poet cleverly alternates a cluster of technical language with simpler diction describing the Ark's wayward course, showing the scene from the double point of view of Noah and his kin, suffering the chaos of the moment, and of an observer, seeing it as a picture; at the same time he shapes the syntax (in lines 421–3, particularly) to create irregular, onomatopoeic rhythms within the alliterative patterning of the lines:

The arc hoven watz on hyghe wyth hurlande gotez,
Kest to kythez uncouthe the clowdez ful nere.
Hit waltered on the wylde flod, went as hit lyste,
Drof upon the depe dam, in daunger hit semed.
Withouten mast, other myke, other myry bawelyne,
Kable other capstan to clyppe to her ankrez,
Hurrok other hande-helme hasped on rother,

Other any sweande sayl to seche after haven,
Bot flote forthe wyth the flyt of the felle wyndez.
Whederwarde so the water wafte, hit rebounde;
Ofte hit roled on rounde and rered on ende.
Nyf oure lorde hade ben her lodezmon,
                    hem had lumpen harde.
                                    (413–24)

In his clear, self-contained narrative, the poet at times follows
Genesis quite closely, though always intelligently judging the effect
of the material, expanding here, condensing there, fusing one
detail with another, selecting, re-ordering, consistently adding
vigour and precision. Anyone reading the account of the Flood
in *Purity* could have no doubt that here was a poet who, had he
had the literary tradition behind him, could have coped with the
great theme of Creation, Fall and Redemption in dignified, forceful
and varied verse. As it is, the tale is a piece of epic writing without
an epic context, a presentation of the ways of God to man where
God is the only individual force, and where the saved and the
destroyed are equally representative of the frailty of the human race.

Though in retelling the story of the destruction of Sodom and
Gomorrah the poet uses many of the same poetic devices, the effect
of the second Old Testament narrative is different. The focus
moves from the anger of God and the suffering of sinful man, to
the filth of sin itself and to the nature and actions of the few innocent
individuals caught up in a moral drama. Instead of the patterned
alternation between formal, divine speeches and panoramas of
destruction, sorrow and release, this tale is presented in terms of
dramatised scenes, each with precise setting, dialogue, tension,
naturalistic speech and reaction. The poet has moved from epic
sweep to novelistic intimacy. So God is no longer a voice from
nowhere but comes as a visitor to Abraham and eats his food; he
no longer sees all from an unplaced above, but sends two angels as
his messengers to spy on the men of Sodom. Where Noah is a
featureless recipient of God's commands, Abraham and Lot are
freer agents, who can discuss the situation with God and his
messengers, who can influence God, advise his angels, and choose
whether they obey or not. The reader's attention is directed to plot
and character, and the movement, by means of narrative, descrip-

tion and dialogue, towards the tale's dramatic climax and reflective epilogue.

The medieval poet is as skilful in the verse-novel as in epic, and never puts a foot wrong in his adaptation of *Genesis*, 18–19. He takes us directly into the first scene and, from the Bible's description of Abraham '*sedenti in ostio tabernaculi sui in ipso fervore diei*' ('and he sat in the tent door in the heat of the day'), creates the lovely scene of the meeting between Abraham and the three-fold God:

> Olde Abraham in erde onez he syttez
> Even byfore his hous-dore, under an oke grene.
> Bryght blykked the bem of the brode heven;
> In the hyghe hete therof Abraham bidez,
> He watz schunt to the schadow under schyre levez.
> Thenne watz he war on the waye of wlonk wyyes thrynne;
> If thay wer farande and fre and fayre to beholde
> Hit is ethe to leve by the last ende.
> For the lede that ther laye the levez anunder,
> When he hade of hem syght, he hyyes bylyve,
> And as to God the good mon gos hem agaynez,
> And haylsed hem in onhede . . .   (601–12)

Following *Genesis* the poet consistently adds animation and naturalistic detail: to Abraham's instructions to Sarah, to the hasty preparation and presentation of food, to Sarah's laughter at the thought that she should at her age bear a child, and to the laconic reaction of God, when she denies her mirth:

> 'Now innoghe, hit is not so', thenne nurned the Dryghtyn,
> 'For thou laghed alow, bot let we hit one.'   (669–70)

This indulgent tact is in tune with the intimate narrative, with its detailed depiction of objects and actions, and leads smoothly to God's revelation to Abraham of the purpose of his visit, and to the most forceful part of the episode, God's condemnation of the sin of the cities of the plain and Abraham's humble pleading for the salvation of the sinless. The poet's conception of this part of the tale as a dramatic scene is clear in the way that he creates a climax by intensifying the speeches of both. He elaborates God's explanation to Abraham by adding to his source a

substantial passage about perverse sexuality and natural sexual
love, a passage as remarkable for its passion as for its clear
presentation of God's hatred of unnatural vice:

'Thay han lerned a lyst that lykez me ille,
That they han founden in her flesch of fautez the werst.
Uch male matz his mach a man as hymselven,
And fylter folyly in fere on femmalez wyse.
I compast hem a kynde crafte and kende hit hem derne,
And amed hit in myn ordenaunce oddely dere,
And dyght drwry therinne, doole altherswettest,
And the play of paramores I portrayed myselven,
And made therto a maner myriest of other,
When two true togeder had tyyed hemselven,
Bytwene a male and his make such merthe schulde come,
Wel nyghe pure paradys moght preve no better,
Ellez thay moght honestly ayther other welde.
At a stylle stollen steven, unstered wyth syght,
Luf-lowe hem bytwene lasched so hote,
That alle the meschefez on mold moght hit not sleke.
Now haf thay skyfted my skyl and scorned nature,
And henttez hem in hethyng an usage unclene.
Hem to smyte for that smode smartly I thenk,
That wyyez schal be by hem war, worlde wythouten ende.'

(693–712)

The imagery and outspoken seriousness convey with striking
power the quality of sexual passion and the joys of the 'flame of
love', and truly have the effect of a revelation of God's inner
feeling and thought; his disgust at the scorning of nature provides,
more realistically than in the earlier tale, a just motivation for
punishment, and the passage gives the reader the sense of the
positive value of the rule of Nature, of the paradisal bliss of love
in an ordered, honest and modest human society. In response to
this, Abraham's pleas for the innocent are also given a more
individualised cast, both in the manner in which Abraham
speaks to God, mingling humility with a friendly reminder of
what is fitting for God, and in the addition of a specific prayer
for his kinsman, Lot.

With a neat transition, leaving Abraham in sorrow while the

Lord sends his spies to Sodom, the poet moves to his second act at
the house of Lot. The treatment remains naturalistic and dramatic, bringing out clearly what is only implied in the Old Testament and adding touches in many places which add to the logic
of the narrative. So the poet describes the beauty of the two angels,
and hence accounts for their sexual attractiveness to the men of
Sodom; he introduces at an early stage the daughters of Lot and
the legend of Lot's wife's salting of the food, so that their later
appearances in the story are prepared for; he puts into words
Lot's sense of shame at the lewd demands of the Sodomites.
Most effectively of all, he builds up the encounter at Lot's door
into a scene of vigorous speech and action, full of specific detail,
both in the dialogue and in the physical touches which create a
sense of place and of the movements of the characters. The poet's
dramatisation of the 'yestande sorwe' ('yeasty filth') of the men
of Sodom not only makes the events seem tense and real, but again
strengthens the motivation and the moral basis of the tale. This is
true also of the least acceptable element, Lot's offer of his daughters,
which the poet inherits from his source. Lot's pimp-like praise of
their virgin ripeness serves, in context, both to demonstrate a
plausible, pliant courtesy in Lot and the extremity to which his
protection of his guests will stretch, and to re-assert the prefer-
ability, even at this expense, of natural to unnatural sex.

The third scene is the escape of Lot and his daughters and the
destruction of the cities of the plain. The account of the destruction
is nearest to the epic style of the Flood, for obvious reasons.
Alliterative poets always take the chance of elaborating a storm
scene and always do storms well. The heavy emphasis of the
rhythmic repetition of sound and a traditional set of words and
phrases give a ready-made surety of, at least, poetic adequacy.
However the passage here is no collection of alliterative storm-
clichés, for this is no ordinary storm; the towers of cloud, the
shower of flakes of fire and sulphur coming down as through a
sieve, the rain which paradoxically roasts and burns, all have the
necessary unusualness, and the climax of the passage makes
striking use of personification and imagery:

> For when that the Helle herde the houndez of heven
> He watz ferlyly fayn, unfolded bylyve.

The grete barrez of the abyme he barst up at onez,
That alle the regioun torof in riftes ful grete,
And cloven alle in lyttel cloutes the clyffez aywhere,
As lance levez of the boke that lepes in twynne. (961-6)

This strong evocation of the powers of heaven and hell uniting,
and adding earthquake from below to burning eruption from
above, shows the poet at his most majestic, but he manages not
to disrupt the intimate narrative style of the rest, since the passage
is sandwiched between Lot's departure with his wife and daughters and their terrified hearing of the cataclysm, as Lot and his
daughters run unlooking away and Lot's wife glances over her
left shoulder and remains a salt stone for the beasts of the field to
lick. The destruction, that is, is presented to us still with reference to the individual characters, and it seems in the spirit of
completing this personalised plot, as well as returning to the point
from which he began, that the poet should follow the Bible and
move from the safety of Lot and the punishment of his wife, back
to the distance from which Abraham looks towards the plain and
sees the devastation:

He sende toward Sodomas the syght of his yyen,
That ever had ben an erde of erthe the swettest,
As aparaunt to paradis that plantted the Dryghtyn;
Now is hit plunged in a pit like of pich fylled. (1005-8)

In the epilogue which rounds off the section this cheerless
scene is turned into explicit symbolism, with the poet's intelligent
adaptation of Mandeville's description of the desolation of the
Dead Sea, its barren bitterness, its legends of death, its contradiction of the laws of nature, and, most suggestively of all, its ashy
fruits.

Whereas the Flood displays the poet's response to the noble
themes of universal punishment and divine repentance, the
effectiveness of the story of the fall of Sodom and Gomorrah
depends upon a different kind of response and creative power.
Here is a dramatic, well-shaped narrative, treating events of
remote history with lively naturalism in scenes of intimacy, and
with poetic sensitivity and originality in those moments when
divine anger is explained and enacted. The moral dimension of

the tale is not asserted but rather shown through speech, action and imagery, in the humility of Abraham, in the courtesy and shame of Lot, in the intimate gravity of God's tone to Abraham, as well as in the violent lewdness of the men of Sodom. Though caught up in extraordinary events, the characters are treated with believable naturalism. The combination in Abraham of meek service to his lord and loving, righteous concern for justice and family, and in Lot of confused honesty and desperation show a sure touch on the poet's part, and he is as sure with the super/ natural figures and the minor characters.

The tale is expertly structured. Its three scenes show the three stages of God's thought and action, suspicion, certainty and con/ sequent punishment, and, at the same time, the three stages in Lot's situation, fear for him and for any innocent, demonstration of his adherence to natural law and of his obedience, and, finally, his fearful preservation. At the level of image and symbol the tale moves from the peaceful wholesomeness of the moment when Abraham meets God beneath the shadowing trees to the sterile devastation of the burned plain. As the men of Sodom have scorned nature and destroyed the paradisal love between man and woman, so the defiance of gravity and of natural sweetness and the ashy fruits of the Dead Sea have replaced the fertile beauty of the Eden/like region. Lifted from its context this is a superb verse/ novel.

The main reason for the variation in narrative manner between the two sections is to be found in the poet's source/material. Indeed, each of the four narratives in *Purity* has its own character/ istic tone, largely because each represents a different type of scrip/ tural writing. The destruction of Sodom is one of the primitive episodes from early accounts of the establishment of the Jewish law, with characteristic anthropomorphism and dramatic inci/ dent, as in the related episode of Abraham and Isaac. The Flood is part of the more intellectually conceived compilation of univer/ sal myths about the creation of the world and the beginnings of mankind. Belshazzar's Feast is part of the chronicles and pro/ phecies of much later Jewish history, which mingle accounts of dynasties and conquests with zeal for the survival of the Jewish race and faith. The parable is representative of the Evangelists' use of illustrative, allegorical fictions for the purpose of teaching. It is one tendency of medieval English poetry, particularly of the alliterative school, to realise its source-material: that is, to introduce or to expand detail which is realistic, pictorial and sensory. Many passages in *Purity* could be cited as examples. But what is surprising in *Purity* is that its tales so remarkably demonstrate the poet's response to the *varying* qualities of their scriptural antecedents.

So his treatment of the Flood remains intellectual and formalised. The poet does not, as he well might have done, give any personality to Noah, or show any leaning towards the 'homely realism' with which Noah the boat-builder, Noah the hen-pecked husband, Noah the simple, honest man rising to the challenge of unique experience, and so on, was endowed by medieval carvers, painters and dramatists. Nor does he, on the other hand, turn the tale into a medieval abstraction by drawing the parallel, as did many a commentator on Scripture, between the preservation of Noah and the Redemption: that is, he is no more inclined to allegorise the tale than he is to naturalise it. What he does do is to realise and interpret the ideas involved in the myth. He does this in two main ways. First he concentrates on the mind of God and compares his treatment of the sins of Lucifer, whom he punished 'In the mesure of his mod' (215), and of Adam, where the vengeance was made 'Al in mesure and methe' (247), with the third punishment, in which 'ther watz malys mercyles' (250). From this he creates a plot in the movement of God's mind from fury, through merciless cruelty, to a rueful recovery of his Measure, recognition of man's weakness, and a repentant promise never again to let loose such wholesale destruction and slaughter:

> For quen the swemande sorwe soght to his hert,
> He knyt a covenaunde cortaysly wyth mankynde there,
> In the mesure of his mode and methe of his wylle,
> That he schulde never, for no syt, smyte al at onez.
>
> (563–6)

Secondly he interprets and extends the legend by applying his poetic, realising gifts to a demonstration of the turbulence unleashed by God's destructive use of the powers of Nature and the horror of universal fear when 'noght dowed bot the deth in the depe stremez' (374). The pity which the poet evokes for the doomed, and even for the preserved, expands the reader's sense of the myth, enlists his sympathy and judgement against God, and encourages a sense of approval at the moral growth in God's nature which his covenant with Noah displays. The poet does not get involved in individual human reactions and character/istics, but remains concerned with general issues, and super/human thoughts and actions, investing the unknowable with qualities which stretch the imagination, and yet which remain within the boundaries fixed by our knowledge of the story and its status as historical and scriptural 'truth'.

In contrast the story of Sodom is realistic and circumstantial. Its structure is determined not by the poet's perception of an arc of moral development in the tale, but by its incidents and scenes. Here the reader is asked to respond to particular moments and feelings, even to minor ones such as Sarah's irreverent mirth and the sullen pigheadedness of Lot's wife. Though the destruction is as violent as the earlier flood, it is a particular, local punishment, not universal cataclysm. Even the addition of apocryphal inci/dent to the tale is characteristic of the difference from the treatment of the Flood: whereas there the additions (the story of Lucifer's fall, the treachery of the raven) are thematic, pointing to the mentality of God and to a symbolic contrast between the black bird feeding on the dead and the white bird bringing promise of new life, the main addition to the story of Sodom (the legend of Lot's wife's putting salt in the angels' food) is particularising, at the level of domestic incident and the contrast of attitudes in Lot's house. Again the poet seems to have responded intelligently and imaginatively to the tone as well as the narrative pattern in the Vulgate. The poet is, in this particular respect, an example of the chameleon artist who takes his colour from his source, and, most remarkably in a medieval poem of this kind, does not dye his source/material to fit into a pattern; he allows the matter to have, and even augments, its own quality of life, and to exist as an independent unit within the larger work.

The story of Belshazzar's Feast, the longest of the narratives, is an example of what one may call romance/chronicle. It presents an elaborate and exotic, supernatural scene within a framework of complicated historical incident. In the English poem the sequence is a composite one, in two related ways. First, the poet has worked together passages from different parts of the Old Testament: *2 Chronicles* 36, *Jeremiah* 52 (and *2 Kings* 24–5), and *Daniel* 1, 4 and 5. Secondly, this amalgam contains different aspects. The historical aspect consists of accounts of bloody warfare as first Jerusalem, under its king Zedekiah, is besieged and captured by Nebuchadnezzar, and then Babylon, ruled by Belshazzar, is captured by Darius, King of the Medes. A providential aspect gives us the confusing view of both conquests as directed by God's punishment of idolatry. A reverential aspect is present in the story of the fate of the holy vessels of the temple of Jerusalem and of the prophet Daniel, both captured by Nebuchadnezzar's captain, Nebuzaradan, both, in a sense, treasured during Nebuchadnezzar's reign, and both brought out to satisfy the whims of his successor, Belshazzar. The dramatic scene of the profanation of the vessels and the interpretation by Daniel of the minatory writing on the wall is the part most relevant to *Purity*'s theme of God's punishment of impurity—here the impurity of desecration—but, though the reader may feel that the poet would have been wiser to go straight to the heart of the matter and begin with Belshazzar, he seems again to think of the narrative as a whole and not primarily of its illustration of an idea. So he supplies the background and accepts the chronicle manner, with its providential overtones, from *Chronicles* and *Kings/Jeremiah* until he reaches the feast, when he passes to the later scriptural book of *Daniel*. *Daniel* is romantic and prophetic in matter and manner, with its accounts of apocalyptic dreams, its exotic, dramatic tales of Nebuchadnezzar's golden image, of Shadrach, Meshach and Abednego and the burning, fiery furnace, of the madness of Nebuchadnezzar, and of Daniel in the den of lions. The English poet responds accordingly.

As an adaptation this part of *Purity* is ambitious and professional. Following the *Kings/Jeremiah* account of the siege of Jerusalem the poet neatly introduces, in their logical place, details from elsewhere: from *2 Chronicles* 36 he adds material about Zedekiah's rebellion against Nebuchadnezzar; from *Daniel* 1 he identifies the prisoners taken by Nebuzaradan; from Jerome, or some intermediary, he adds the explanation that Nebuchadnezzar was not punished for taking the holy vessels because he revered them

and placed them in his treasury. He makes a smooth transition to
the feast of Belshazzar by emphasising the influence of Daniel on
Nebuchadnezzar, giving, on the basis of the last sentence of
Daniel 4, a brief account of Nebuchadnezzar's death, and
characterising Belshazzar, with among other things, details from
the later parts of *Daniel* 5 and from comments in *Jeremiah* on the
worship of false gods. The feast itself is a vastly expanded version
of *Daniel* 5, drawing on Mandeville for details of the adornment
of the holy vessels, and again showing literary and logical intelligence in its exclusions, particularly of Daniel's initial rejection
of Belshazzar's reward, and its relevant use of details from elsewhere (the introduction of Nebuzaradan's name in the queen's
reminder of Daniel's capture, and the amplification of Daniel's
reference to Nebuchadnezzar's transformation by elements
postponed from *Daniel* 4). The tale is an excellent demonstration
of the poet's technical competence as an adaptor and translator,
full of evidence of working directly from his sources, thinking
about them, dovetailing details from separate places, giving them
an over-all narrative shape and keeping in the reader's mind
the aspects that he wants to emphasise.

But is technical competence enough? The intractable dullness
of the events in the siege of Jerusalem seems to lay a leaden weight
on the only part of this narrative that kindles the imagination of
poet and reader, the feast itself. In the earlier part the poet keeps
trying, rather too obviously, to give the material some bite. He
tries the sharpening effect of oxymoron as he shows God helping
the heathen Chaldeans to conquer the land of the true faith:

> And thay forloyne her fayth and folwed other goddes,
> And that wakned his wrath and wrast hit so hyghe,
> That he fylsened the faythful in the falce lawe
> To forfare the falce in the faythe trwe.   (1165–8)

This sort of verbal ingenuity draws too much attention to itself.
He tries to enliven the account of the siege and conquest by expanding the details of fighting, famine and bloodshed:

> Nabizardan noght forthy nolde not spare,
> Bot bede al to the bronde under bare egge;
> Thay slowen of swettest semlych burdes,

Bathed barnes in blod and her brayn spylled,
Prestes and prelates thay presed to dethe,
Wyves and wenches her wombes tocorven
That her boweles outborst aboute the diches,
And al watz carfully kylde that thay cach myght.

(1245-42)

This vaguely arouses sympathy for the defeated and condemnation
of wanton cruelty in the conquerors, but eventually the passage
seems gratuitous since neither the pity nor the condemnation is
developed by later events. Similarly the poet elaborates the list
of the holy relics. His most effective device is repeatedly to put into
antithesis the present and the past and to point the sudden reversals
of fortune; about this I shall have more to say below. In spite of
these rhetorical flourishes the introductory part of the story remains competent, pains-taking and dull.

After nearly two hundred lines of this journeyman stuff,
the poet passes to the material from *Daniel*, and his greater response
to the romantic narrative is apparent from the start, in his invention, as introduction to the feast, of a sketch of the character of
Belshazzar:

Bot honored he not Hym that in heven wonies,
Bot fals fantummes of fendes, formed with hondes,
Wyth tool out of harde tre, and telded on lofte,
And of stokkes and stones he stoute goddes callz
When thay are gilde al with golde and gered wyth sylver,
And there he kneles and callez, and clepes after help.
And thay reden him ryght, rewarde he hem hetes,
And if thay gruchen him his grace to gremen his hert,
He cleches to a gret klubbe and knokkes hem to peces.
Thus in pryde and olipraunce his empyre he haldes,
In lust and in lecherye, and lothelych werkkes;
And hade a wyf for to welde, a worthelych quene,
And mony a lemman, never the later, that ladis wer called.
In the clernes of his concubines and curious wedez,
In notyng of nwe metes and of nice gettes,
Al watz the mynde of that man on misschapen thinges,
Til the Lorde of the lyfte liste his abate. (1340-56)

This passage shows three of the poet's skills working in harmony together. First, he has intelligently selected suggestions from various parts of the Bible to build up a picture of Belshazzar's nature and idolatry, extrapolating details from his behaviour at the feast, from Daniel's subsequent reproof, and from Jeremiah's prophecies of punishment for the idolatry of Babylon (especially Chapter 50 where specific comparison with Sodom and Gomorrah is made). Secondly, he connects Belshazzar with other examples of uncleanness by portraying him as a man who, like the men before the Flood, like the men of Sodom, perverts nature and the forms which God has created. Thirdly, he finds vivid phrases and images, with suggestive physical detail, which project the type of man he has perceived in the tale; his instances illustrate in a sharply focused, condensed way Belshazzar's idolatry, waywardness, violence, lust and decadent, jaded appetites. Portrayals of tyrants in romances and of Herod in drama may have provided some suggestions.

With this characterisation the narrative begins to come to some sort of life, and it becomes obvious that what had attracted the poet to this story was the opportunity it offered for the creation of a scene of magnificent splendour, with a display of objects and attitudes heightened and exaggerated, animated by a satisfying current of emotion from boastful luxury and pride, through fear and rage to moral rectitude and retribution. From one point of view, it is pure Hollywood, with fine opportunities for the art-director and parts for a young Donald Wolfit, Charlton Heston and some bosomy specialist in abused queens. This is not said in denigration; the feast is patently and enjoyably melodramatic and sensational. From four verses in *Daniel* 5 the poet creates, by colourful expansion, lines 1357–1528. First he builds up anticipation of the feast, describing the guests invited, the stronghold of Babylon (whose medieval curtain-wall is an obvious example of the medieval romance-writer's heightening by anachronism) and the assembling in the hall. Then the food enters, on horseback, on richly decorated platters, with flourishes of music and banners. The narrative moves with swift precision through Belshazzar's drunken dotage and his command that the holy vessels be brought forth, to the next feast of description, the vessels themselves. The history of the vessels is obligatory but lacks the impact of the subsequent massing together of details of rich materials and fine workmanship, with ornamentation of leaves and branches, birds in the branches, and flowers and fruit made of exotic jewels:

> For alle the blomes of the boghes wer blyknande perles,
> And alle the fruyt in tho formes of flaumbeande gemmes,
> And safyres, and sardiners, and semely topace,
> Alabaunderynes, and amaraunz, and amaffised stones,
> Casydoynes, and crysolytes, and clere rubies,
> Penitotes and pynkardines, ay perles bitwene. (1467–72)

The rich adornment in the description as a whole borrows some of its glory, such as the artificial birds, from Mandeville's accounts of the wonders of the palace of the Great Chan and of the land of Prester John. The resonant embellishing of the verse with exotic words and images leads to a fine crescendo of emphasis on the holy use for which the vessels were intended and the horror of the sacrilege, which is brought sharply to the reader by bathos:

> Now a boster on benche bibbes thereof,
> Tyl he be dronkken as the devel, and dotes ther he syttes.
>
> (1499–1500)

As Belshazzar cries 'Weghe wyn in this won –Wassayl!', into the feast, as into the more genial banquet in *Sir Gawain*, stalks supernatural horror, here from the start in the form of a severed limb, and the poet follows *Daniel* in not making it clear until later that the hand comes from God, concentrating on the visual manifestation and the terror it causes. Belshazzar's fear, then his rage at the inability of his wise men to understand the writing, and the pompous proclamation of reward for the man who can interpret lead to another climax of massed, exotic words, this time a list of interpreters, also ending in anti-climax.

The latter part of the tale is dominated by Daniel's long speech (lines 1642–1740) of reproof and interpretation, the dramatic interest of which is increased by the inclusion of the story of Nebuchadnezzar's pride and punishment. There are again echoes here of the mystery plays in the king's boasts:

> 'I am God of the grounde, to gye as me lykes,
> As he that hyghe is in heven his aungeles that weldes.'
>
> (1663–4)

God's curse, however, has even greater dramatic force:

'Now is alle thy pryncipalté past at ones,
And thou, remued fro monnes sunes, on mor most abide,
And in wasturne walk, and wyth the wylde dowelle,
As best byte on the bent of braken and erbes,
Wyth wrothe wolfes to won and wyth wylde asses.'
(1672–6)

The 'mad', transformed Nebuchadnezzar is brilliantly visualised,
by a massing together of grotesque physical detail and effective
imagery, as the product of some hideous miscegenation of cow
and bird of prey: the ingenious inventiveness of the poet goes
far beyond what was needed to make the moral point that 'Thus
he countes hym a kow that watz a kyng ryche.' The horrific
humbling sends its force through the rest of Daniel's reproof to
Belshazzar, for his 'bobaunce', 'blasfayme' and 'frothande
fylthe', and echoes in the closing words of the interpretation of the
writing, as Belshazzar, like Nebuchadnezzar, is told:

Departed is thy pryncipalté, depryved thou worthes,
Thy rengne rafte is the fro . . .   (1738–9)

All that remains is the fulfilment of the prophecy, atmospherically
developed by description of the dark night in which Darius and
his army deal to Belshazzar a fitting end:

Baltazar in his bed watz beten to dethe,
That bothe his blod and his brayn blende on the clothes;
The kyng in his cortyn watz kaght bi the heles,
Feryed out bi the fete, and fowle dispysed.
That watz so doghty that day and drank of the vessayl,
Now is a dogge also dere that in a dych lygges. (1787–92)

Despite the longueurs of its historical introduction, the tale of
Belshazzar's Feast eventually works well enough, though in ways
which, by comparison with the earlier Old Testament tales,
seem at times crude, even vulgar. Here we have a conception of
action as pageant and of character as a series of attitudes and
gestures. So the 'bolde Baltasar', the 'boster on benche', with his
decadent seeking after new thrills, is represented in a succession

of exaggerated postures of pride, drunken boast and folly, fear and anger. He is pictured as invaded by surges of emotion:

> Thenne a dotage ful depe drof to his hert (1425)

and

> Such a dasande drede dusched to his hert,
> That al falewed his face and fayled the chere . . . (1538–9)

The suggestion that the feeling is born outside him and then animates his puppet nature effectively conveys the instability and essential nonentity of the figure. The degraded corpse, dragged in a curtain by its heels, belongs to the same world of reversals of for﹨ tune and emblematic tableaux. The other characters are even more obviously pasteboard and functions of the plot; Daniel and the queen are wheeled on at the appropriate moments, utter, and are wheeled off again. Such a conception of the characters is, however, consistent with the style of the whole; any depth of portrayal or suggestion of complexity and continuity of motive would conflict with the essentially arbitrary nature of the world which they inhabit.

The arbitrary quality, which is one of the features that identify romance, is present not only in the galvanised actions of the charac﹨ ters. This part of *Purity* makes particularly frequent use of the sudden reversal, as Spearing points out; he says, 'the very texture of the narrative evokes a world in which sudden reversals of fortune are the common order of things'.[3] The tale begins in paradox with God's direction of the heathen conquest of the faithless city of faith, and presents examples of degradation in terms of antithesis of what was and what is, at regular intervals through the tale. So the Jewish prisoners

> sytte in servage and syte, that sumtyme wer gentyle;
> Now ar chaunged to chorles, and charged wyth werkkes,
> Bothe to cayre at the kart and the kuy mylke,
> That sumtyme sete in her sale syres and burdes. (1257–60)

In similar terms the poet describes the capture of the holy vessels by Nebuzaradan (1285–6), the death of Nebuchadnezzar (1329–32), the degradation of the vessels (1444–50 and 1497–1500), the madness of Nebuchadnezzar (1685) and Belshazzar's end (1791-2, quoted above); there are several other passages, particularly in Daniel's speech, which make us conscious of the transience of glory, the debasement of what was great and the folly of pride.

I find it difficult to agree with the implications of Spearing's comment on these reversals, however: 'Such reversals are ultimately the work of God, the manifestation of his power.'[4] He sees more sense of purpose in this patterning than is really apparent as one reads. The reversals indeed seem indirectly to work against any sense of an intelligent power, by cumulatively building up a world of instability and chance, in which kings can become cows and imprisoned Jewish prophets princes in the twinkling of an eye. God's own ways do not appear very different from those ascribed by Daniel to Nebuchadnezzar:

> Who so wolde wel do, wel hym bityde.
> And quos deth so he dezyre, he dreped als fast.
> Who so hym lyked to lyft, on lofte watz he sone.
> And quo so hym lyked to lay, watz lowed bylyve.
>
> (1647-50)

Within the confines of the tale the poet does not invite us to judge God's actions, however, nor to apply logic to them. What we are invited to do is to accept the arbitrariness of fortune and action as the quality of the world in which unstable, mortal kings exist, and to sit back and watch, with appropriate feelings of wonder and horror, a series of tableaux in which history is seen as a rising and falling of kings, and where kings themselves are presented in postures of pomp and pride on the one hand and humiliation on the other. The four kings involved in the tale are all presented in the traditional symbolic position of power. Zedekiah, who 'sete on Salamones solie, on solemne wyse', is succeeded by Nebuchadnezzar, 'noble in his chayer', Belshazzar 'dressed upon dece' on a bejewelled throne, and 'Dere Daryous that day dyght upon trone'. The first three are all degraded, both by being deprived of their kingdoms and by death, and, though Nebuchadnezzar is allowed to die in peace after recovering God's favour, death is still presented as a bringing-down of pride:

> Bot al drawes to dyye wyth doel upon ende;
> Bi a hathel never so hyghe, he heldes to grounde.

And so Nabugodenozar, as he nedes moste,
For alle his empire so highe, in erthe is he graven.

(1329–32)

Darius, triumphant at the end, waits his bringing-down, but the narrative implies that it will come. The pattern impresses us less with the power of God to bring about such falls, than with the waste and meaninglessness of it all, if we are unwise enough to pursue the thought that far.

The poet's conception of human actions as ritualised gestures and arbitrary shifts is of a piece, too, with the importance of description in the tale, the halts in the action while objects are richly depicted, and the consequent emphasis on static effects and surfaces. Even the descriptive methods themselves make, at times, a very superficial appeal to eye and ear, depending rather on the reader's stock response to grouped images of a traditional, alliterative type. I would again, as with the melodramatic action and the two-dimensional characters, defend this as appropriate to the poet's choice of style. Spearing says of the jewelled description of the holy vessels, quoted earlier, that 'this then degenerates into a mere catalogue'.[5] But are catalogues always mere? It depends what they are catalogues of, to some extent, and where they occur. Lists of words as beautiful in themselves and referring to objects as beautiful as *alabaunderynes, casydoynes, peritotes,* and *pynkardines,* or later, as beautiful and baleful as *sathrapas, walkyries, devinores of demorlaykes, sorzers* and *exorsismus,* are very different from the catalogues of the gold hair, white and red cheeks, small waists etc., of medieval heroines. The exotic quality of such words gives them in themselves emotional overtones, and piling them together suggests endless richnesses of the beautiful and strange, to be wondered at, or shuddered from, or in their turn degraded. Obviously the poet cannot work by lists alone, and the longer such lists are, beyond a certain point, the less effect they are likely to have, but in combination with other descriptions, such as those of the ornamentation and workmanship of the vessels, they work well to create for the voyeur-reader a picture of accumulated wonder and unreality.

I suggest, for these various reasons, that the tale of Belshazzar's Feast was seen by the poet as romance-chronicle in kind and that he consciously applied to it the treatment which such a kind demanded, focusing the reader's attention on the ups and downs of fortune, violent extremes and excesses of character and action, and rich, visually detailed pictures of objects and scenes of heightened unreality. So the hideous butchery and pillage of the conquest of Jersualem, as Nebuchadnezzar has Zedekiah's sons killed before his eyes and plucks out Zedekiah's eyes, as Nebu-zaradan spills children's brains and women's bowels, strikes off the heads of priests and loots the temple, occur at the same moral level as Belshazzar's lusts, rages and drunken dotage, Nebu-chadnezzar's vainglory, Darius' slaughter of Belshazzar, and the appearance of the supernatural hand. In descriptive terms the intricate elaboration of the dishes with their over-arching pergolas of paper on which food for the feast appears has as much beauty as the elaborate decoration of the holy vessels. This is a style of writing which levels things and creates a world in which any-thing can happen. The angle of vision is such that, as we read the tale, it does not seem impossible that Belshazzar should be converted and repent and become an example of a different sort of melodramatic reversal, except that the material is 'historical' and that such speculation is held in check by our knowledge of the outcome. It is as difficult for such a narrative to make serious moral points as it is, for example, for Beaumont and Fletcher's type of tragi-comedy where it is the play's aim to wring the last drop of emotional blood from the teetering piquancy of the con-trived situations, precisely because distinctions are blurred by the extremes of feeling and style. The vision of the hand lacks the awesome force it ought to have, for the poem's theme, because it seems no more strange than the other moments and actions in the tale; it is presented as a 'grand guignol' object stimulating horror and fear. The beauty and splendour of the vessels do not distin-guish them in aesthetic or moral terms from the other splendid objects—the stronghold itself and the unsanctified dishes. The hand is one manifestation of the expected poetic justice which rounds off the tale, and the vessels one manifestation of power and riches.

The conception of God in the tale is as a *deus ex machina*, a manipulator of men, whose ends justify his means. The means are as arbitrary as those of Nebuchadnezzar, as the poet shows by expanding the consequences of the conquest of Jerusalem, performed by Nechuchadnezzar, instigated by God. That God should later be sickened by heathen lips touching a holy cup, after contemplating, presumably with righteous satisfaction or at least equanimity, the sadistic slaughter of the priests and virgins of the temple, displays as precious a scale of values as that of Belshazzar, but the end, the quelling of idolatry, is all. God's purpose receives fitting emphasis in Daniel's speech, particularly with the vivid narrative of the humbling of Nebuchadnezzar, and the tale ends, as brutally as it began, with another salutary and purificatory letting of blood. The conception of God and of the narrative as a whole, as with the tales of the Flood and of Sodom and Gomorrah, shows the poet working within the confines of his selected episode, and developing a style appropriate for its particular events, rather than appropriate to the illustrative pur, pose for which it is professedly told.

The three Old Testament tales make up almost all the narrative in *Purity*, and account for more than three-quarters of the poem as a whole, and the poet regards them, as his epilogue makes clear, as his three illustrations of God's punishment of impurity. The variety of style, tone and thought in the three demonstrates the wide range of the poet's competence and his ability to respond to the qualities of differently conceived narratives, but it will by now be obvious that my view of these differences among the tales is that they create problems for the reader and, more particularly, that the poet's response to the quality of the individual tale gives each story an independence of its surroundings, even to the extent of conflicting with its context. The reader's problems and the poet's conflicts are at their most extreme in the first, the shortest and the least clearly characterised of the narratives, the parable of the Wedding-Feast, which is told less as an example than as a development of the introductory presentation of the idea that God is offended by moral filth.

The story is introduced through the imagery of clothing, seen as representative of man's spiritual state; in his role of homilist, the poet advises us:

Forthy hyy not to heven in haterez totorne,
Ne in the harlatez hod and handez unwaschen.

For what urthly hathel that hygh honor haldez
Wolde lyke if a ladde com lytherly attyred,
When he were sette solempnely in a sete ryche,
Abof dukez on dece, wyth dayntys served—
Then the harlot wyth haste helded to the table
Wyth rent cokrez at the kne, and his clutte traschez,
And his tabarde totorne, and his totez oute,
Other ani on of alle thyse, he schulde be halden utter,
With mony blame, ful bygge a boffet, peraunter,
Hurled to the halle-dore and harde theroute schowved,
And be forboden that borghe to bowe thider never,
On payne of enprysonment and puttyng in stokkez . . .

(33–46)

This lively, cogent passage, with a relevant illustrative narrative told in the compressed manner of a passing instance and yet with striking detail and all the essentials for the reader to imagine the dramatic scene, is the best example of narrative used to make a point in the whole poem. It is based on a readily appreciable, social image which is also traditional. Matthew's parable of the man without a wedding garment is implicit in the passage and all the qualities of the parable are preserved: simple, effective symbol-ism and angry revulsion, natural if intemperate, project the mind in the right moral direction. The parable, which is a type of imagery, has been transformed into the imagery of a dramatised instance; it has been absorbed and recreated by the poet. The only trouble is that the poet has composed this passage as an introduc-tion to a full narration of the parable itself, which becomes, as far as the argument of the poem goes, completely redundant; all that needs saying for the theme of God's rejection of the unclean has been said.

This might be seen simply as evidence of unsure workman-ship. At first sight the poet seems to have attempted a natural introduction to his first exemplum, and to have overdone it by conveying the idea before the tale which was supposed to embody it. Didactic writers are liable to over-emphasis and many medieval writers treat their audience as nitwits, but concessions to the slow-witted, unfortunately necessary in a prose sermon, are not acceptable in an alliterative poet, whose choice of form indicates that he is not merely dealing out our weekly dose of moral improvement. But is this a case of such over-insistence? Elsewhere the poet avoids repetition: he cuts out repetitive verses from the account of the Flood in *Genesis*, for instance; even when he has to repeat ideas in the transitions from one tale to the next he finds varied ways of expressing them, and the same is true of the series of Abraham's pleas to God for the salvation of fifty, forty-five, forty, thirty, twenty and ten possibly righteous men in the cities of the plain. It seems doubtful, therefore, that the poet was merely hammering home his point, more likely that he has more complex aims in juxtaposing a homiletic statement of the idea of the parable and the parable itself.[6] The 'introduction' is a complete, though condensed, statement of an illustrative example. The succeeding parable is a parallel treatment of the same idea which suggests to the reader, at this early stage of the poem, that narrative and homily are separate. The differences between homiletic use of narrative and narrative for its own sake emerge clearly from a comparison of the prologue with the story itself; the poet's treatment of the tale introduces confusions which the summary does not indicate.

The conflicts within the story are produced by the poet's decision to combine two versions of the parable, the story of the supper which, after the refusal of the first-invited guests, was offered to the poor, the maimed, the halt and the blind, taken from *Luke* 14, and the longer tale, from *Matthew* 22, which adds the rejection from the feast of the man without a wedding garment. In outline this sounds characteristic of a careful poet who, as in his version of Belshazzar's Feast, seeks out the various relevant parts of the Bible in search of comprehensiveness of view and fullness of detail. In the part of the parable which the two evangelists have in common there are obvious places where one supplements the other. In particular, Matthew says of the guests who refuse to come to the feast:

> . . . they made light of it and went their ways, one to his farm, another to his merchandise.

Luke is more specific:

> And they all with one consent began to make excuse. The first said unto him, 'I have bought a piece of ground, and I

must go and see it: I pray thee have me excused.' And another said, 'I have bought five yoke of oxen, and I go to prove them: I pray thee have me excused.' And another said, 'I have married a wife, and therefore I cannot come.'

The poet naturally takes the livelier, fuller version of Luke and with it Luke's conception of the guests as wrong but observing the outward forms of politeness. So he rejects Matthew's state-ment that others of the invited scorned and killed the servants who came to bid them to the feast, and the subsequent wrath of the lord, which leads to his armies killing the unwilling guests and destroying their city. The poet seems to be deliberately expanding the tale by his combination but he is, at this point, making choices between the two versions and not just adding one to the other. He also, as one would expect, makes his own elaborations, as in the speech of the lord at the beginning, where Matthew's 'my oxen and my fatlings are killed and all things are ready' becomes:

> 'For my boles and my borez arn bayted and slayne,
> And my fedde foulez fatted wyth sclaght,
> My polyle that is penne-fed and partrykez bothe,
> Wyth scheldez of wylde swyn, swanez and cronez—
> Al is rotheled and rosted ryght to the sete;
> Comez cof to my corte, er hit colde worthe.'   (55–60)

Such amplificatory treatment is lively and attractive enough, but further consideration suggests that it is contrary to the spirit of parable, the allegorical interpretation of which depends upon a simple narrative outline; the more detailed and realistic the telling becomes, the less it works as parable, since the allegory gets embroiled in irrelevancies. The poet's method is that of a man more interested in imagining the fictional situation than in moral or doctrinal meanings, but that in itself would not complicate the tale so much, were it not for the fact that Luke's version of the parable has a different meaning from that given by Matthew. *Luke* 14 concentrates on Christ's teaching of two ideas: first, that 'whoever exalteth himself shall be abased and he that humbleth himself shall be exalted' and secondly, that 'whoever he be of you

that forsaketh not all that he hath, he cannot be my disciple.'
After two exhortations teaching humility, that one should take
the lowest seat at a feast and that one should offer hospitality to
those too poor to pay it back, Christ uses a third supper to make
a bridge between the idea of humility and his second theme; so
the lord who bids his servants invite the poor, maimed, halt and
blind to his table is connected to the preceding instance of generous hospitality, and the behaviour of the invited guests, too
bound up in their worldly concerns to come to the feast, leads to
the succeeding idea that one must give up all personal and
worldly consideration to follow Christ. This is *why* Luke is so
specific about the refusals, since they demonstrate the kinds of
concern which must be abandoned. Luke's story thus expresses
two desirable qualities: the need for humble generosity to the
poor is expressed through the openness of the feast to all; the
exclusion of those who will not subdue their own concerns
expresses the need to give up all for Christ. Both refer implicitly
to the kingdom of heaven.

Matthew's version concentrates on the idea of worthiness for
the feast (so the first bidden are slain as unworthy), and fitness to
partake of it (so the man in foul clothes is punished). The parable
is explicitly about the kingdom of heaven and the sequence of
thought is mainly exclusive in nature, leading to 'For many are
called but few are chosen.' Matthew elevated the importance of
the feast by making it a marriage-feast given by a king for his son,
and so gives a very different impression to the refusals and to
the idea of dressing in a fitting way. Matthew, uninterested in the
generosity theme, gives little detail about furnishing the wedding
with guests; the servants simply went out 'into the highways
and gathered together all as many as they found, both bad and
good' and this leads immediately to 'And when the king came
to see the guests, he saw there a man which had not on a wedding-
garment', and the subsequent reproof and punishment.

The medieval poet, by amplifying what we may call the 'ex-
cluding' parable of Matthew with details from the humbler
'including' portions of Luke, imports a lack of logic into the
tale, which he makes more extreme by adding details of his own.

Thus, when he reaches the point at which the servants have
to find guests in the streets, he first uses Matthew's version,

condemning the first-bidden as unworthy, and instructing the servants to bring

> The wayferande frekez, on fote and on hors,
> Bothe burnez and burdez, the better and the wers . . .
>
> (79–80)

and then uses Luke's fuller and more detailed sentences as the basis of an account of what the servants do, their report to the lord and the second orders given to them. The whole incident, as a result, has much more weight than in either source and the identity of the guests has more emphasis, more variety and more complication. The servants first bring

> bachlerez . . . that thay by bonkez metten,
> Swyerez that swyftly swyed on blonkez.
> And also fele upon fote, of fre and of bonde.
>
> (86–8)

They are arranged in order of rank, and the lord then instructs his servants to go into the fields to fetch more:

> 'Waytez gorstez and grevez, if ani gome lyggez,
> What-kyn folk so ther fare, fechez hem hider . . .'
>
> (99–100)

The servants do as they are told and bring 'peple of alle plytez', who were 'not alle on wyvez sunez'; those who are 'bryghtest atyred' are placed highest, but there is room for those 'soerly semed by her wedez'; few are 'clene men', but all are 'served to the fulle'. Now this amplification fulfils Luke's idea that all should be welcome very well, but the more detail the poet gives following that train of thought, the more he focuses on realistic points and on the idea of the generosity of the lord to all, no matter how poor, how base, how unclean. As a result, the lord's re-jection of

> A thral thryght in the throng unthryvandely clothed,
> Ne no festival frok, bot fyled with werkkez.   (135–6)

seems inhospitable, unfair and contradictory. The suggestion that peasants and tramps in 'gorstez and grevez' should have a clean garment handy in case somebody forced them to go to a wedding is an idea one can only accept if one abandons the literal fable and translates the garment into its allegorical equivalent, but the poet, by being realistic and dramatic, does not encourage one to make this desperate breach of decorum. The lord's protest

'How watz thou hardy in this hous for thyn unhap neghe,
In on so ratted a robe?'   (143–4)

is absurd, given what has gone before, and he emerges as quixotic and tyrannous. Though the poet wrenches us back to the doctrinal level in his interpretation of the parable, and though as experienced readers we can check the impulse to object by reminding our-selves that the clothes are symbolic and that we have known from the start that the point of the tale was rejection of the unclean, the damage has been done. The initial and concluding statements of the meaning of the parable do not say the same thing as the narrative itself. The poet has confused the issues by entering energetically and imaginatively into amplification of the literal level of the story.

What then are we to make of this? Is it that the poet keeps his argument in one hand and his narrative in the other and does not let the right hand know what the left is doing? If we simply 'take the fruit' of the tale and forget the rest as interesting but irrelevant, then we have an allegorical presentation of two themes, the gener-osity of God (and man's poor response to it) and the anger of God against uncleanness. These two themes are certainly built on in other parts of the poem and the parable could be seen as an initial presentation of the central issues of the rest. Pamela Gradon sees the poem in this way: 'The structure of the poem thus consists of a number of juxtaposed exemplary narratives which develop a number of themes implicit in the initial parable.'[7]

On the other hand, is there not greater imaginative truth in the poet's recognition of the contradictions within his composite narrative? The assertion of the parable's meaning before the tale and the interpretation of its symbols afterwards provide a doctrinal frame within which the actual experience of thinking through the events exposes its oversimplifications. Since the poet was intelligent enough to remove one sort of contradiction between Matthew's fable and Luke's, we have to assume that he was capable of seeing others and are thus entitled to surmise that his reason for putting the two stories together was not purely to make a longer tale but to bring two aspects of God together, his generosity and his anger, and to express these in enough detail to make us aware of the antithesis between them. God in this tale is a Janus-headed God whose one mouth says 'Come in' and whose other says 'Get out'. The tale shows that the antithetical presentation of 'fayre formes' and 'kark' is not just a treatment of men's actions and destinies but a recognition of the opposites in the nature of a God who gives with one hand and takes away with the other.

However one resolves the difficulties, with this first narrative in *Purity* we meet the problems of relating homiletic and narrative parts. The solution of the problem, for the poet, would have been to cut straight from line 50 to line 169, but that would be to assume that he wanted to concentrate on argument, and the main thing betrayed by this part of the poem is that the poet is com-mitted to narrative for its own sake, and not because it is a good way of illustrating a point. His treatment of the parable proceeds from a desire to use the imagination to amplify, particularise and dramatise within a borrowed outline. This desire, even more in evidence later, is inherently incompatible with the use of narrative merely for exemplifying purposes, because it repeatedly seizes opportunities to envisage things which are incidental to the tale's exemplary character. As a result, any simple allegorical effect or single message is dissipated and compromised by being en-meshed in a mass of circumstance. In the parable it is not only the cross-currents created by combining Luke and Matthew that diversify the moral force of the tale, but even such passages as the description of the food and the detailed replies of the first-bidden guests offer images and circumstances which complicate the reader's reaction. They create a wider-ranging representation of life than can be contained by the tale's original meaning, and the interpretation of the tale comes to seem a simplification, or even, as here, a distortion of the picture of life offered to us as the sequence of action unfolded.

Critical judgement of the conflicting elements depends on one's order of priorities. Those who see the homiletic theme as the most important, the 'serious' aspect of *Purity*, tend to blame the poet for being irrelevant and letting the exuberance of his imagin-ation run away with him. Thus Menner, though he praises the

poet otherwise, says, 'He becomes so engrossed in his narrative
that he forgets that his stories are not being written for their own
sake, but as illustrations of a particular theme.'[8] Dorothy Everett's
view is that 'he tends to tell his stories at disproportionate length',[9]
which implies the same standard of judgement, and Spearing
finds several instances in the narratives where 'the poet has been
carried away by the vividness of his imagination'.[10] On the other
hand it seems equally possible, since many readers have found that
the Old Testament narratives are the most impressive part of the
poem, to take the view that the homiletic passages are provided to
link the tales together and that they at times cramp or oversimplify
the sense of the tale. The opposing opinions pinpoint the relationship of homily and narrative as the central critical problem of
Purity as a whole.

3. The poet as homilist

Purity begins in a curiously tentative manner:

> Clannesse who so kyndly cowthe comende,
> And rekken up alle the resounz that ho by right askez,
> Fayre formez myght he fynde in forthering his speche,
> And in the contrare, kark and combraunce huge. (1–4)

The effect of this piece of disguised *occupatio* is to suggest that
the poet is unwilling to commit himself to the theme of cleanness,
and is rather nervously dipping his toe into it. The rhetorical
formula, in which the name of any virtue could be substituted
for the opening word, focuses on the poet's intention, to praise
purity and set its beauty against the ugliness of its contrary, rather
than on the idea of purity itself. The reader's sense of what
cleanness means to the poet and what are the 'fair forms' which
might fittingly commend the virtue, remain nebulous for a long
time, except insofar as they are indicated by their contraries. The
poet assumes that the reader will provide a stock response to the
idea, obliquely presented, that purity is beautiful; he is nudged,
at intervals in this opening passage, to keep this stock response
going, first by assertion of God's cleanness:

> He is so clene in his corte, the kyng that al weldes,
> And honeste in his housholde and hagherlych served

With angelez enorled in alle that is clene,
Bothe wythinne and wythouten, in wedez ful bryght . . .

                                        (17–20)

then by citation of the Beatitudes:

The hathel clene of his hert hapenez ful fayre,
For he schal loke on oure Lorde wyth a bone chere.

                                        (27–8)

The imprecise presentation of purity (let alone the feebleness of
the suggestion that we are to be impressed by the contents of God's
linen/cupboards) reflects the poet's treatment for most of the
poem. The contrast of 'fayre formes' and 'kark and combraunce'
becomes a contrast between two unequal qualities: purity, whose
attributes are briefly referred to or merely assumed, and impurity,
whose attributes begin to be identified and illustrated. The poet
explains the 'combraunce' as the result of God's anger against
filth, as in the case of dishonest priests, and later moves quickly
from the Beatitude to restatement in negative form and the
imagery of torn and dirty clothes, quoted above. The argument
of the first fifty lines is urbane and sensible, as far as it goes, but
neither penetrating nor particularly cogent; it alludes rather than
states, illustrates rather than identifies, and slides quickly from
one aspect of the subject to another—a style of writing nearer to
the anecdotal than the dialectic. The most definitely stated things
are the instances of uncleanness; the graphic pointedness of the
description of the 'ladde' with his torn stockings, shoved out at
the hall/door, makes strongest impact, but the passage on priests
also makes its commonplace point with some vigour, provided
by contrast and balanced phrasing. The passage is put together
smoothly and the poet has imposed a consistent tone upon it, a
tone of reasonableness which appeals to the judgements of
common sense by its antitheses, simple graphic examples and
quotation of scripture. But beneath the reasonable surface there is
no actual reasoning, at least not a continuous reasoning, but
rather an assembling of aspects of the idea of purity and its
opposite, with subsidiary impressions of God as all/powerful and
severe, and the purity of man as honest courtesy towards God.
These aspects are the threads which are to run through the poem

to bind its parts together; the threads of man's impurity and God's anger are the strongest. The tentative imprecision of some parts suggest that the poet is feeling his way and thinking more of the introductory function of the passage than of expounding a homiletic theme. The sermon elements are there (Biblical text, explanation of theme, exhortation to avoid vice, etc.) but make less impression than the more fully developed instances of wrong-doing.

Even from this opening passage it seems clear that *Purity* cannot be thought of as 'a homily'; the poet borrows elements from the sermon's style and subject-matter to form, not a reasoned exposition, but a patterned grouping of motifs. The grouping is repeated in the other parts of the poem and, though details vary, the pattern remains the same. Greatest space is given to exempli-fication or 'proof', usually by means of narration but also by the brief instance, imagery, symbolism and quotation. The exempli-fication is almost entirely of the punishment of impurity but the poem's only continuously 'positive' treatment of purity (1057–1132), is also dominated by pictorial and allusive treatment of ethical qualities. The illustrative passages, the full-length nar-ratives and the briefer examples, are preceded by statements about man's impurity, which are placed in antithesis to the need for purity, and about God's hatred of impurity, placed in antithesis to his own purity and his love of it in man. They are succeeded by summary, reiteration or interpretation of the theme of the illustration, and exhortation either to be pure or, more often, to avoid filth. The fullness of illustration and the continual recalling and regrouping of a small number of related ideas give to *Purity* the over-all quality of a set of variations on a theme, or of pictures grouped on the basis of common subject-matter. The poem pro-ceeds by accumulation. We could still accept it as a poem if it stopped at line 176, or at line 556, or at line 1056, or at line 1132, or, as it does, at line 1812, or, if other examples were added, at some later stage; this is why, earlier, I compared *Purity* to the linked compartments of a train. It is the stories which determine the poem's form and its stages, not the development of an argu-ment working towards its conclusion. Indeed the 'argument' has the air of being shaped principally to provide an introduction to the next story rather than having a necessary progress of its own which naturally brings an instance to mind, though this fact is disguised.

The first two transition passages show the bridging technique clearly. The transition between the parable and the episode of the Flood (161–248) consists of:

1. 161–76 *Leading out* of the parable by interpretation of its symbols (feast = kingdom of heaven; clothes = deeds), repetition of God's hatred of filth, and consequent exhortation to be clean if we wish to see God.

2. 177–92 *Middle of the bridge*: the idea of man's sinful deeds amplified by a dreary list of sins in the old-fashioned homiletic manner of *Sermo Lupi ad Anglos*.

3. 193–248 *Leading into* the Flood by distinction of impurity from all other sins as the most hated and most severely punished, and more lengthy illustration of this by the moderation of God's punishment of Lucifer for presumption and Adam for disobedience.

The technique is similar in the passage between the Flood and the story of Sodom and Gomorrah (541–600):

1. 541–56 *Leading out* by summarising comment and consequent exhortation to avoid 'fylthe of the flesch'; if one wants to see God one must be as spotless as beryl or pearl.

2. 557–80 *Middle of the bridge*: a backward-looking summary of God's anger and the remorseful covenant with man leads to the forward-looking qualification that God did subsequently punish 'wykked men' for the same 'vycios fylthe'.

3. 581–600 *Leading into* the tale of Sodom by a reminder that God sees all and examines mankind, rewarding the pure and punishing the unclean; this clearly prefigures God's appearance to Abraham and his sending of spies to Sodom and sparing of the pure.

The two passages are both neatly shaped for their structural function; in particular the lead-in to the Sodom episode prepares for God's actions in an effectively cryptic way, which does not become a pre-statement of the plot, but suggestively leads up to the threshold of the tale. The overlapping, too, is done cleverly so that there is a point where the two currents merge, though, as I said, there is also a point where one could stop the flow without a sense of incompleteness. Such development in the argument as there is, is clearly the result of matching one tale's logic with that of the tale that follows.

The longest transition passage, between the tales of Sodom and Belshazzar's Feast (1049–156), is more ambitious in its range of poetic expression but not essentially different in function. It is still a bridge but one crossing a wider river, from buggery on one bank to sacrilege on the other. The poet has, for the first time, to analyse purity and impurity in order to make a smooth transition from one type of impurity to the other. The passage has the features which appear in the other two, however; there is the same sort of leading out section (1049–56) with comment on the significance of the Dead Sea symbols and consequent exhortation to be clean if we wish to see God, and the same sort of leading in section (1133–56) with warning that one should not sin again after shrift since what is once God's is always his, even a basin or a bowl, as the example of Belshazzar shows. The difference from the other two passages is in the greater length and variety of the 'middle of the bridge' section (1057–132).

First, in this passage, he enlarges the reader's idea of purity and strengthens his hitherto vague positive advice on pure behaviour; characteristically he combines illustrative devices and a web of ideas touched on earlier in the poem, here amplified. He makes a prop by quoting from an unexpected secular source, Jean de Meun's portion of *Le Roman de la Rose*, advice to the lover that he should woo the beloved by observing her ways and tastes and then imitating them; this illustration is then applied to man's expression of love towards God. This leads to consideration of God's purity, again presented by means of instance, here of Christ's conception and birth which is expansively coloured by imagery, then God's antipathy to filth, illustrated by Christ's healing of the sick. The three illustrations have followed an antithetical course of thought which is familiar from the introduction to the poem and elsewhere, but the length and variety of the illustrations give a new air to the themes and create a wide gap between the end of one tale and the lead-in to the next. The blurring of our sense of what impurity has hitherto meant is completed by the poet's only bit of 'intellectual' analysis of his subject, when he brings out a different sense of the word *clene* itself, in the example of Christ's breaking bread with his fingers as cleanly as men do with a knife. He then further amplifies the sense of cleanness in fuller development of the symbolism of the pearl (already referred to at lines 556 and 1068). The domination of the passage by illustrative features shows, as in the introductory section of the poem, that 'argument' of any length is conceived of by the poet as a linking of different images and instances, and that direct homiletic statement is used to create context and pattern. In such things the reader finds that *Purity* is unmistakeably a poem, not a sermon. As in the introduction the illustration is well done and stands out from its flatter surroundings; the passage on the purity of Christ's birth is particularly fine:

> Watz never so blysful a bour as watz a bos thenne,
> Ne no schroudehous so schene as a schepon thare,
> Ne non so glad under God as ho that grone schulde.
> For ther watz seknesse al sounde that sarrest is halden,
> And ther watz rose reflayr where rote hatz ben ever,
> And ther watz solace and songe wher sorw hatz ay cryed;
> For aungelles wyth instrumentes of organes and pypes,
> And rial ryngande rotes, and the reken fythel,
> And alle hende that honestly moght an hert glade,
> Aboutte my Lady watz lent, quen ho delyver were.
>
> (1075–84)

The tight patterning of the series of antitheses, pointed by alliterative stress, and then opening out into the vowel alliteration of 'aungelles wyth instrumentes of organes and pypes', mimes, with sensitive euphony, the rise and fall of joy and sorrow and the release from bondage of the Saviour, salvation and joy, which music here symbolises. The passage also obliquely prepares the way for the story that follows by presenting the purity of the Nativity as a reversal, from bad to good, the contrary to the reversals of fortune later emphasised in the fall of Belshazzar. The juxtaposition of unclean and clean elements runs through the rest of the section with the example of Christ's transformation of filth and sickness into wholesomeness by his touch; the sin of man and the cleansing power of shrift and penance; the purity of the pearl's round whiteness and the cleansing of a discoloured pearl by dipping it in wine. The series of examples of making clean the unclean turns quite naturally, in this poem of contraries, to the idea of making unclean the clean, and so to the sacrilege of Belshazzar.

This trickiest of the transitions in the poem is, in poetic terms, the most successful; the poet has risen to the challenge of the width of sense between his two tales and imaginatively juggled in antithesis, reversal and word-play with the reader's sense of the poem's theme. But the passage remains a clever piece of bridging, not an inevitable development of ideas. Logically Christ's clean breaking of bread and Belshazzar's unclean bibbing of wine have little, if anything, to do with one another, but at the associative level of imagery the two make a suggestive antithesis, and it is at this level that the poet works most creatively and intelligently.

The brief, concluding passage, which sums up the process of the poem, combines once again the poem's leading motifs:

> Thus upon thrynne wyses I haf yow thro schewed,
> That unclannes tocleves in corage dere
> Of that wynnelych Lorde that wonyes in heven,
> Entyses hym to be tene, teldes up his wrake.
> And clannes is his comfort, and coyntyse he lovyes,
> And those that seme arn and swete schyn se his face.
> That we gon gay in oure gere that grace he uus sende,
> That we may serve in his syght ther solace never blynnez.
>
> (1805-12)

This summarising, almost perfunctory, whipping together of the threads that run through the poem shows the poet in his assumed role of demonstrator, reminding his audience of what his tales exemplify. But the reminder is so brief that we are struck more by the obvious structural function of the passage, to round off the series, than by any moral force in the expression; 'gay in our gere' takes us back to the imagery of clothing with which the poem began, but the reference seems arbitrary after the long story of Belshazzar, in which to be 'gered ful gaye in gounes of porpre' was merely a sign of worldly reward.

The homiletic sections of *Purity* are not ineffective. They reveal three positive merits in the poet: skilful use of illustration; evocative reference to images and traditional Christian symbols;

and an exceptionally neat use of homiletic motifs to effect the transition from one narrative example to the next. But they reveal also that the poet is no homilist in any real sense. He makes no memorable moral statement outside his examples and images, and such statements and exhortations as he does make, often commonplace to start with, are weakened rather than strengthened by repetition, since the repetition is not an essential part of a developing argument, but merely echoing of earlier statements to create a unified texture in the poem as a whole. The failure to subordinate his examples to his propositions means that *Purity* reads as a collection of tales connected together by homiletic threads, rather than as a set of principles made effective by ex-empla. This is not, however, to say that *Purity* has no unity, or that it lacks coherence. It is a question of what kind of relation-ship one perceives between the tale and the framework, not a question of whether there is a connection at all.

4. Themes versus instances

The author of *Purity* worked hard, perhaps too hard, to weld his tales into a smooth sequence. Not only are the intermediate homiletic passages shaped to provide a natural movement from the end of one tale to the beginning of the next, but also the poet repeatedly brings out connections between his narratives. God's love of purity and his punishment of impure behaviour, and the pure man's hope of sight of God as opposed to the impure man's banishment therefrom, are obviously the main links in the chain,[11] but there are other links, parallels and thematic sequences, though these are sometimes partial sequences rather than ones that run with consistent strength through the whole poem.

First identified in Luke's parable of the supper is the theme of generosity, ingratitude and punishment. God's generous pro-viding for man is represented first by the symbolic banquet, the 'frelych fest' to which man is invited. The symbolism draws on the traditional Biblical and romance associations of the court and the quality of courtesy, present in divine terms in the ceremony of the court, the hierarchy of the seating at the banquet, the richness of the offered food, the generous condescension of God's inviting all to the feast; by contrast courtesy is shown as lacking at the human level in the failure of unclean priests, and in the refusals of the first-bidden guests, as well as in the double pre-sentation of the man in foul clothes. The anger of the lord is aroused by the failure to accept the obligations which the generous conferment of benefit demands. As I have suggested earlier, this particular group of ideas and images serves, whether by accident or design, to display God as two-faced; the impression the poet manages to create is of God as an elderly rich relative whose whims have to be indulged if he is not to change his will. The theme of generosity is asserted but made equivocal rather than convincing, because the poet wants to make us aware of man's subordination and the vagaries of his lot as well as his sin. The connected ideas of generosity, ingratitude and punishment are elevated in importance and poetic effectiveness when, instead of the imagery of banquet and court, the poet substitutes images of paradise and shows God's generosity in the gifts of beauty and perfect joy. Lucifer, 'attled the fayrest', Adam, 'ordaynt to blysse', and the descendants of Adam, 'the fayrest of forme and of face', to whom God had 'geven alle that gayn were,' all make poor returns for the generosity and are punished in moderation or in anger according to the nature of the fault, but all are cast out from the bliss of the particular paradise they have been given, heaven, Eden and the world of nature. God's remorse is expressed in a second giving of the earth to Noah and the preserved beasts:

> he blessez uch a best, and bytaght hem this erthe. (528)
> The fowre frekez of the folde fongez the empyre.   (540)

The paradisal imagery re-appears, more fleetingly, in the story of Sodom and is adapted to the new set of circumstances. Here natural sexual love is presented as a gift of God of such surpassing beauty that 'Wel nyghe pure paradys moght preve no better' and the ingratitude of Sodom's perversity has its punishment in God's own destruction of the natural beauty he had created and given:

> That ever hade ben an erde of erthe the swettest,
> As aparaunt to paradis that plantted the Dryghtyn.
> (1006–7)

The theme of generosity and gratitude also appears in reversed form when Abraham, in a paradisal setting of shady leaves, provides food for the threefold God and is thanked and rewarded for his courtesy, and for what it stood for, by God's promise that Sarah shall bear a son; Sarah's disbelieving laughter is checked but not punished, since God, unlike man, keeps his promises and pays back what he owes:

> 'And yet I avow verayly the avaunt that I made,
> I schal yeply ayayn and yelde that I hyght.' (664–5)

God's preservation of Lot and his earlier saving of Noah can also be seen as acts of gratitude which stand in contrast to his punishment of those who had themselves shown no response to his generous love. This theme develops the idea of the generous feast offered to God's creatures and God's response when it is rejected, or abused. The sequence is not, however, carried beyond the story of Sodom, unless one regards it as implicit in subsequent images of beauty (the birth of Christ, the pearl, the holy vessels), in the God-given kingly power of Zedekiah, Nebuchadnezzar and Belshazzar, in the reversal and perversion of the banquet-image in the scene of Belshazzar's Feast, and in the fact that worship of false gods means that 'hym that alle goudes gives, that God thay foryeten' (1528). The thread is, therefore, a sub-theme developed out of the symbolism of the parable, making use of obvious, almost obligatory, aspects of Old Testament myth, and used as a link between parts of the poem. It remains an aspect of the poem's material rather than a controlling meaning, but one which, in displaying God as giver and depriver, develops the antithesis of reward and punishment from which the poem starts.

Working in a similar way is the overlapping theme of Nature or 'Kynde', which flashes through *Purity* without coming to dominate it. The sequence begins with the descendants of Adam who, given the earth to inhabit and fill, were left free without masters to rule them, and 'ther watz no law to hem layd but loke to kynde' (263). Their offence of filth of the flesh is condemned because it is an offence against natural law: they 'controeved agayn Kynde contrare werkez' (266). The men of Sodom are later damned because they 'scorned nature'. Nature thus appears primarily in terms of God's gift to men of the earth and of the power to multiply, fill the earth and enjoy its fruits, and God's establishment of natural order and natural law, represented in the succession of the seasons, the hierarchy of the world of men and animals, and a pious sense in man of custom and right, of what is owed to God and what is seemly for men. When men break the law by their unnatural vices, God himself reverses the natural order and uses the power of tempest, flood and earthquake as his instruments of punishment. The tales of the Flood and the destruction of Sodom both end with powerful natural images: the Flood episode with the restoration of natural order; the story of Sodom with symbols of reversal in the contrary properties of the Dead Sea, which is 'corsed of kynde'. In the later parts the theme occurs in isolated passages, as if the poet wished to con-tinue the thread where he could. So the passage on the purity of Christ's birth, whereby womb and shippon are both turned into enclosures of wholesome beauty leads to:

> Thenne watz her blythe barne burnyst so clene
> That bothe the ox and the asse hym hered at ones:
> Thay knewe hym by his clannes for Kyng of Nature.
> For non so clene of such a clos com never er thenne.
>
> (1085–8)

But this reference to a traditional idea is not built on. Similarly Belshazzar is linked to earlier examples of unnatural vice by being portrayed as a man whose jaded appetites can no longer be satisfied by the natural and seemly, but thereafter the theme disappears underground, present only insofar as it is implied in the connections between the earlier breaches of natural law and Belshazzar's breaking of the law of sanctity, between earlier mis-uses of the richness of the natural world and the idolatrous worship of gods of stone and metal, and between earlier reversals of nature and God's reversal of natural hierarchy in his punishment of Nebuchadnezzar who must 'in wasturne walk and wyth the wylde dowelle/As best', and who himself becomes a perversion of Nature.

Menner identified what he called the 'second theme' of trawthe, with the suggestion that, 'Besides the three main instances of God's vengeance on men for sin against purity, four other incidents of punishments inflicted by Divine justice are recorded. . . Lucifer is represented as a traitor; Adam "fayled in trawthe"; Lot's wife becomes a pillar of salt "for two fautes that the fol watz fonde in

mistrauthe"; Jerusalem fell because the people were found "un‑
trwe" in their faith.'[12] Charles Moorman carries this further and
produces a comprehensive pattern whereby each Old Testament
narrative is accompanied by two shorter ones 'illustrating a failure
in *trawthe* (i.e. disobedience or unfaithfulness) in Lucifer and
Adam, Sarah and Lot's wife, and Zedekiah and Nebuchad‑
nezzar'.[13] Each group of three, in his view, shows God's more
severe punishment of uncleanness than lack of faith. I think that
both Menner and Moorman, especially the latter, rather overstate
the case as part of an argument for the poem's unity. In reality
there is again only a partial sequence apparent as one reads. Lucifer
is punished for vainglory and is not reconciled with God 'so
proud watz his wylle'; Adam is punished for disobedience. The
point of the two examples is that their faults were different and
show God's 'moderate' punishment of more than one sin other
than the fleshly filth for which his immoderate rage is reserved.
The same sort of distinction of degrees of punishment is made
only with reference to Nebuchadnezzar, who was not punished
for accepting the spoils of the temple because he revered the holy
vessels, and who was punished for Lucifer's sin of vainglory but
released when he recognised God's power. The instance of
Lucifer, therefore, may be said to introduce a partial sequence of
the humbling of pride, which, as we have seen, the poet emphasises
in his treatment of Belshazzar's Feast. One could suggest others in
the connection of Adam's disobedience and the double disobed‑
ience of Lot's wife, in the connection of Sarah's laughter with
the foolishness of those who believe that God does not hear all
and Belshazzar's confrontation with the hand of God. Pamela
Gradon identifies a sub‑theme of 'coyntyse' or wisdom in the
poem,[14] and Charlotte C. Morse argues that the image of the
vessel is a unifying theme in *Purity*.[15] These ideas, and others,
such as the symbol of the pearl and the imagery of clothing, which
occur several times in the poem, are threads which float out from
the resemblances between tales, from the poet's circling round the
same set of ideas, from continual antitheses, repeated metaphors
and so on. Cumulatively they add to one's sense of *Purity* as a
poem with a rich variety of patterns and parallels.

A different sort of connection, presumably intended further to
bind the parts together, is a very simple use of number linking.

The number involved, as in *Sir Gawain*, is three, and it occurs in each of the four stories. In the parable there are three refusals from the first-bidden guests. The Flood is presented as the third offence against God and the tale refers, obviously, to Noah's three sons and their three wives. Abraham meets God in triune form; three measures of meal are used to make three cakes; there are three saved from the cities of the plain. Belshazzar gives to Daniel the position of third lord in the kingdom in return for the conversion of the three words on the wall into the threefold warning. The poet finally sums up by pointing out that he has demonstrated 'upon thrynne wyses' God's anger against impurity, and we may suspect that the phrase means not only 'in three ways' but also 'in threes'. This looks like a surface decoration, a seeking for a kind of external, unifying definition of form, a further sign of the poet's realisation that the diverse material of *Purity* might, if he wasn't careful, come apart at the seams.

The parts of *Purity* are thus linked in many ways, so many, in fact, that one feels constrained. Had the poet devised a looser framework one would not be so conscious of the disparities and over-simplifications. The four narratives are presented as examples of God's relationship to man, but the treatment means that we perceive at least four different human views of God. If we make comparisons among the tales, as the poet by his insistent thematic linking encourages us to do, then we cannot accept that the God who ruefully makes covenant with Noah is the same being as the one who plays ducks and drakes with the kings of Judah and Chaldea, nor that the God who responds to Abraham's reminder that destruction of the innocent is unfitting to his great and gracious ways, can stimulate war in which innocent women and children are butchered. There are many other points at which such disparities occur. The tales are connected by themes and by recurrent motifs and symbols, but in stylistic, historical and logical terms they are separate. The fact that the poet's narrative method is to project his imagination into the story means that the tales not only preserve the differences of style and of aesthetic and moral appeal which they had in the Vulgate, but have these differences augmented. The only way in which we can read them as one whole is to accept only that part of the narratives which serves the supposed theme, and to quell our response to effects irrelevant to it; since those effects are the ones which readers tend to find the most vigorous and striking, this is not easy, nor, in my view, desirable. If, on the other hand, we attempt to cater for the varia-tions in a total interpretation of *Purity*, then the only interpretation big enough to hold them is that the poet was portraying a God and a world of total arbitrariness.

If one accepts the element of medley in the poem, then *Purity* may best be regarded as linked in kind with Gower's *Confessio Amantis*, *The Canterbury Tales* and the Middle English version of *The Seven Sages of Rome*, as a collection of independent tales linked together by a continuously running frame. The difference between *Purity* and these other collections marks it as a less successful attempt at the mode. In *The Canterbury Tales* Chaucer has accounted for differences of style and outlook by giving the stories to different narrators, and deliberately displaying con-flicting views, of love and marriage in particular; in *Confessio Amantis* the ebb and flow of the discussion between the lover and his confessor and the comprehensive moral scheme of the work create distinctions and shifts of emphasis which enable stories, even when several are grouped together as exemplifying the same moral idea, to reflect differently on the fictional situation; even in *The Seven Sages* the contest between the sages and the queen provides a framework which can include changes of attitude. The author of *Purity* does not use any distancing technique by which the reader may hold the tales at arm's length, and the voice assumed in the link-passages does not seem to allow the reader such freedom, but the composition of the tales shows that the poet was actually giving it to us when he spoke as story-teller.

The critics who have discussed *Purity* are few in number but they nevertheless present a variety of solutions to the poem's problems, and those who have published discussions fairly re-cently provide a fair range of critical opinion. Charles Moorman offers the least questioning view of the work; he accepts the 'com-plex sermon structure' as defining the poem's meaning and suggests that *Purity* is 'the poet's first attempt at thematic fusion' whereby he 'not only relates the groups of stories employed in the poem chronologically by treating them as parts of the same running narrative, but . . . he has given them . . . a new thematic relation-ship by allowing the themes of impurity and disloyalty to overlap and complement each other'. For Moorman the 'charges of lack of proportion and design that have been brought against the poem . . . are seen to be baseless when the overall design of the poem is grasped'.[16] A. C. Spearing also argues that the structure is complex (though both Moorman and Spearing seem to mean by 'complex' mainly that the series of consecutive parts is unusually long) and he argues, persuasively, that the 'principle of structure is not a plot but a homiletic purpose, to which narrative is subordinate'.[17] But when he comes to analyse the realisation of Scripture in the tales themselves, Spearing does not disguise the disparity between the homiletic purpose and the fully imagined scenes and is forced to suggest, more than once, that 'when we consider the purpose of the episode as a whole . . . we must agree that the poet has been carried away by the vividness of his imagination'.[18] This is the argument, mentioned earlier, that the homiletic purpose is over-riding, though compromised by the exuberance of the poet's over-long elaborations.

J. A. Burrow takes an alternative view. While arguing that *Purity* is typical of late fourteenth-century uses of narrative for exemplification (though unusual in combining several episodes, which links it with other tale-collections) Burrow concludes that the poet has failed to create a clearly defined over-all form, leaving 'the exterior form of his poem somewhat rambling and unsatisfactory'.[19] This is to put emphasis on the tales rather than the frame; the stories have been selected 'on thematic principles' and the poet is obviously trying, 'with elaborate care' as Menner says, to form his stories into a unity, but the linking remains clumsy and forced. Pamela Gradon's solution is to see *Purity* as an example of a 'paratactic' medieval structuring which does not see the need to make full connections between parts, but juxtaposes and intertwines themes, images and narratives which reflect on one another: 'The function of the paratactic structure of homiletic exhortation and exemplary narrative is thus a means by which the poet explores the implications of both the meaning of the parable and the implications of the word "cleanness".'[20]

It seems, from the views of Spearing, Burrow and Gradon, to be fair to say that readers find conflicts in *Purity* that need accounting for, and that there is probably no completely satisfactory way of doing it. Either the frame does not neatly fit the tales, or the tales do not neatly fit the frame. Either there is a unity perceptible to modern readers except that the poet does not consistently observe it, or there is some special medieval type of structure for which the modern reader has to make allowances.

Purity seems to me the work of an extremely talented, ambitious and ingenious poet who has failed to control and harmonise completely two opposing intentions. In the narratives the poetry is mainly expressive of the interests of a born story-teller. The poet treats the tales as if they had never been told before, and wants to show the stories as they happen, to make the moment live again so that it is held in the reader's senses to be lived through and savoured; even with the garish caravanserai of Belshazzar's Feast, it is his desire to make us watch the pageant passing. So the tales are filled, in varying degrees, with vigour, complexity, realism, feelings, individuals, scenes, drama, images, speech and multiplicity. With one hand the poet is making each tale as particular as he can. With the other he is trying to hold them together and so to persuade us that the tales are, in some sense, the same. The didactic and the pattern-making impulses treat the tales as examples from history and holy writ, simplify them to moral ideas, remove their particularity and show them as they appear from a distance. The reader of *Purity* is asked to respond both to the impulse which particularises and envisages, and to the impulse which generalises and abstracts. As I have suggested earlier, the double response would have been possible, if the poet had devised a more flexible framework, which allowed for some distance and ironical relationship between the voice of the narrator and the tales themselves, but, as it is, the reader has to choose whether to accept the logic of each separate story, conflicting with the logic of others, or the logic of the narrator's voice. The choice is not difficult to make because the homiletic passages do not have the force to stand by themselves, but prove, on examination, to be shaped according to their function as introductions, transitions and conclusions, and so to be the servants of the narra-tive sections rather than their masters. In any case the most forcefully expressed portions of the homiletic sections are the instances and images, not the moral statements or exhortations; this again tends to subordinate the didactic element to the illus-trative.

Because there is uneven workmanship in *Purity*, and because
the poet has not shaped the whole in a way which accounts
completely for the parts, one cannot but surmise that this poem is
a 'transitional' work. He is moving towards pure fiction but has
not yet fully realised that the process of exemplification is itself a
fictional strategy; he had realised this by the time he wrote
Patience. Several times in *Purity* the reader senses that the poet is
fumbling towards an effect not completely achieved. In some
places there is an implicit, not fully articulated, irony, by which
the homiletic presentation of an idea is set off against, rather than
supported by, the narrative treatment of the idea; we are made aware
in the story of complexities, conflict and dramatic feelings which
have their own kind of truth, ignored by the simplifying use of
the tale as a moral example. It is difficult not to believe, in some
parts of the poem, that the poet had the intention of showing the
disparities in God's nature and of revealing the vulnerability of
man in a world whose mutability is a projection of the contrary
aspects of God's Absolute Power. Man is seen in the poem
mainly in moments of suffering and humiliation, God in rapid
switches from generosity to more lengthily presented punishment
and destruction; by his sympathetic, imagining treatment of
man, the poet upsets the balance and makes us see God from the
point of view of those harassed by his vengeful dealings. That this
impression is not an accidental product of the differences between
medieval and modern views of God is made clear by an aspect of
each of the four narratives: in the parable the poet makes the great
lord's behaviour appear unreasonable by adding Matthew's fable
of exclusion to Luke's fable of openness, and by expanding both;
in the Flood episode he expresses the bewildered suffering of
doomed men with great poignancy and gives stress to the modification of God's mind; in the story of Sodom he greatly expands
the conversation between God and Abraham so that we have a
powerful sense of God as a sentient and thinking being who is
influenced to greater mercy by his loving servant; in the tale of
Belshazzar he creates a sense of reversal and arbitrariness at both
human and divine levels. Certainly the poet's choice of the
'negative' method by which the idea of purity is used as a framework for a treatment mainly of impure acts suggests that it was
antithesis and conflict which the poet was mainly interested in.

The solid realisation of fictional worlds full of weakness and evil, set in a context of more nebulous assertions of righteousness and beauty, is another facet of the poem which sets up ironies and cross-currents. We are encouraged to read in antithetical terms and to see continual contrasts and contradictions, to see likenesses with difference, and differences with likeness. Again we seem in contact with an exploring, imaginative mind, a mind interested in what art can do, not primarily in subordinating it to an instructive purpose.

As I said at the outset, *Purity* seems to me an unsuccessful poem, for reasons which I have fully indicated, but there is no doubt that its author was a man of great poetic gifts, even if they are not here fully matured or controlled. To say that a fourteenth-century poem is marred by a plethora of imagination and talent, by an over-ambitious attempt to combine several styles of writing and levels of meaning, hardly amounts to a very damning criticism.

4. Patience

1. Introduction

The third and shortest of the four poems consists of 531 unrhymed, alliterative long lines, the last of which is virtually the
same as the first.[1] Enlarged capitals divide it into five sections.
An introduction commending the virtue of patience and briefly
citing Jonah as an example of angry refusal to accept the inevitable
(lines 1–60) precedes a full-scale retelling of the tale of Jonah,
based on the Vulgate text and divided into four scenes. Discussion
of the poem has, therefore, to focus on questions of translation
and expansion, not just in the interest of historical accuracy,
but because one is able to measure what the poet is doing by
reference to the matter from which he started; one can more surely
here (and with similar material in *Purity*) gain some feeling of
working alongside the poet than in either *Pearl* or *Sir Gawain*.[2]

The Book of Jonah is a curious work, a brief tale, laconic in
style. The few indications of place, time, motive and feeling
serve but to expose the general lack of circumstantial detail, and
the reader is continually nagged by questions. The narrative
seems unsure and includes some strange statements and sequences.
When the lot has fallen upon Jonah and the sailors ask him who
he is and where he is going, he replies, 'I am an Hebrew and J
fear the Lord, the God of heaven which made the sea and the
dry land.' This does not answer all the questions posed, but does
answer a question not asked, and provokes the unexpected
response, 'Then were the men exceedingly afraid and said unto
him, "Why hast thou done this?" ' Covering the lack of logic,

the Old Testament writer adds an explanation: 'For the men knew that he fled from the presence of the Lord, because he had told them.' When had he told them? Why not say so at the appropriate point in the story? In this part of the tale there are other signs of muddle, unexpected omissions, and some actual repetition (e.g. I. 11–13). Not surprisingly, the poet of *Patience* changes the order to produce a coherent sequence, removes the inconsistencies, and tidies it all up. At a later point comes a more significant inconsistency (if that is what it is): Jonah's protest at the Lord's mercy to Nineveh begins: 'I pray thee, O Lord, was not this my saying, when I was yet in my country?' Since Jonah had said nothing, the reader inevitably mutters 'No, it wasn't,' and is left wondering whether to read this as an attempt at hind-sight justification on Jonah's part or whether the writer is in-competent. The narrative looks, in places, like a confused summary of an earlier tale. It remains memorable not only for the great fish, but also for its demonstration of the mercy of God towards a Gentile city, and for its presentation of a rare protest against God's right to change his mind. But it is clear that this version is cutting down detail about Jonah and leaving in only those portions which express God's power and the need for submission to it. So the side-issue of the conversion of the sailors is fully expressed, but the writer has insufficient interest in the individual fate of Jonah to tell us whether he in turn submitted or not, preferring to leave his tale with God's rhetorical question: 'And should I not spare Nineveh, that great city, wherein are more than six score thousand persons that cannot discern between their right hand and their left hand; and also much cattle?' In a sense, of course, the very peculiarities seem to readers of a much later age part of its essence. Because it is ancient and oracular, one accepts the unexplained and the unrealised. Any attempt to imagine in naturalistic terms is likely to seem a weakening of the tale's preternatural forcefulness. This is, nevertheless, the attempt the poet of *Patience* makes.

Because it was a cryptic story, it was not often used by medieval homilists; nor did it achieve a standard meaning and use for medieval commentators. Jonah was sometimes interpreted as a type of Christ and emphasis put upon his success in bringing Nineveh to repentance and his prefiguring of Christ's descent

into Hell; this was because of the reference to Jonah in *Matthew*
XII. 40-1.[3] Jerome was the source of a tradition which justified
Jonah's actions as the result of fear for the downfall of Israel,
if the Gentiles were saved.[4] On the other hand, Jonah was sometimes blamed, and the fact that Tertullian's *De Iona* uses Jonah
as an example of futile flight from God's command is one of
the reasons why it has been thought that the English poet may
have made use of the Latin poem.[5] The story of Jonah did also
occur as an example of the patience of God.[6] The lack of one
accepted meaning gave to the imaginative writer a story with the
authority of scripture, but with much left out and with some
ambiguity of sense; with these qualities it is by no means an
obvious illustration of patience. Rejection of the traditional
exemplar of patience, Job, in favour of this equivocal tale suggests
that the literal interest of the story itself was more important than
its exemplary force.[7]

The over-all impression of the poet's treatment is that it was
his main concern to amplify, realise and dramatise the tale by
adding details of visual appearance, physical actions, feelings and
motives. Close comparison of the two shows that the degree of
amplification does, however, vary considerably. At one end of
the scale the poet translates or paraphrases, making those additions
concomitant upon turning the material into English and into
a traditional metre. At the other end he invents passages which
are necessary to his own interpretation of the tale. Between the
two extremes the poet colours his source by expanding, explaining and re-ordering.

The longest continuous passage where *Patience* follows the
Vulgate closely is Jonah's prayer to God from the belly of the
whale. Here one can see how a medieval maker of alliterative
verse used the sounds as well as the sense of his source-material
as his skeleton. The poet tends to use one phrase or clause of
the Vulgate as the basis of a line of verse, and one verse of the
Bible as the basis of a quatrain. Quite often he uses one word of
his Latin unit as the foundation of the alliterative pattern of his
line. This and other characteristics of the treatment can best
be observed by looking at a portion of the two texts side by
side.

Vulgate, Cap. II. v. 3–7 (Authorised Version in brackets)

Clamavi de tribulatione mea ad Dominum,
(I cried by reason of mine affliction unto the Lord;)
       Patience 305–24
       Lorde, to the haf I cleped in carez ful stronge

From the start the English poet uses a direct vocative and the second person for God, adding intensity and taking the reader into the imagined moment of the prayer.

et exaudivit me: de ventre inferi clamavi, et exaudisti vocem meam.
(and he heard me; out of the belly of hell cried I, and thou heardest my voice.)
       Out of the hole thou me herde of hellen wombe;
       I calde and thou knew my uncler steven.

In place of the Vulgate's repetition with variation and modulation into the second person, the adaptor creates a development by using two new verbs, instead of repeating *cleped* and *herde*; the Lord first heard and then knew, and the addition of 'unclear' invites the reader to imagine this recognition in terms of the muffled tones of the prophet coming up from the depths of the sea. Again the moment is evoked, while the sense of patterned expression is retained.

Et proiecisti me in profundum in corde maris.
(For thou hadst cast me into the deep, in the midst of the seas;)
       Thou diptez me of the depe se into the dymme hert,

The imitative quality of *diptez* and the colouring added by the adjective *dymme* together realise and heighten the moment; *dymme* echoes both the sense of *uncler* and the sound of *diptez* and so binds the lines together.

et flumen circumdedit me: (and the floods compassed me about:)
       The grete flem of thy flod folded me umbe;

The line obviously grew from *flumen* as the following one does from *gurgites*.

omnes gurgites tui et fluctus tui super me transierunt.
(all thy billows and thy waves passed over me.)
       Alle the gotez of thy guferes and groundelez powlez,

> And thy stryvande stremez of stryndez so mony,
>   In on daschande dam dryvez me over.

The water is given life in a series of amplifications of the meaning
and sound of the Latin words; a crescendo of surging movement
breaks in the onomatopoeia of 'on daschande dam'. In counter-
point to the alliterative patterns within the lines run echoing
sounds across the line-divisions, such as *stryvande/dryvez*, and the
echo of *dymme* running through *flem, umbe, stremez* to *dam*; the
effect is of a rich weaving together of images and sounds, developed quite appropriately from the Vulgate's own rhetorical use of
repetition.

> *Et ego dixi*:
> (Then I said,)
>   And yet I sayde as I seet in the se bothem:

The reader is again encouraged to envisage the actual moment
of prayer and Jonah's situation.

> *Abiectus sum a conspectu oculorum tuorum*:
> (I am cast out of thy sight:)
>   Careful am I, kest out from thy cler yyen,
>   And desevered fro thy syght;

Here the English poet imitates the Latin order, throwing emphasis
on *Careful* by disturbing the ear's expectation of normal alliterative positioning of strong stress; he translates both the literal
and the metaphorical sense of *Abiectus*; he adds the word *cler*,
making a contrast between the unclear voice of Jonah and the
clear sight of God and so confirming the impression that *uncler*
had moral as well as sensory implications.

> *verumtamen rursus videbo templum sanctum tuum.*
> (yet I will look again towards thy holy temple.)
>   yet surely I hope
>   Efte to trede on thy temple and teme to thyselven.

The substitution of *trede* for *videbo* may be because of the alliterative pattern but it is consistent with the poet's tendency to use,
where he can, physical words which envisage Jonah's experience;
to see the temple again involves being on *terra firma*, which Jonah

longs for and so his hope is expressed as a hope for solid ground beneath his feet. The possessive idea of *tuum* is given fuller emotional weight by being translated into a clause, *teme to thy selven* ('belong to you').

> *Circumdederunt me aquae usque ad animam;*
> (The waters compassed me about even to the soul:)
>> I am wrapped in water to my wo stoundez.

Again the poet chooses a mimetic, physical verb, and develops *ad animam* by thinking what the soul must have experienced, translating the idea into the actual effect of sorrow.

> *abyssus vallavit me,*
> (the depth closed me round about,)
>> The abyme byndes the body that I byde inne,

The idea of *vallavit* ('surrounded with a rampart') is translated into an image of imprisonment, made threatening by the insistent echoing in *abyme, byndes, byde*.

> *pelagus operuit caput meum.*
> (the weeds [sc. *flood*] were wrapped about my head.)
>> The pure poplande hourle playes on my heved.

Here the poet deserts close translation for the onomatopoeia and the vigour of *pure poplande hourle* and the suggestiveness of *playes*, which the consonants of *pelagus* probably put into his head.

> *Ad extrema montium descendi:*
> (I went down to the bottoms of the mountains;)
>> To laste mere of uche a mount, man, am I fallen.

Because *mere* means both 'sea' and 'boundary' the line has more intense reference to Jonah's situation, and the plangently rhetorical interjection and inversion of *man, am I fallen* colours the line with a sense of his present state; he is fallen man in both literal and allegorical senses.

> *terrae vectes concluserunt me in aeternum:*
> (the earth with her bars was about me for ever:)
>> The barrez of uche a bonk ful bigly me haldes,
>> That I may lachche no lont,

In *ful bigly* one finds one of the very few weak phrases in the passage, used merely to fill out the sound⁄pattern.

et sublevabis de corruptione vitam meam, Domine Deus meus.
(yet hast thou brought up my life from corruption, O Lord my God.)

and thou my lyf weldes.
Thou schal releve me, renk, whil thy ryght slepez,
Thurgh myght of thy mercy that mukel is to tryste.

Here the poet departs from his text, clearly because, in his view, it is not appropriate that one should think of Jonah as free from corruption; he substitutes a recognition of God's power and an interestingly ambiguous statement which I shall comment on later.

By such close comparison one can appreciate how the poet gradually built up a texture of expression which transforms the source into something more intensely pictured, more varied and complex. Even when he follows the Latin closely, he creates a different effect, always amplifying slightly, if only to augment the emotional quality. There are only occasional signs that he deliberately filled out the alliterative lines, in some addition of adjectives and adverbs, and there are hardly any obvious tags. The situation of Jonah is emphasised throughout by touches of physical placing and lyrical and rhetorical force are added too. An intimate and fervent quality is given by the frequent use of personal pronouns, especially in the succession of possessives in 'thy flod', 'thy guferes', 'thy stremez', 'thy cler yyen', and 'thy syght', where the English poet adds to the number of such refer⁄ences already present in the Latin. Most important, the poet introduces touches which remind us of the nature of Jonah as he has been portrayed in the earlier part of the poem; though here at his most humble and obedient, he has not changed character and, though he may have learned from his experience, there is a flavour of expediency about the prayer, particularly in its later parts.

In the rest of the tale the additions are lengthier and more far⁄reaching, but even here it is obvious that *Patience* is a trans⁄formation rather than a translation, which augments literal senses and effects in particular. The treatment indicates that it was not a simple illustration of a point that the poet had in mind, since such amplification consistently complicates moral points by an excess of emotional and sensory detail. The poet's modifica-tion of the structure of *Jonah* seems to confirm this.

The narrative in *Patience* is, as is the Vulgate text, divided into four sections, but the second of the four, dealing with Jonah in the whale, is mainly the poet's invention. Most of the material of the Vulgate's second chapter is run together with the third chapter in the section that follows. The re-division of the matter means that the sections more strikingly correspond to Jonah's various states of mind and to moral and emotional aspects of the tale. Section I (lines 61–244) has the ship as setting and deals with Jonah's crime; it shows him in panic and flight, pursued and captured. It is full of incident, violence, dramatic interchange and a changing situation, with emphasis on character and motive and pictures of desperate action. It has its own complete narrative form in the sequence of flight, capture, and recognition of guilt, and shows Jonah, though he is portrayed with some sympathy, as wrong in all directions and heedless of the fate of others. As Section I concentrates on crime, so Section II (lines 245–304) isolates Jonah's punishment. It too has its own vividly realised setting, the belly of the whale, and shows Jonah alone, entombed and given his own private hell, surrounded by filth and evil, the emblems of his sin. By putting Jonah's prayer and release into the same section as the story of what happens in Nineveh, the poet creates, in Section III (lines 305–408), a unit of all the parts of the tale dealing with repentance, and presents, with the city as the main setting, a series of images of submission to God. The repentance of the Ninevites reflects and yet contrasts with Jonah's recognition of obligation, and the penitential sequence culminates in God's own restraint. In Section IV (lines 409–523) the bower is setting for the fourth movement of the action, Jonah's relapse into anger and petulant excesses of childish joy and violent protest. This section is dominated by dramatic dialogue and by the image of the woodbine, which acts not only as the symbol by means of which God teaches but also as an emblem of Jonah's self-destructive fury.

The structure is one, therefore, which suggests that the poet saw the tale as a dramatic sequence of contrasting phases, develop-ing one from another. His visualisation of the four settings and his division of the material according to dominant moods and dramatic reversals again suggest an author more interested in exciting the reader's interest in feelings and in suggestive images than simply in illustration of a moral argument. However, the poem does proclaim itself an examination of patience and the narrator says that he means to guide us; in order to test how far the narrator is to be trusted, the poem must be taken in sequence, and so one must begin with *Patience*'s curious prologue.

2. The prologue

Pacience is a poynt, thagh hit displese ofte.

The thoughtful, balanced opening line of *Patience* presents the theme of the poem as a debating point, but in simple, intimate style. The obvious sense, 'Patience *is* a virtue (though it may often displease),' is underlined by a suggestion of knowing reassurance: 'there is some point in being patient (though you might not think so)'. The lines that follow (2–7) build up an initial impression of a voice of reason speaking of general truths based on experience and weighing one thing against another:

For quoso suffer cowthe syt, sele wolde folwe.
And quo for thro may noght thole, the thikker he sufferes.

(5–6)

The neat patterning has an almost Augustan quality, with the combination of chiasmus, pointing of the sense by repeated sounds, and the witty contrast of the two meanings of *suffer*. The poet clearly is thinking in terms of the paradox of hateful good and his later linking of patience and poverty shows that his line of thought is similar to Chaucer's traditional presentation of poverty through the mouth of the old hag in *The Wife of Bath's Tale*.[8] The paradox is exploited by the play on words which contrasts sufferance and suffering, as well as in the basic antithesis of virtue and discomfort which is used in each of the four sentences in the first eight lines of the poem. The neat introduction of first-person pronouns in the eighth line increases the sense of an intimate voice speaking from the ripeness of personal experience and the balance of reasoned judgement; nowhere in Middle English outside Chaucer is there an opening so urbane:

Pacience is a poynt, thagh hit displese ofte.
When hevy herttes ben hurt wyth hethyng other elles,
Suffraunce may aswagen hem and the swelme lethe.
For ho quelles uche a qued and quenches malyce.
For quo-so suffer cowthe syt, sele wolde folwe,
And quo for thro may noght thole, the thikker he sufferes.
Then is better to abyde the bur umbe-stoundes,
Then ay throw forth my thro, thagh me thynk ylle.   (1–8)

The truth of experience is succeeded by the truth of authority
as the poet paraphrases the Beatitudes, but authority is given a
familiar, personal ring by being communicated as part of the
speaker's own experience:

I herde on a halyday, at a hyghe masse,
How Mathew melede . . .   (9–10)

The speaker, that is, is no preacher but an ordinary man like
ourselves summarising what he has heard. This intimate modulation of the authoritative text is continued in the sixteen lines
devoted to the text itself. First, by devoting two lines to each
Beatitude with a regular alternation of 'Thay arn happen' and
'For' as line-openings, the poet modifies the declarative force of
the words of St. Matthew and makes a pattern out of them.
Secondly the frequent occurrence in the English of possessive
phrases ('alle her wylle', 'her harme', 'her mede', 'her savyour',
'her pese', 'her hert') gives a strongly personal, even cosy, tone to
the whole. And thirdly the choice of the word 'happen' to render
beati puts more emphasis on the good fortune of the reward than
the blessedness of the state that deserved it. The cumulative effect
is a softening of the force of the original, which brings the
scriptural text into harmony with the tone of the rest of the prologue, intimate but detached, combining friendliness and wit.
The poet's interpretation of patience as the quality of those who
'con her hert stere' gives a broad basis to the theme of the poem,
combining sufferance with self-control.
    In the lines that develop from the scriptural text the speaker
again ingratiates himself with his audience by associating himself
with us ('the happes . . . that uus bihyght weren'), and gives

an informal, even playful, aspect to the Beatitudes by personifying
them as a company of allegorical dames, with two of whom he
proposes to have a romp:

> Dame Povert, Dame Pitee, Dame Penaunce the thrydde,
> Dame Mekenesse, Dame Mercy and miry Clannesse,
> And thenne Dame Pes and Pacyence put in therafter.
> He were happen that hade one, alle were the better.
> Bot syn I am put to a poynt that poverté hatte,
> I schal me porvay pacyence and play me with bothe.
>
> (31–6)

'How happy could I be with either, if t'other dear charmer came
along too' seems to be the spirit; the 'play' is, of course, intellectual
cultivation, but the implicit comparison between following a
virtuous pattern of life and admiration for a woman creates a
humorous undertone which, in combination with the chatty
reference to the speaker's own situation, tends to undermine the
serious aspects of the passage. Intellectual play is even more
strongly apparent in the lines that follow, which are pure
university wit:

> For in the tyxte there thyse two arn in teme layde,
> Hit arn fettled in on forme, the forme and the laste,
> And by quest of her quoyntyse enquylen on mede,
> And als, in myn upynyoun, hit arn of on kynde.
>
> (37–40)

By way of a pun on *teme*, in the senses of 'theme' and 'team',[9]
which makes one apprehend the virtues simultaneously as allotted
their place in the theme and as coupled in harness, the poet makes
an emblematic pattern from the first and last of the Beatitudes.
As with the first and last lines of *Patience* itself, so with poverty
and patience, the beginning and end together define oneness and
wholeness. I think Jay Schleusener is probably right when he
suggests that the idea has its origin in Augustine's view that each
Beatitude is a maxim, that together the maxims form a seven-
rung ladder to perfection, and that the eighth 'returns as it were
to the beginning; it presents and approves something consummate
and perfect.'[10] I would not agree with Schleusener, however,

that this is to be taken very seriously in *Patience* or that it has much
to do with the rest of the poem. It seems an obvious example of
local wit and love of intellectual ingenuity. The poet is seeking
reasons for linking poverty and patience and finds them at three
levels: the level of common sense and experience (that they are
alike in quality); the level of the logic of the textual authority
(that Matthew allots them the same reward); and the abstract
level of symbolic form (that, by being first and last, they are fixed
together in a mould). The play on the two senses of *forme* in line
38 points the witty quality of the thought. It juxtaposes the two
meanings 'formula' and 'first', but the repeated sound creates a
sort of double-take effect which makes one see that within the
common phrase 'the forme and the laste' are two hidden nouns.
Since the word *last* can mean 'form', 'mould', 'print', 'trace'
(from OE *last*), 'load', 'cargo', 'content' (from OE *blæst*), and
'sin', 'vice' (from ON *lostr*), there are plenty of interesting ambiguities available. The pattern-making and word-play turns
one's mind in the direction of intellectual sport, and other features
in the prologue to *Patience* confirm the feeling that this introductory
section is not fully committed to a point of view, but belongs to
the sphere of 'play'. Certainly there is nothing which could be
called an exposition of the theme of patience; rather the poet
allusively and ingeniously sports with it, and aims at an intimate
and lively reasonableness.

When the poet turns from pattern-making to speak of his own
poverty, he speaks with self-deprecating, equally urbane rueful-
ness, introducing instances and rhetorical questions which are the
first obviously persuasive devices in the prologue, though they
continue in the same common-sense voice, with its touches of
colloquialism, intimacy and humour. The instances are invented
to make a smooth transition to the tale of Jonah, and they fore-
cast what is to happen, but that the instance of patience is the
obedience of servant to liege-lord is significant; it emphasises the
fact that there is one law for the rich, another for the poor. That
patience is expedient for those who will get nowhere by being
impatient is the level at which the poet's message is made applic-
able to daily life. This provides the neat bridge to the introduction
of Jonah as an example of a fool lacking the sense of the narrator
and treated therefore with scorn and ironic wit:

Did not Jonas in Jude suche jape sum-whyle?
To sette hym to sewrte, unsounde he hym feches.

(57–8)

What then does this prologue amount to? It is not a homiletic setting-forth of the nature and operation of patience, nor an ex-hortation. It presents different aspects of its subject in a reasoned, intimate, and at times playful tone. It is best described as a dramatic monologue, in the sense that the poet acts out the attitude of mind which he is recommending. He presents himself in a trying situation as capable of a controlled attitude to difficulties; he is aware of the resources of humour, and of the balanced play of mind around ideas and words; he is sober and sensible and open to the reassurance of scriptural teaching; he knows how to use authority and experience to make a virtue of necessity, and how to do it in a civilised way. The prologue is modelled on the vision-poem's use of a first-person narrator who mediates between the reader and the narrative and I suspect that it has learnt something of its urbane, intimate quality from Chaucer's ex-ample. That its effect is eventually rather cynical is, I think, deliberate and is confirmed by the epilogue. Sweet reasonableness and humble acceptance are not necessarily attitudes with which the reader is completely in sympathy, and his choice of narrative, as well as his beginning and ending with antithesis of virtue and the difficulty of adopting it, shows that the author knows it. The polished obliqueness of the prologue does not encourage us to identify the speaker as the authoritative, disinterested author, let alone the wise preacher, in spite of his promise: 'I schal wysse yow.' He is a fictional character whose own attitude is given to us as a touchstone. The prologue does not read like something which can fairly be described as a 'homily', and by being articulated in a voice with an identity separable from the author's, it provides a freer basis for the poet's ironies than does the framework of *Purity*.

3. Story and epilogue

The poet begins with a brief tale-teller's formula, placing the action and identifying the central character, and then proceeds to the Biblical matter. Lines 63–88 are developed from the first two verses of *Jonah* I which state simply that the word of God came to Jonah. The poet characterises God's command as harsh, suggesting the relationship of liege-lord and vassal already referred to in the prologue, and indicates from the start the reaction of Jonah, about which the Vulgate has nothing. The message itself, by its personalising of the Ninevites ('hit arn so wykke . . . her malys is so much') is much more dramatic and frightening and it is phrased so as further to characterise God as furious, vengeful and impatient:

> ' I may not abide,
> Bot venge me on her vilanye and venym bilyve.'
>
> (70–1)

Jonah's reaction therefore seems not unnatural, and it is clear that the poet's first major addition to his text, the feelings of Jonah, was the result of wondering why Jonah fled as soon as he heard the word of God. His invention of a reaction (line 73ff.) has led him to colour the actual issuing of the command with elements that might cause fear and hence to imagine the nature of a God who could inspire such fear. So God's angry description of the evil of the Ninevites leads to Jonah's visualisation of the possible effects of his carrying out the command:

> 'I com wyth those tythynges, thay ta me bylyve,
> Pynez me in a prysoun, put me in stokkes,
> Wrythe me in a warlok, wrast out myn yyen.' (78–80)

This current of thought runs quickly to rejection of the message and an instinctive decision that his own safety matters more. The only reason for the message must be that 'my gaynlych God' wishes his death, which is another good reason for going 'sum other waye' so that 'he letes me alone'. Lines 89–96, based on *Jonah* I. 3, take him to Joppa 'ay janglande for tene', resentful that God sits too high to care if he is captured, stripped and crucified in Nineveh.

The initial impression of Jonah and his situation is a mixed one. There is some justification for his fear and his foreseeing of difficulties. Commands from imperious divinities are traditionally troublesome and if Jonah is a coward, he is not the first or the last and wouldn't most of us be in such circumstances? The poet suggests this reaction by presenting Jonah's thoughts in what we may call average human terms. 'This is a mervayl message a man forto preche' (81) expresses with nice colloquial irony that resentful sense of inadequacy for superhuman tasks. One's heart hardens against him as the poet shows fear developing into self-pity and reminds one that the prophet had an obligation to do something in return for the protection that he expects God to provide. Also Jonah's vivid imaginings of punishment and torture have a neurotic, though truthful, note which culminates in the comic petulance of:

> ay janglande for tene
> That he nolde thole for no thyng non of those pynes.
>
> (90–1)

However, even as one condemns Jonah's want of a sense of obligation, of obedience, of reason, one understands him. The poet has invented a character for Jonah and begins to display it, mainly in direct speech. One's recognition of a weak, fearful and imaginative man, moved by fear to petulance and flight creates a kind of sympathy, which makes one's disapproval affectionate and self-analytical.

The rest of the first section of the tale (97–244) is dominated by the poet's skilful creation of a dramatic and realistic narrative out of the Vulgate's bare account of Jonah's taking ship, the storm, the casting of lots and the casting overboard of Jonah. A flurry of technical language contributes to the impression of movement and speed in the flight; this leads to Jonah's relief, which is quickly checked by the narrator's ironic comments:

> Lo, the wytles wrechche, for he wolde noght suffer.
> Now hatz he put hym in plyt of peril wel more.
>
> (113–14)

and a reminder of God's all-seeing power, supported by the quotation from Psalm XCIII (94 in AV) that is used for the same purpose in *Purity*. This leads in a smooth, natural narrative sequence to God's pursuit ('For the welder of wyt . . . at wylle hatz he slyghtes') and rousing of the winds. Unlike many another alliterative poet's depiction of a storm at sea, this one spends only a short time (137–44) on violent images of turbid water and moves quickly to the effect on the ship and the people in it. Several changes of order in the Vulgate's matter increase the sense of logical and dramatic sequence. First, we are made to follow the seamen's actions and thoughts, so that we have a developing account of their difficulties, attempts to remedy them, their fear and superstition, and their anger towards Jonah. Secondly, by placing the sailors' belief that there is a villain among them ('I leve here be sum losynger, sum lawles wrech') before the picture of the sleeping Jonah, the poet increases the ironic sus-pense and the sense of moving towards an inevitable end. And, thirdly, the poet makes a dramatic and moral point out of Jonah's absence from the scene—with all this desperate action on deck, Jonah has fled and is discovered huddled by the rudder-board, a repellent image of sloth, dead to responsibility and the lives of others:

> Slypped upon a sloumbe-slepe, and sloberande he routes.
>
> (186)

In place of the courteous questions of Scripture, Jonah is greeted by violent reproach, more taut, intense and naturalistic in its reflection of the resentment of Jonah's unregarding slumber:

> 'What the devel hatz thou don, doted wrech?
> What seches thou on see, synful schrewe,
> With thy lastes so luther to lose uus uchone?
> Hatz thou, gome, no governour ne god on to calle,
> That thou thus slydes on slepe when thou slayn worthes?'
>
> (196–200)

Jonah's reply is filled with sorrowful dignity and a recognition of God's power and his own sin. The poet increases the effect by cutting out the sailors' successive questions and bringing all the material into Jonah's own words, both directly (205–12) and indirectly (213–14). The sailors' instinctive attempt to get away from something they don't understand is fruitless, and they have no choice but to do as Jonah has suggested:

> Thenne nas no coumfort to kever, ne counsel non other,
> Bot Jonas into his juis jugge bylyve.   (223–4)

The pun on *juis*, in the senses of 'justice' or 'doom' and of 'liquid', gives a sardonic bite to the passage. Jonah has himself pronounced sentence as well as earned it and it is right that he should be jugged in his own juice. The poet then follows the actions of the sailors, and brings the section to a close by four lines of comment (in the manner of the end of the first part of *Sir Gawain*), contrasting them and Jonah and preparing for what follows:

Thagh thay be jolef for joye, Jonas yet dredes;
Thagh he nolde suffer no sore, his seele is on anter;
For what-so worthed of that wyye fro he in water dipped,
Hit were a wonder to wene, yif holy wryt nere.　(241-4)

In this first section the poet's attention is given mainly to bringing the narrative to life. He creates a physical world around the events, and often shapes the rhythm and sounds of the alliterative line to imitate movements and sensory aspects of the scene. The vividly depicted action is controlled by the poet's careful dovetailing of his material so that, from God's words to Jonah to the casting overboard, all unfolds in a consecutive sequence, punctuated by intense moments of suspense, action and speech, but moving towards an inevitable end. The events continually reflect on character and motive and are the outer aspects of the dramatic inter-play of the four voices present in the section, those of God, the sailors, the observing narrator and Jonah himself. The first three have each a characteristic tone: God's imperious asperity, expressed through his commands and the action of wind and water at his bidding; the sailor's fearful and resentful anger; and the narrator's superior judgements and detached ironies. Together they accumulate into a solid weight of different kinds of righteousness against the weak and guilty prophet. Jonah's voice is, in contrast, shifting, even at times shifty, but capable at last of self-criticism:

'Alle this meschef for me is made at thys tyme,
For I haf greved my God and gulty am founden;
Forthy berez me to the borde and bathes me theroute.
　　　　　　　　　　　　　　　　(209-11)

This stage of Jonah's drama shows his first chastisement and his learning of a first saddening lesson—that he cannot escape.

The narrator's comments are all devoted to emphasising the futility of Jonah's acts, both in that God is all-seeing and all-powerful
and in the ironic fact that it is Jonah's attempts to escape that have
brought him into greatest danger. The initial impression in
Jonah of a contemptible but understandable vulnerability is
fostered by the narrator's irony, which simultaneously displays
him as a fool and as a victim doomed to undergo trials and
punishments. For Jonah, at this stage, as for the sailors 'the lyf is ay
swete', though in time it will cease to seem so, and the reader has
some sympathetic reaction to the underdog aspect of the character,
with all men, God, Nature, and even the teller of his story
ranged against him.

The second section of the story (lines 245-304) is devoted to
Jonah's incarceration in the belly of the whale; it is almost
entirely the poet's invention, based on the material of only the
first two verses of *Jonah* II. In the invented portions the poet
weaves together several emotional and moral strands: Jonah's
misery and fear, God's preservation of Jonah, Jonah's awareness
of his fate, of God's sweetness, of his own fault and his first prayer
for mercy. These elements are held together by the physical
images of the startling experience of being in a whale and under
the sea. The imaginative visualisation of the scene is again very
effective; though depicting a totally strange and miraculous event,
the poet is concerned to make the literal narrative as convincing
and real as possible. So the section is full of sensory words,
emphatic, vigorous phrasing and similes, and lines whose rhythm
and sound mime the actions described. So, for instance, Jonah is
seen:

> Ay hel over hed hourlande aboute
> Til he blunt in a blok as brode as a halle.   (271-2)

The grotesque horror of these roads and halls, slippery with
stinking slime, envisages Jonah's experience for us, but the poet
can even enter into the whale's feelings as he depicts the frantic
wallowings and suggests that

> that mote in his mawe mad hym, I trowe,
> Thagh hit lyttel were hym wyth, to wamel at his hert.
> (299-300)

The diminution of Jonah is utter in his reduction to something
as small

> As mote in at a munster dor, so mukel wern his chawlez.
>
> (268)

which serves only to make a whale feel sick. The most powerfully
suggestive image of all is used to lead into Jonah's fervent prayer
to God for his release, as the poet imagines what Jonah hears of
the world beyond his own wallowing hell-mouth:

> Ande as sayled the segge, ay sykerly he herde
> The bygge borne on his bak and bete on his sydes.
>
> (301–2)

Together with these physical images goes a pointed expression
of moral ideas and of Jonah's state of mind, for which the poet
turns to those 'strong' rhetorical figures which give to the alliterative line something of the quality of the heroic couplet: inversion,
balance of one half of the line against the other, antithesis, and
irony.

> Lorde, colde watz his comfort, and his care huge
>
> (264)
>
> Ther watz bylded his bour, that wyl no bale suffer
>
> (276)
>
> ay thenkande on dryghtyn,
> His myght and his merci, his mesure thenne;
> Now he knawez hym in care, that couthe not in sele.
>
> (294–6)

The irony of 'ther watz bylded his bour' continues the detached
strain in the narrator's commentary, and the same irony later
makes a specific connection with Jonah's hiding in the bottom
of the ship. If Jonah thought the bottom of a boat was deep
enough to hide from God, what of his safety now?

Running through this section is another kind of irony, dependent upon the poet's reminders of the traditional hellish and devilish
associations of the whale. He comes 'fro the abyme', sent not by God
but by 'wyrde'; its belly stinks as the devil and 'savoured as helle'.
Jonah enters the whale as one sinking into a hell-mouth and is
preserved in 'Warlowez guttez' only through the protection of
'the hyghe heven-kyng'. The poet is making use here of the
parallel between Jonah's sojourn in the whale and Christ's

descent into Hell, just as his earlier reference to crucifixion had reminded us of Jonah's typology, but it is the piquancy and irony of the parallel that this poet is conscious of, not its appropriateness. Though, in a sense, a victim and later a scapegoat, this Jonah is no redeemer. Ironically he comes nearest to God when furthest from him; ironically too his purgatory becomes an oratory and the comparison of the whale's jaws to a minster door not without point. The parallel of hell enlarges the significance of Jonah's bizarre punishment, which is identified thus as symbolic and not just evidence of the malicious sense of humour of an irritated God. Jonah *is* made into a comic object as he reels about 'hele over hede', but we are made conscious also of the real horror of his punishment, of an element of dignity in his frightened penitence, and of the moral significance of the sojourn, as

> in a bouel of that best he bidez on lyve,
> Thre dayes and th[r]e nyght, ay thenkande on dryghtyn.
>
> (293–4)

The quality of Jonah's repentance and submission is expressed in the lengthy prayer which begins the third section of the tale; the poet has introduced earlier a shorter prayer (282–8), probably to justify the logic of the Vulgate's past tense *Clamavi*. As I pointed out above, the only significant change in the poet's paraphrase of the psalm in his version of the seventh verse of *Jonah* II. His rejection of the Vulgate here suggests that he does not wish to show Jonah as free from corruption, but rather to bring out the fact that Jonah is attempting to influence God. Submissive though the idea that God's justice is being neglected may be, there is an undercurrent of hypocritical ultimatum about it, which taints the humility of 'thurgh myght of thy mercy that mukel is to tryste' with a touch of expedient flattery. These under-currents are briefly suggested again in the later parts of the prayer. Though at his most humble and obedient here, Jonah has not, the poet seems to hint, changed character. There is a note of self-preserving caution about his promise

> 'to do the sacrafyse, when I schal save worthe'   (334)

and a touch of bribery about his promise to

> 'offer the for my hele a ful hol gyfte.'   (335)

Since God apparently is willing to release Jonah on the basis of this prayer, the mixture must be presumed to be effective in the poet's view, a view which not for the first time in the poem has a strain of cynicism woven into it.

Jonah's release from the whale is coloured by three additions: God's manner is characterised as still stern; the poet sets the seal on the irony of Jonah's futile flight by bringing him to land in the very place he had tried to avoid; and, in an ironical understatement, the poet suggests, through the familiar imagery of soiled clothing, that Jonah comes to shore still clad in the mantle of sin. Jonah is at last ready to fulfil God's command and we return to the beginning of the tale as, with the same brusque imperiousness, God again orders Jonah to warn Nineveh. He immediately does so and the tale goes on its inexorable course to God's change of mind. The poet's main elaborations here are, first, to add an ungracious bowing to the inevitable to Jonah's submission:

> 'Yisse, lorde' quoth the lede, 'lene me thy grace
> Forto go at thi gre—me gaynez non other.'   (347–8)

Secondly, he gives two warning speeches to Jonah and increases their forcefulness. Thirdly, he greatly augments the reaction of the Ninevites, both by emphasising their immediate fear and awe and by intensifying their penitent actions with physical details and rhetorical expansion of the king's speech:

> 'Sesez childer of her sok, soghe hem so never,
> Ne best bite on no brom ne no bent nauther,
> Passe to no pasture, ne pike non erbes,
> Ne non oxe to no hay, ne no horse to water.
> Al schal crye, forclemmed, with alle oure clere strenthe;
> The rurd schal ryse to hym that rawthe schal have.'
>
> (391–6)

The effect of this expansion, in particular, is to exaggerate the king's speech to such an extent that the rhetoric seems false, and when Jonah, a few lines later, protests that the people of Nineveh have gained forgiveness 'Wyth a prayer and a pyne', the reader cannot but feel that he has a point. The King of Nineveh's speech would, one feels, have been recognised by Goneril and Regan.

In this third section the poet consistently complicates and blurs one's moral judgements, with the intention, I suggest, of prevent‑ ing the confrontation of God and Jonah in the last part of the poem from seeming a matter of simple issues. Jonah is repentant, performs his allotted task with success and is, as we know, doomed to be unthanked for it. On the other hand, he is still self‑regarding, as the undercurrents of his prayer reveal, and sly, and he performs his duty only because 'me gaynez non other'. We can not approve of him but neither can we simply condemn him. The nature of God is also shown as equivocal. His just anger is flavoured with an unnecessary harshness, and his mercy with a suggestion that he is amenable to fair speech, particularly in the form of repetitive rhetoric. The poet, that is, makes one aware of the way the acts of God appear to human judgement, so that it is still necessary for God to justify himself if he is to be understood by Jonah and within the world the poem creates. The latter part of the third section presents a double narrative reversal, the 'right' action of Jonah after he has been so long in the wrong and the change of God's mind. So in classical nar‑ rative terms the tale moves to its climax in the fourth section.

The last part of the poem begins with the anger of Jonah, and the expression of it ('he wex as wroth as the wynde') is a reminder of God's earlier anger against Jonah, when he summoned the winds as his instruments of punishment. The image makes us conscious both of the parallel between the two, in that Jonah is now accusing God of not fulfilling obligations, and of the futility of Jonah's anger against the all‑powerful. When Jonah proceeds to self‑justification, the rhetorical question 'Watz not this ilk my worde . . . in my cuntre?', brings, as in the Vulgate, the answer 'No' to the reader's mind, but whereas in the Bible this is because no explanation had been given for Jonah's reluc‑ tance, in *Patience* it is because the poet has supplied reasons for flight and this was not one of them. The effect, therefore, is of duplicity and self‑righteousness, which leads to the poet's inven‑ tion of Jonah's scornful condemnation of the ease with which Nineveh has got off the hook. This suggestive and imaginative development of the material identifies both an element in Jonah's psychology, by which his resentment of his own harsh treatment expresses itself as a wish that others should suffer too, and also an ethical and theological aspect of the situation. Jonah's standards are revealed as narrower than God's and he sets his own judge-ment above God's, thinking nothing of repentant words and a return to right action. Jonah, more clearly than in the source, blames God for being soft, and the preceding lines (e.g. 'Wel knew I thi cortaysye, thy quoynt soffraunce') take on an ironic tinge in retrospect, since it becomes clear that to Jonah 'cortaysye' is no recommendation in a god, and, in any case, he has known other divine qualities. The ideas are developed further in the following elaboration of: *Domine, tolle quaeso animam meam a me; quia melior est mihi mors quam vita.*

> 'Now, lorde, lach out my lyf, hit lastes to longe;
> Bed me bilyve my bale stour and bryng me on ende,
> For me were swetter to swelt as swythe, as me thynk,
> Then lede lenger thi lore that thus me les makez.'
>
> (425–8)

To Jonah the rules have been broken and the only path open to him is to resign, both from the service of God, and from life itself. As the poet has developed the matter, the whole system of belief is rejected. Though earlier he had submitted to the inevitable, now, the poet suggests, he reverts to self-regard never fully over-come but, at the same time, shows a consistent logic which is a development of character and motive within the tale. Jonah's experience has taught him not the quality of mercy but God's harsh and relentless pursuit of the sinful man. Now what he has learnt from his own punishment is, apparently, undermined. In the face of the inconsistency of absolute power, by which Jonah is made nothing and his words turned into a lie, the life which once seemed sweet now seems pointless; death is sweeter.

As in the first section of *Patience*, when the poet is dealing with Jonah's 'tene', the impression is mixed. He invites condemnation of Jonah's putting self first, of his weak attempts to justify his wrong-doing and of his proneness to accidie. But the bitter force of the expression of feeling also carries conviction; the poet found some of his most pointed and memorable phrasing for the speeches of his central character. As a result, one understands exactly how Jonah could regard himself as a wronged man, who

has been made use of and who is ill-treated and unthanked.
There is an *element* of tragedy in this picture of a weak man who
has eventually performed a difficult office and who sees the great
act of his life brought, as it seems from his egotistical point of view,
to nothing. He has been put in a false position, diminished and
made into a lie (both are indicated by 'thus me les makez').
Again he receives only reproof and not unnaturally goes out
'joyles and janglande'.

In the passage that follows the poet elaborates the scene of the
bower by adding a day to the action, picturing the construction
of the bower from hay, ever-fern and other plants, and creating an
impression both of Jonah's affection for the thing he has made
and of God's provision of favour. From the three bald sentences
of *Jonah* IV. 6 the poet develops lines 443–66, envisaging the
bower as an object of beauty in such terms as to promote aesthetic
appreciation which the reader shares with Jonah:

> When the dawande day dryghtyn con sende,
> Thenne wakened the wyy under wod-bynde,
> Loked alofte on the lef that lylled grene;
> Such a lefsel of lof never lede hade . . .
> The gome glyght on the grene graciouse leves,
> That ever wayved a wynde so wythe and so cole;
> The schyre sunne hit umbe-schon, thagh no schafte myght
> The mountance of a lyttel mote upon that man schyne.
>
> (445–8, 453–6)

This is the only image of loveliness and pleasure in the bleak
world of the poem. Jonah's response is sympathetically described,
again with a mixture of what is understandable and shareable
and a note of excess in Jonah's childish joy, the opposite extreme
to his over-readiness to grief and anger. The further evidence that
Jonah is not one who can 'steer his heart', as he lies 'loltrande' in
the booth, not bothering to eat, and yet still wishing for the further
satisfaction of being able to possess the booth and take it home
with him, brings the mind back to the poem's theme; but the
childish grasping of pleasure is softened by innocent pathos.
The didactic point of the episode is made when, after the impression of beauty, we feel a pang at the worm's destruction of the
creeper; this works, as it should, as an image preparing the

way for God's lesson. But the main point is, because of the
poet's elaborations, accompanied by ironic and disturbing under‑
tones. We are shown Jonah once again asleep, a picture of sin‑
fulness and of vulnerability. The all‑powerful God is once more
demonstrating that 'at wylle hatz he slyghtes', and his resources
here seem to include tricks that tease in order to create suffering.
Jonah is, in such a moment, the epitome of man seen as hapless,
weak and lost. Though the reader subdues to the moral tenor
of the action his emotional reaction to the cruelty of letting a man
sleep in happiness while the source of happiness is destroyed,
yet the colouring given to the situation is designed to prevent an
over‑simple moral view which completely ignores suffering. The
scene of the booth, of Jonah protected in the shade, watched over
in sleep by God, and of the coming of the worm provides as a
sort of parody of the Garden of Eden, a series of ironies. God is
not acting as protector of the sleeping prophet but as chastiser;
the worm is not the enemy working against God but a tool
working for him; Jonah has no right to his situation of happy
innocent joy, is both self‑deluded and has been tricked into his
state of mind as he is to be tricked out of it; he does not, by choice,
eat of the tree of knowledge but has knowledge thrust upon him.
If Jonah is in a fool's paradise, yet it is one provided by God as a
lure.[11] The aesthetic appeal given to the bower by the poet's
elaboration also works ironically. It is seen almost as a work of
art and Jonah's feeling for it is not merely a selfish pleasure but an
appreciation which presupposes some sensibility in his nature,
consistent with earlier moments in *Patience*, such as his fearful
imagining of what the men of Nineveh might do to him. Imagina‑
tion and sensibility are not qualities which the reader will
necessarily think should be held in 'mesure'. In the destruction
of the bower, therefore, there is an element which exposes the
fact that there is a blur in the parallelism between the *wodbynde*
and the men of Nineveh; the parallel works in general terms of
the creator not wanting the destruction of what he has created,
but the poet's entering into detail makes us aware that a thing of
beauty has a different kind of value from the lives of men and
cattle.

In what follows it is the pathos of Jonah's awakening that the
poet stresses, and the expected development of this sorrow is a

further burst of fierce anger, echoing Jonah's earlier rejection of
God, but expressed even more strongly and tragically:

> 'A, thou maker of man, what maystery the thynkez
> Thus thy freke to forfare forbi alle other?
> With alle meschef that thou may, never thou me sparez.
> I kevered me a cumfort that now is caght fro me,
> My wod⁄bynde so wlonk that wered my heved;
> Bot now I se thou art sette my solace to reve.
> Why ne dyghttes thou me to diye? I dure to longe.'
>   (482–8)

God's rhetorical questions in response are as forcefully and justly
expressed:

> 'Is this ryght⁄wys, thou renk, alle thy ronk noyse,
> So wroth for a wod⁄bynde to wax so sone?
> Why art thou waymot, wyye, for so lyttel?'   (490–2)

and bring a reply superbly indicative of the poet's imaginative
penetration into the character he has created:

> 'Hit is not lyttel,' quoth the lede, 'bot lykker to ryght.
> I wolde I were of this worlde, wrapped in moldez.'
>   (493–4)

This exchange is the dramatic, if not the moral, climax of
Patience. God's words are just, controlled and pointed and put
Jonah firmly in his place, and yet Jonah is given words of
splendid dramatic truth and conviction. Petulant his expression
remains, for the poet maintains the skilful characterisation of this
foolish and vulnerable man, but the bitter resentment and the
sense that it is a matter of *principle* have a tragic ring of truth.
In this unequal combat Jonah can not win and might as well be
dead; the poet's development of the Vulgate's cryptic account
makes us feel the justice in his point of view.

God's final speech begins in a tone of calm reason and reproof,
expressing judgement of Jonah much more explicitly than the
source. From the last verse of the Vulgate text the poet develops
a lengthy passage (lines 501–23) bringing out the parallel,
implicit in the Bible, of creation, with emphasis on God's
regard for his creatures and the sorrow destruction would cause.

The poet adds pathos to the account of the helpless people and dumb beasts, and moves to a fine expression of the moral point:

'Why schulde I wrath wyth hem, sythen wyyez wyl torne.
And cum and cnawe me for kyng and my carpe leve?
Wer I as hastif as thou, heere, were harme lumpen;
Couthe I not thole bot as thou, ther thryved ful fewe.
I may not be so malicious and mylde be halden,
For malyse is nogh[t] to mayntyne boute mercy withinne.'

(518-23)

The nature of God is here most fully and sympathetically explored, with a New Testament spirit of love, mildness and mercy which is not in tune with some earlier actions and speeches in the tradition of the awesome Jehovah. The moral point of the parallel is firmly and effectively made, and the lack of discipline, measure and pity in Jonah clearly exposed.

It is clear that Jonah is wrong, but then we knew all along that he was wrong; it is not his rightness but his suffering that has been impressed upon us. The antithesis of sufferance and suffer-ing is turned at the end into a comparison between God and Jonah and the poet does not, any more than his source, suggest the effect of God's speech upon the rebellious prophet, leaving us with a firmly made moral point but an unresolved dramatic situation. Jonah, the melancholic and self-regarding man, is offered as a warning, but his feelings have been entered into with enough sympathy for his case to be disturbing. The poet makes artistic capital out of the open ending, since it provides an opportunity to move from God's speech to his short epilogue, with a slight change of tone, and relate the tale to his theme. Jonah has not replied and so is still in need of advice and remains, in a sense, the audience's representative. However, the poet is subtle enough to want the unresolved ending, whereby attitudes remain in conflict, for its own sake.

The epilogue echoes the tone of the prologue; the voice is calm and reasonable, colloquial with folk-wisdom, assured with recipes for content in affliction. But the return to the beginning in the final line:

That pacience is a nobel poynt, thagh hit displese ofte.

leaves us with the antithesis we started from; patience is a virtue but alas for the man who has need of it. The irony is obvious; though the reasonable voice may be an echo of God's it has not his authority and the self-consciously kindly note, tolerant, slightly patronising, brings the poem to an equivocal conclusion. If life is horrible, full of poverty and affliction, then it is expedient to submit, to avoid trouble, to compromise and make the best of it, but it is possible to question the necessity for sorrow and the things that displease oft. Jonah's is the voice of the fool who does, wrongly and neurotically, and to no profitable end. If this poem teaches, then it does so in the most complicated and truthful way, by making the reader aware of the complexity of issues, by involving him in a debate, finally unresolved and essentially irresolvable.

4. The dangerous edge of things

From the spare outline of *Jonah* the poet creates a sequence of scenes: the ship, the whale, Nineveh and the bower. Against these backgrounds he weaves together an outer drama of action and an inner drama of human weakness opposed to divine power. To the outer drama the poet adds physical detail which convinces us of the reality and historicity of the tale. He also adds structural and logical elements, such as his initial placing of the story 'in the termes of Jude' and the transition from the sailors, who are followed to port to complete the action of the first section, to Jonah at the beginning of the second. The effect of such devices is to bring the tale out of an ancient world of myth into a world of circumstance, history and probability. At the same time the inner drama is intensified by the poet's provision of images and symbols which colour the motives of the central character and our judgement of him. Among these are the 'slucched clothes' of Jonah as he comes to shore, the association of the whale and Hell, and the references to Jonah's traditional typology, but the most suggestive ones are the succession of Jonah's 'refuges', the hold of the ship, the cleanest corner of the whale's belly and 'his lyttel bothe'. Through these the poet identifies Jonah as one who seeks safe enclosures as hiding-places, thus adding a psychological undercurrent to his actions, and deepening one's understanding of the neurotic element in his excesses of feeling. Jonah is given characteristics both of childhood and of old age. To the lack of self-control and the vulnerability of these two ages of man, the poet adds a strong element of fear of life itself. This is symbolically represented in the pictures of Jonah huddled asleep in the darkness of the hold, sitting 'safe' in the dark whale's belly, and lolling in his bower looking out at the world. The reader's sense of God is also focused through these images, since it is his role to remove Jonah's refuges and to force him into the current of a life full of fear and threat.

The result of the development of the material on more than one level is not only that *Patience* has a wider range of feeling and thought than the Old Testament *Jonah*, but also that the relationship between human and divine becomes more complex. This can best be seen in the treatment of the two central figures.

One effect apparent in the presentation of God is that the poet involves him in the world of circumstance and gives him a character. In the Vulgate God is merely a mouth: '*Et factum est verbum Domini ad Ionam. . . dicens. . .*' But in English he 'with a roghlych rurd rowned in his ere'. In the condemnation of the Ninevites he displays anger and lack of sufferance and the poet takes the opportunity to emphasise these qualities again in God's second command to Jonah:

> Thenne a wynde of Goddez worde efte the wyye bruxlez:
> 'Nylt thou never to Nunive bi no kynnez wayez?'
> 'Yisse, lorde,' quoth the lede, 'lene me thy grace
> For-to go at thi gre; me gaynez non other.'
> 'Ris, aproche then to prech, lo, the place here!
> Lo, my lore is in the, loke, lance hit therinne!'   (345–50)

God's tone of schoolmasterly irritation and exasperation is in piquant contrast to Jonah's meek and patient suffering of the inevitable, and the pricks and scorns which Jonah has to endure are ironically provided by the same agency through whom, when their roles are reversed, the necessity for calm and merciful tenderness to the weakness of others is preached at the close of the poem. Thus God in *Patience* is, in one sense, brought to the same level as Jonah in that he is subject to the same emotions, and distinguished from Jonah not by a different nature but by applying emotions more discriminatingly, and, of course, by his greater power. The poet's treatment of God has the effect of making the extremes in his nature further apart; because the poet has in-tensified his anger and power, his mercy and forbearance seem a great dramatic reversal. So, while God's overcoming of anger and his access of mercy and sufferance are set against Jonah's relapse from submission into undisciplined rage, joy and despair, at the same time Jonah's logic and concern for fairness and prin-ciple, weak, narrow and petulant as they may be, are set against a sense of arbitrariness in the nature of God.

The fuller treatment of Jonah works in the same way, and it is a way which, in my opinion, is the inevitable result of the poet's using his imagination to interpret and to realise equally all the actions and moments of a cryptic and ambiguous tale. By projecting his mind into Jonah's separate actions the poet has produced a character study of great penetration and complexity. He is provided with motives where the Old Testament has none, but his irrational moments are also intensified. Jonah, therefore, becomes a more contemptible character than in the Vulgate, and is guilty of a worse collection of sins, including hypocrisy, ex-pediency, sloth, disregard of the safety of others, a too ready despair, and an inability to see the parallel between himself and the men of Nineveh. The reader's sense of Jonah's wrongness is increased by the narrator's distancing ironies and he is laid open both to condemnation and to scornful, dismissive laughter. But if Jonah's wrongness is intensified so are the 'sympathetic' elements in his nature and situation. His weaknesses are realised in terms of everyman's human failings. He is pictured in pathetic and moving littleness and frailty against the forces of storm, hellish whale and burning sun. The references to his Christ-like role do not work entirely against him because they remind us that, though completely inadequate for the part of saviour, he is type-cast for the part of victim and scapegoat. Neither, in my view, is Jonah's rebellion against God something which, as A. C. Spearing suggests, 'for the medieval poet can only be comic';[12] it is comic, but it is not only comic, because the medieval poet has entered sufficiently into Jonah to make us see from his point of view as well as the narrator's. The words of Jonah are not all self-pitying and wayward but sometimes have force and dignity.

The combination of different, intensifying currents in the poet's presentation of Jonah goes beyond simple realism and penetrates into inward nature. By using a sensitive imagination to explain and fully to articulate the changing moods of Jonah, the basic outlines of which are provided by the source, he reaches intuitively into a more complex and more questioning view of human nature than is evident in the work of his contemporaries. He has per-ceived in Jonah a man who wants the reassurance of strict rules for living, and who feels the need for protection, yet resents the obligations which the protector lays on him. A brilliant portrait emerges of one of life's resigners, who is both worse and better than his Biblical original.

Though at the level of universal truth the story of Jonah is an example of God's patient dealings, at the realised level of human experience it is a tale of suffering. The poet is not inter-ested exclusively in one of these, but in the antithesis which they form, even in the sheer *drama* of the juxtaposition; the poem is as much an exploration of what makes patience displease oft as of patience as a noble point. The poet leaves us with the confronta-tion of God and Jonah—not with capitulation but antithesis, which leads to the advice to take the better part, but leaves it open to us to realise the force of the worse. The poet, using irony and antithesis as his tools, creates a sense of potential tragedy within comedy. The thought lying behind the conception seems to me akin to, and possibly influenced by, the thought of some fourteenth-century sceptic philosophers, particularly William of Ockham. Gordon Leff epitomises Ockham's combination of empiricism and contingency as follows: 'At the immediate point of human experience, only the individual is real: at the summit of all existence, God's will is the only arbiter.'[13] (The arbitrary quality in the poet's view of God could also be based on the Ockhamist view of God's Absolute Power.) But, whether or not the poet knew of sceptic views, he seems to be trying to use poetry to explore that complex middle ground between the two extremes, the area where human experience comes into conflict with the supernal, and where the reality of the individual possesses one kind of truth, the will of God another. By inviting us to respond in terms of realised actions, feelings, sights and sounds, the poet makes us judge in a way appropriate to such terms, and thus view

Jonah in the light of ordinary human behaviour. Given his character (which the poet does everything he can to develop, illustrate and make consistent), Jonah was bound to behave in the way he did; the tale, thus, becomes a tragedy of character, dominated by images of man's life as a futile attempt to find refuge from harsh reality. But, of course, it remains a piece of 'divine comedy' if it is viewed from the point of view of the hard-shelled urbanity of the narrator's voice.

If one attempts to sum up *Patience* it is difficult not to conclude that, while the poet ostensibly tells the story of Jonah as an exemplum to teach the virtue of patience by displaying the dis-comforts of the impatient man, in fact both the prologue and the narrative contain elements which complicate any initial impression of a simply conceived poem. 'Patience,' as one of Ivy Compton-Burnett's characters puts it, 'contains more impatience than anything else', and at the end of the poem we know more about impatience than about how to contain it. Of the use of negative exempla, in both *Patience* and *Purity*, J. J. Anderson claims that 'although examples of "patient" and "pure" lives might suffice to demonstrate the desirability of the two virtues in question, only the method adopted by the poet will enable him to present them as *necessary*; the negative approach is the more forceful'.[14] I can only say that I do not find it so. The works of art which most forcefully suggest that patience is a virtue and a necessary thing are, to my mind, those which show the noble endurance of adversity. One needs to be shown that

> There is a comfort in the strength of love;
> 'Twill make a thing endurable, which else
> Would overset the brain, or break the heart.

or to be made to experience the moment when impatient protest is quelled and

> Me thoughts I heard one calling, Childe:
> And I reply'd, My Lord.

If the author of *Patience* really thought that after reading his poem we would all resolve to 'be preve and be pacient in payne and in joye', then he was a fool, and there is plenty of other evidence that he was not. A poem can not mean what is opposite to the weight of experience within the poem, no matter what the poet may *say*, and the weight of shown experience in *Patience* is Jonah's experience of suffering. The narrator's experience is light-weight in comparison and his comfortable references to his poverty carry little moral force. As David Williams puts it, there is 'a calculated discrepancy between the truth expressed by the homilist and that revealed by the narrative.'[15] The only other explanation of the mixture of elements in the poem is that the poet's choice of tale was naive.

There seems to me an accumulation, as the poem proceeds, of evidence leading to the conclusion that the choice of a tale with inbuilt irony and conflict was a deliberately subtle one of the difficult case which tests and strains the maxim it supposedly supports. The choice of tale and its treatment are not those of the homilist but of the creative writer, who has used his imagination to amplify and interpret the nature of Jonah, and, in so doing, has aroused and satisfied that taste of which Browning speaks in *Bishop Blougram's Apology*:

> Our interest's on the dangerous edge of things.
> The honest thief, the tender murderer,
> The superstitious atheist, demireps
> That love and save their souls in new French books—
> We watch while these in equilibrium keep
> The giddy line midway. . .

After watching Jonah on his particular tightrope, and watching partly through the eyes of a worldly-wise and ironic narrator, our feeling is hardly that 'Patience is a nobel poynt', but some-thing more complex and equivocal, in the spirit perhaps of Cleopatra:

> All's but naught:
> Patience is sottish and impatience does
> Become a dog that's mad.

The effect of *Patience* is not to persuade but to illuminate and enlarge our understanding, and it thus identifies itself as a work of mature artistry, showing the poet as more ambitious and boldly intelligent in his interpretation of Scripture than he was with even the most effective parts of *Purity*.

5. Sir Gawain and the Green Knight

1. The literary sophistication of *Sir Gawain*

There is a marked difference between the last poem in the manuscript, *Sir Gawain and the Green Knight*, and the other three.[1] Its
material is the secular stuff of chivalry and marvellous adventure.
The story is therefore set in a framework of the mutability of
history, a more shadowy realm than the areas of virtue and vice or
of death and salvation within which the poet's other narratives
are placed. The voice which the poet adopts is also consonant
with his choice of matter, a voice mingling the professional patter
of the court entertainer and the manipulative arts of the all-
observing narrator. The narrator is, for the most part, the servant
of the tale, who speaks as moralist only in the passage explaining
the pentangle and otherwise keeps his distance, reminding one
of his stance in the other poems only when he regards his hero
with ironic detachment similar, in some ways, to the narrator's
comments on Jonah. There is no insistence that one should relate
what the poem says to one's own sense of life, nor that one should
see the tale as illustrative of a moral maxim. Any sense of exempli-
fication is only in what the reader may discern in the working out
of the fable.

At first reading, one accepts the story on the narrator's terms,
as an Arthurian adventure in which Gawain, Arthur's nephew
and leading knight of the Round Table, takes on a challenge to
the honour and reputation of Camelot, is tested and found to be
'On the fautlest freke that ever on fote yede', though he 'lakked a

lyttel' and falls below the ideal standards of knightly perfection, proving to be as subject as all men to 'the faut and the fayntyse of the flesch crabbed'. The poem is indisputably 'a romance', but it has an unexpected ending, employs more mystery, trickery and jesting than is common in romance and shows a more realistic sense of conduct and motive than one would accept as normal to the romance mode. The art which one recognises as the *Gawain*-poet's concern here is that of writing a sophisticated, literary romance which inhabits the same imaginative world as the one variously represented in the tales which Chaucer gave to his Knight, Squire, Franklin and Wife of Bath.[2]

Literary sophistication is present in many minor qualities of the poem and in at least three major aspects of the poet's handling of the subject-matter and the genre. First, *Sir Gawain* shows a n art-conscious sense of form and structure.[3] The larger capitals in the manuscript indicate that the poem is divided into four main parts, which correspond to the four stages of the action: the Green Knight's challenge at Camelot; Gawain's journey and reception at the Castle; the three days of Gawain's exchange-bargain with the Lord, who goes out hunting each day while Gawain is tempted by the Lady; the second meeting with the Green Knight and Gawain's return to Camelot. The disposition of the material is at once natural, in its following of a single narrative sequence, dramatic, in its focusing on the main encounters which define the poem's stages, and patterned, in its use of the traditional journey and return of the hero, in its beginning and ending at Camelot, and in the virtual repetition of the opening line as the last allitera-tive long line of the last stanza. Like *Pearl*, it has a hundred and one stanzas; to the symbolic qualities of the number, complete-ness combined with continuity, may be added the suggestion that it corresponds to the year and a day which the main action occupies. Similar evidence of studied craftmanship is found in the poet's choice and handling of metre. The stanza, rare in having an unfixed number of alliterative long lines before the five shorter lines of the bob-and-wheel, combines a sense of pattern with an impression of freedom and flexibility, since it is able to expand or contract according to the needs of the moment. The alternation of long and short lines creates a rhythmic balance between expan-sive expression and condensed; the long lines tend towards amassing of detail, complex sentence/structure and elaborate expression, while the short lines tend towards simple sentences, antithesis, summary and sententiousness. Though the poet some/ times reserves crucial or surprising information for the wheel and so exploits the break between stanzas, more noticeable is a tendency to open a stanza with a slight overlap, and even, at times, to echo a word or phrase and so to create a bond between stanzas. At other points too he carefully bridges gaps, even when there is a change of subject/matter, as can be seen in Part III of the poem. Each time the scene changes from hunting/field to bedroom, or the reverse, the poet binds together the two sets of events, either by continuing the alliterating sound over two or more lines (1178–80, 1560–1, 1893–4), or by some word/echo, parallel or contrast, such as the internal rhyme in 1468–9, the word/echo of *game/gamnez* and the parallel of rising moon and setting sun in 1313–21 and the repetition and alliterative echo in *morne* in 1729–32. These transitions are signs of a careful narrative art and of a desire on the poet's part for a feeling of fluid con/ tinuity even when the action is simultaneous rather than con/ secutive. From such details one receives a cumulative sense of a writer with professional and discriminating technical control.[4]

The sense of unified form and the impression of controlled fluency seem the more remarkable once one begins to analyse the material from which the poem is made, for the second main aspect of the poem which shows the poet's complex sense of art is his ambitious inter/weaving of narrative strands. Though *Sir Gawain* is full of conventional romance motifs, such as the challenge, the arming of the hero, the questing journey, the hero's stay at a strange castle, and the climax of a single combat, the poet has combined them in an ingenious 'new' plot of his own invention. The newness is, of course, in the combination, for the fable may be broken down into at least three narrative elements found separately in Celtic and French analogues, and known as the Beheading Game, the Exchange of Winnings and the Temptation.[5] The choice of these particular stories and the way in which they have been linked together means that within the unified plot of the poem there is a curious mixture of effects, considerable ambiguity, and a sense of intertwined and subtle richnesses of detail. The qualities inherent in each of the separate

motifs are played off against one another and shifting impressions
are thus created in the reader's mind. Among them the three
episodes cover a wide range of the possible colourings of romance.

The Temptation story shows romance at its nearest to fabliau;
though the tone is courtly, the scenes between Gawain and the
Lady belong to the world of sexual intrigue and are full of irony
and equivocation.[6] Their quality is intimate and comic; chivalry
is treated in the boudoir terms of elegant conversation and the
etiquette of love. By choosing the wiles of a woman as the means
by which Gawain's honour and self-command are tested, the
poet indicates a basically comic view of Gawain's failure, and
introduces a note of parody into the poem. The receiving and
giving back of Gawain's gains, the kisses from the Lady, both
expose him to ridicule: as receiver Gawain is a parody of the
youthful, chivalrous lover as he lies in bed using his wits to fend
off the importunities of the bold, provincial lady; as giver Gawain
is made to look a ninny as he solemnly plants kisses on the Lord's
teasing face. The vigour and virility of the accompanying hunts
seem equally to throw Gawain's knighthood into comic relief.
The sexual temptation turns out, in a sense, to be a blind; it
merely leads to the real trap, another exchange and another
promise from Gawain. The belt is ostensibly a love-gift having a
private meaning, as far as we know, only for the hero. It is later
clear that this element in the poem is a deliberate piece of misdirection. Gawain's attention is focused on sex and the dilemma
of balancing the demands of courtesy against those of loyalty,
but the Lady's success is in finding a way for Gawain to express
his fear of the Green Knight's axe. By doing no more than hint
at the possible significance of the bedroom scenes, the poet encourages the reader to enjoy them at the level of social comedy,
but later makes him feel that he has been wrong to do so; the
need to revise one's judgement creates an ambivalence in the
mind.

The same may be said of the Exchange of Winnings. Its main
purposes are to examine Gawain's conduct, to put the Temptation into a framework of promises, to subordinate the Lady to
the authority of the Lord and to continue from the Beheading
Game the theme of paying back. The atmosphere of the scenes
involving this part of the plot is one of good fellowship and

masculine fair play. The story is a courtly version of archetypal contests between heroes and brothers involving gratuitous bets and tests of honour, carried out in a spirit of teasing mirth, though mirth may be a thin covering for a real contest for superiority. In *Sir Gawain* misdirection is again involved for both hero and reader. As the Lord cries

> 'Make we mery quyl we may and mynne upon joye,
> For the lur may mon lach when so mon lykez.'
>
> (1681–2)

Gawain is encouraged by the reminder of the particular 'lur' waiting for him on the next day, to be as free and joyful as can be in the time left to him; only a boor would reject the challenge. The reader sees further, alerted to suspicion by scattered hints and the sense that all the doings at the Castle cannot be merely an interlude, but even the reader cannot see far enough to recognise the courtly game as possibly a matter of life and death.

The Beheading Game is inherently more heroic, although the challenge offered by the Green Knight is essentially arbitrary. It is an 'aventure' which will test the Round Table's spirit but which is necessitated only by the custom of challenge and honourable response. The emphasis on the challenge as a 'Crystemas gomen', in a sense, only confirms what one already knows about the world of chivalry, that acts are performed according to an artificial set of rules and performed for renown and 'nobelay'. The episode is characterised by that watered-down version of epic attitudes of masculine stoicism in the face of danger, of boasting speech, of ceremonial displays of high courage and so on, which one recognises as characteristic of medieval romance.[7] The attitudes remain from older epic traditions without the national or tribal motives which gave rise to them, and are valued for their own sake. Though presented as a game, therefore, it is clear that life is at stake and courage and honour are on trial. The story sets the events at the Castle in an embracing context of honour, obligation and fear. Misdirection works in the reverse way here, since what was apparently the main challenge proves to be dependent on the other tests and when Gawain comes to the Green Chapel he comes not to his supreme test but to a post-mortem on his behaviour. Again the reader has to revise his sense of what has occurred.

In the interweaving of the stories the poet shows intricacy of intention. The Beheading Game encloses the Exchange of Winnings which encloses the Temptation. Counterpointing this closed symmetry is the linear narrative sequence whereby the three plots are made mutually dependent: the outcome of the Beheading Game proves to depend on the hero's conduct in the Exchange of Winnings, which in turn depends upon his reaction to the Temptation. The Lady proves to be working under the direction of the Lord, who is the Green Knight, who in turn is working under the direction of Morgan la Fay, who is the old lady at the Castle, and, moreover, Gawain's aunt. Once one has read the poem the scattered clues to the relationship of the plots are apparent: the green and gold colouring of the belt, the hints that the Lady knows more than her apparent identity warrants, the irony in some of the Lord's speeches to Gawain, the parallel between Gawain and the treacherous fox, and so on. The effect is clever and complex; the poem makes a more concentrated and organic impression of a single adventure than is common in medieval narrative, and yet retains a pleasurable variety of inci/dents and scenes. The parts of the poem which may have seemed to be an interlude to the main action prove not have been digres/sive. The serious nature of the Beheading Game justifies in retrospect the serious view of the tests at the Castle, but the cheerful atmosphere of the scenes there fuses with the game aspect of the Green Knight's challenge and justifies the comic anti/climax of the scene in the desolate valley. The poem's end, insofar as it consists of a dispersal of mystery and a resolution of suspense, belongs to the idea of adventure fiction as a sequence of strange events whose logic is not apparent at the time they occur; the kind of unravelling which the poet provides pre/supposes one's expectation of a completion of the sequence, an untying of knots and a tying/up of loose ends. The revelation of Morgan as the villainess has seemed inadequate to many readers, 'a bone for the rationalising mind to play with',[8] but some such explanation had to be provided and the sense of anti/climax is made part of the artistic effect. On one level *Sir Gawain* is a medieval mystery story, though in modern terms it cheats by using magic, in which the first crime, the attempt on Guenevere's life, is foiled by Arthur's secure courage and power to re-assure, and the second crime, the attempt to lure Gawain into wrong-doing so that he could become the victim of justifiable homicide, is foiled by Gawain's own virtue and strength of mind. The Green Knight is allowed to be free of condemnation at the end because the motive for the crimes, malicious jealousy of Guenevere and the reputation of Camelot, is all ascribed to Morgan, as useful a tool to medieval romance-writers as the felonious butler and the mysterious woman-with-a-past were later to be to writers of detective stories. That this aspect of the poem may carry with it a sense of triviality is covered by the poet's comic conception of the whole. The poem tells an absurd story of plotting and secrecy, which yet has been given some depth of meaning; Gawain's adventure is a testing of knighthood and of an individual man, which yet turns out to be an anti-climax. The poet's creation of a chronological, consequen-tial narrative out of his several plot-elements thus makes the reader respond at different levels, that of the mysterious adventure-story and that of the testing and education of the hero, even if, for the moment, one ignores the further complexities of level which the poet introduces in his treatment and colouring of the tale.

The over-all impression of a unified poem telling a single story of adventure and shaped into a neat circle of action is, therefore, a triumph of illusion. The actual material of the poem consists of separate episodes which are to some extent arbitrary and absurd in themselves, and which have been joined together in a way which involves the chivalric hero in a comic and con-fusing tangle, and misleads the reader about the significance of what he reads. But, though the professionalism of technique is impressive, it is not simply as a triumph of structural craft over unworthy material that one would praise *Sir Gawain*. Its capacity for being read again and again with enjoyment lies rather in the richness with which the material has been adorned. The descrip-tive and dramatic powers of the poet, the command over tones of speech, the interweaving of moments, scenes and moods and of the serious and comic, the variety of settings and the combina-tion of brilliantly visualised actions and intricately subtle convers-ations, together create from the basic narrative a poem with a great range of expressiveness. Any anthologist of Middle English poetry would be likely to turn to *Sir Gawain* for the best examples in the period of idealised descriptions of court life, of realistic depiction of nature, of civilised conversation, of lively depictions of hunting and of physical action, of dramatic dialogue and of social comedy. The poetry has tremendous power to please the imagination, mainly, though not entirely, by the sense of a poet's eye dwelling in delight on objects and scenes. The settings are precisely depicted and used imaginatively to build up the dramatic effect of action and speech, and to create a sense of extreme contrast between a wintry outdoors and an indoor world of bodily comfort and courtly civilisation. The poet has, that is, imagined a world for his tale to inhabit, and it is arguable that the poem's true success is the world it depicts rather than the tale it tells, let alone any 'message' that the tale contains.[9]

Sir Gawain is not an assertive poem; it allows the reader some freedom of response, a freedom which, though it has often been abused, lies at the heart of its power to survive longer than most of the romances contemporary with it.[10] There are many in-dividual places in the poem where the reader is encouraged to speculate. Such instances are signs of the over-all uncertainty created by the poet's combination of a narrative framework which is traditionally romantic and unnaturalistic with a treatment which seeks, in varying degrees, to make the events seem real and plausible. The result is that *Sir Gawain* occupies a world which is simultaneously real and unreal, where the high ideals and exemplary forms of chivalry are continually being undercut by naturalistic details, sympathetic human feelings and the complexity of experience, but where, on the other hand, real behaviour is continually being confused by having to exist in the context of fantasy, symbolism and pattern. J. A. Burrow describes the combination as a mixture of modes, a combination of an older, romantic mode and a newer, realistic one which scales down and levels the experience of romance: 'The cumulative effect is to create in the reader a degree of uncertainty about the rules or laws governing the *Gawain*-world.'[11] It is my belief that such uncer-tainty is not an accidental product of a poet's re-treating in a new spirit tales which were originally differently conceived, but a designed effect, by a poet who loved to explore contraries. This combination of romance and realism is the third major aspect of the poem where the poet shows sophisticated artistic intention.

The combination of romance and realism in *Sir Gawain* identifies the audience for which it was designed as sophisticated enough not simply to take on trust the events of the tale. The poet indicates the taste for which he is catering in Arthur's desire to hear of 'sum mayn mervayle, that he myght trawe'; to be truly satisfying, marvellous adventure must be credible. The story is inevitably 'romantic', not only because it involves magic, but also because the poet uses a stylised narrative pattern, stock romance ideas, such as the value of courteous knighthood, and a conventional Arthurian background. Initially he takes up the stance of the court entertainer who assumes our interest in 'an outtrage awenture of Arthurez wonderez' and assumes our acquiescence in his loving picture of Camelot at feast-time, peopled by

> The most kyd knyghtez under Krystes selven,
> And the lovelokkest ladies that ever lif haden,
> And he the comlokest kyng that the court haldes.
>
> (51-3)

The idealised luxury and the ceremonial conduct of the scene in Camelot's hall are cast in a literary mould; there is never any possibility that we should mistake the scene for a slice of life. But within the frame the poet simultaneously depicts events in terms of plausible attitudes. The challenge is delivered in a way designed to cause anger and there is, therefore, a naturalistic reason for Arthur's acceptance of the 'foolish' bargain. One knows that a formal tradition decrees that Arthur is honour-bound to accept the challenge, even honour-bound to show a kingly anger, but the poet provides just cause for anger, and so imagines it as natural behaviour; the naturalistic and the formal work together and re-inforce one another. Similarly the presentation of the beheading and its aftermath combines precise physical detail and plausible conduct with the strange and marvellous. The disconcerting effect of the Green Knight on the court is another thing expressed in subtly naturalistic ways. The surprise of his actual appearance is shown through the courtiers in general, who are astonished and frightened. Arthur and, by implication, the other named heroes of the Round Table, are exempt from the naive wonder of 'the folk'. Arthur is himself, however, to be disconcerted and so the poet infuses a certain smugness into his treatment of the challenger and characterises him as youthful, cocksure, rather reckless, touchy and even pompous, as in his certainty that if Gawain does his job properly the challenger will not be alive to offer any return blow. The poet thus lays him open to the accusation of stupidity voiced later by the court; he is asking to be startled out of his self-assurance, and he is, but the poet makes subtle capital out of his astonishment by expressing it in relieved laughter and by using it further to display Arthur's self-command and his sense of fitting public behaviour.

All this obviously develops from the poet's considering his plot in terms of plausibility. He could have dealt with it as something given, belonging only in an unreal world of idealised and exem-plary motives, but this is not good enough for a discriminating poet writing at the end of the fourteenth century for a sophisticated audience.[12] The *Gawain*-poet's method is to create a web of inter-action which is complex enough for us to accept it and, as a consequence, to accept the whole scene as 'real'. In the middle of the cross-currents Gawain's entry into the action, though not without its own ironic aspects, has an acceptability it might otherwise have lacked; Arthur has responded to the challenge and Gawain is therefore free from any taint of pride or heedless-ness; his motive is the generous and seemly one of freeing his liege lord of a silly, unfitting affair.

Some readers have leapt upon the 'unfavourable' aspects attributed to Camelot and to Arthur and seen them as evidence that the poet is making moral criticisms of the court as a place of pride and hedonism, where courtesy is skin-deep, if that, and whose values are exposed by those of the other court at Hautdesert.[13] But to say this is to solidify what in the poem are only suggestions and hints, imagined as part of a dramatic scene; the hint of self-satisfaction in Arthur is a device of plausibility, highlighting the surprise of the talking head, and is set against other qualities in the king which identify him as a worthy master of a worthy house. Through such imagining of character and reaction and through the distinctions of tone between Arthur's addresses to the Green Knight, to Gawain, to Guenevere and to the court, as well as the command of appropriate speech displayed in the words of the Green Knight and of Gawain, the poet builds up an impression of Camelot as a far more real society than it seems in any other medieval English romance. By so doing he creates an effectively piquant and, at times, amusing contrast between the believable if partly idealised human society and the incredible, ambiguous and puzzling figure, who startles, taunts and challenges Camelot, but leaves it ultimately undeterred.

The presentation of events in terms of plausible feelings is one kind of colouring which the poet has applied to his plot. The sense of actuality and lifelikeness is the most striking aspect of his realisation of the narrative. Much of his attention is devoted to straightforward depiction of settings, activities, sights and sounds, which create an impression of a normal current of life going on apart from the extraordinary incidents in which the hero finds himself involved. The most extended realisation of this type is found in the vivid hunting-scenes, from which one can even acquire factual knowledge of how to organise a deer-hunt and how to cut up the quarry into joints of meat. The sense of real actions happening in real time and real places is strongest in the scenes at the Castle, which is pictured as a well-organised, upper-class, Christian household shaping its life according to mass-times, meal-times and bed-times, engaging in suitable occupations, lighting torches when they are needed, cleaning armour and looking after horses properly. Lifelike human reactions fit naturally into such a background, and scattered through the poem are many moments of sympathetic and pleasingly 'true' behaviour, such as the flattered pleasure of the courtiers at the Castle at having Gawain as a Christmas guest, Gawain's lying in bed pretending to be asleep while he wonders what the Lady is up to, the Green Knight's leaning on his axe as he watches Gawain with tolerant amusement. The pleasure and pungency of such touches depends on the unexpectedly honest impression of the narrator's reporting; characters do not behave according to a standard pattern and we have the feeling that the poet is exposing truthful intimate details which other romance-writers are inclined to ignore or suppress.

But however striking such verisimilitude is, it is not the only type of colouring which the poet uses. At some moments what he thought appropriate was a romantic and mysterious quality and the reader is invited to respond not in terms of recognition of 'real' behaviour, but in terms of wonder and speculation. An instance of this is the treatment of Gawain's journey from Camelot and his arrival at the Castle.

The winter journey forms part of that alternation in the poem of indoor and outdoor scenes by means of which the poet creates an effect of variety and inclusiveness, highlights the qualities of court and country, and provides images which enhance and sharpen one's sense of the tale. For reader and hero the poem's adventurous nature is experienced as a journey into the unknown, a leaving behind of normality, and a consequent exposure to the disconcerting qualities of a new environment. The journey is an exploration of places which turn out to be half familiar, half strange, occupying a landscape compounded of identified geographical locations at one extreme, and suggestively depicted but anonymous places at the other. The story begins and ends in a Britain of literary tradition, founded long ago by Felix Brutus, where dynasties have risen and fallen, where Lear and Cymbeline keep company with Arthur and the rest; this national legend, inherited by the alliterative poets from Geoffrey of Monmouth and the corpus of medieval chronicles, Latin, Celtic and English, provided a historical-cum-patriotic framework for legendary narrative. This Britain we accept as real in the sense that we have met it before and familiarity has given it honorary historical truth, even when we know its facts are fiction. So 'the ryalme of Logres' and Camelot are places vouched for by tradition. Nor is it strange that Camelot and Logres should be on the same map as the one which identifies the stages of Gawain's journey north; it is a version of those maps on which London, Avalon and 'here be dragons' appear as equal facts:

> Alle the iles of Anglesay on lyft half he haldez,
> And farez over the fordez by the forlondez,
> Over at the Holy Hede, til he hade eft bonk
> In the wyldrenesse of Wyrale. . . .   (698–701)

Such localisation is found in other romances, though here it is neither as naive as that in *Sir Orfeo* ('For Winchester was cleped tho/Traciens, withouten no'[14]) nor as deliberately local and naturalistic as the use of Grimsby and Lincoln in *Havelok*

the Dane. The place-names assure the reader that he is in recognisable country, and the poet's use of this sort of localisation can be
seen as part of his levelling realism; Burrow goes so far as to say:
'A hero who passes through one's home town on the way to an
adventure is . . . rather less likely to succeed in it than one who
does not.'[15] It is not, of course, quite as simple as that, because
the poet's identification of particular places comes just at the
moment when his hero is going to leave 'real' country behind
and pass into the 'here be dragons' part of the map. From line
709 onwards ('The knyght tok gates straunge/In mony a bonk
unbene') Gawain and we are geographically lost; there are no
more signposts with familiar names, but only features of landscape: *klyf, warthe, water, mount, knarrez, felle*. Instead of undecorated
references to places, now the poet depicts; as the landscape becomes more unknown Gawain's experience of it is more exactly
and feelingly envisaged as that of discomfort and threat. The
suggestiveness of the description that follows belongs to a realm
no longer geographical but on the map of the imagination;
Gawain has left even the road travelled by such fictional tourists
as Higden and Mandeville, but rides in company with Childe
Roland and Auden's questers:

> Bi a mounte on the morne meryly he rydes
> Into a forest ful dep, that ferly watz wylde,
> Hyghe hillez on uche a halve and holtwodez under
> Of hore okez ful hoge, a hundreth togeder;
> The hasel and the hawthorne were harled al samen,
> With roghe raged mosse rayled aywhere,
> With mony bryddez unblythe upon bare twygges,
> That pitosly ther piped for pyne of the colde.
> The gome upon Gryngolet glydez hem under,
> Thurgh mony misy and myre, mon al hym one. . .
>   (740-9)

Though this is recognisable as a piece of rhetorical amplification,
intended to convey to us the hero's loneliness and anxiety,[16] its
effect is not so much to draw us close to Gawain as to make us
suspicious that something is about to happen. In such a forest,
with its suggestions of the difficult place where many a hero has
ridden into danger and of the wild wood where even the ancient

trees may be malicious, anything could happen; we would accept the hostile knight at the ford, the ferocious troll, or even the Giant Despair. The suggestiveness of the landscape colours our view of what follows.

As far as our sense of Gawain himself goes, the desolate scene represents his anxiety that he will not find a place to make the proper Christmas observances:

> . . .mon al hym one,
> Carande for his costes, lest he ne kever schulde
> To se the servyse of that syre, that on that self nyght
> Of a burde watz borne oure baret to quelle.   (749–52)

The emphasis here carries through to the appearance of the Castle as an answer to prayer, something which seems miraculous in a Christian sense, and for which Jesus and St Julian are to be thanked. The reader looks further, encouraged by the description to expect the sinister, and recognising, with the knowledge of hindsight, that Gawain was destined to find the Green Knight's home at this time, wherever he had got to. The Castle is the first fulfilment of that promise 'me for to fynde if thou fraystez, faylez thou never' (455), and the reader is conscious that agencies other than those thanked by the hero may be responsible for its appearance. The description of the Castle itself works on both levels. We are shown it from Gawain's point of view, both in panorama and close-up; the careful maintaining of his view adds to the intensity and impressiveness of the scene. The resemblance to Chrétien's presentation of the arrival of Perceval at the castle of the Fisher King and to medieval versions of St John's vision of the heavenly city (as used in *Pearl*) adds both to the Christian significance of the marvellous sight for the hero and to the mythic suggestiveness of the scene for the reader.[17] As Gawain sees the Castle shimmer and shine through 'the schyre okez' which were, only a few lines before, grey, we are conscious that beauty and significance are in the eye of the beholder, and the poet's reassurance that the Castle is indeed solidly there ('The wallez were wel arayed,/Hit dut no wyndez blaste.') seems to presuppose our suspicion that it is a mirage, a castle whose ingeniously elaborate construction is too good to be true. We know that it is a piece of stage scenery, and whether or not the poet meant

to suggest that it was insubstantial when he said 'that pared out
of papure purely hit semed', the line gives to the passage that
quality which explains why readers have more often been reminded of the pictures of the Brothers Limbourg than of any
actual medieval building.

The second of Gawain's journeys and predestined arrivals is
treated in a somewhat similar, but more fully articulated, way.
When Gawain leaves the Castle with his attendant guide, he
rides through a landscape made solidly and vividly present to the
reader's imagination as a place existing in reality outside the world
of the poem and looking as it should at that season of the year.
With the aid of insistent alliteration, of words indicating violence
and physical effort and of onomatopoeia, the poet conveys the
thisness of the place and the moment:

> Thay bowen bi bonkkez ther boghez ar bare,
> Thay clomben bi clyffez ther clengez the colde.
> The heven watz uphalt, bot ugly therunder;
> Mist muged on the mor, malt on the mountez,
> Uch hille hade a hatte, a myst-hakel huge.
> Brokez byled and breke bi bonkkez aboute,
> Schyre schaterande on schorez, ther thay doun schowved.
>   (2077–83)

From the solid, real sense of landscape we gradually move towards
mystery and ill-defined suspicion. The physical effort now is
Gawain's and the precise depiction (in the stanza beginning at
line 2160) of a succession of actions is done in such a way as to
make one experience the difficulty, the bewilderment and apprehension, the sense of being trapped in an enclosed space and
possibly riding into ambush, and the fearful imagining of evil and
doom, from the hero's point of view. The landscape is treated
in a way which simultaneously convinces the reader that it is a
real though unidentified place and shows it as part of the hero's
consciousness, but the combination is more nightmarish than
realistic. The hero's uncertainty as each new impression strikes
his eye, the anti-climax of 'nobot an olde cave', and the melodramatic twist of imagined devilry represent a kind of heightening of the material which is moving away from realism towards

mystery and fantasy; the reader is being asked here not so much for a satisfying recognition of plausible feeling, though there is something of that present, but rather for an excited uncertainty, a readiness to be thrilled and surprised, or even possibly to be amused, if the build-up proves, as it does elsewhere in the poem, to be leading to a let-down.

It is possible to distinguish other types of colouring in addition to the realistic and the mysterious, though they tend to be colour-ings of particular moments or aspects of the action. At times the poet invests passages with a sense of heightened meaningfulness, displaying actions as symbolic and illustrative of general ideas.[18] So Gawain's departure from Camelot is shadowed by the idea of the mutability of human life, brought to one's mind by the description of the passing seasons. The interpretation of the pen-tangle is a self-conscious digression from the narrative, making Gawain appear temporarily in a representative role. The descrip-tions of the Green Knight and of the young and old ladies at the Castle similarly hold up the action and invite us to surmise and to attempt to attach to the figures moral and emblematic signifi-cance. In some of these passages the poet goes outside what one would think of as normal romance modes and uses images, ideas and expressions which bring into the Arthurian world echoes of moral lyrics, sermons and personification allegory, as well as reminders of medieval iconography. At other moments the height-ening is completely within the romance mode, as when the poet masses together elaborate and decorative detail, intended to en-hance our escapist pleasure in an idealised fictional world. In fact one cannot view *Sir Gawain* as a 'realistic' poem because the real is constantly counter-pointed by the inherently unrealistic and stylised quality of the narrative pattern and of the story's content, and because the poet invites response to the romantic quality of adventure, to the ceremonial aspects of its courtly setting, to the excitement of mystery and wonder, and to a sense, only partly to be grasped at any particular moment, of meanings larger than the individual actions and figures, which loom behind the actuality so vividly depicted.

The poet, at times, goes so far as to play off one sense of the action against another, where he makes the reader conscious that different views are possible. One is not able simply to dismiss the common sense of the courtiers of Camelot at Gawain's setting-out as a typical 'low' reaction of the 'lewed' folk, because the common sense is supported elsewhere in the poem. The practical, bourgeois moral that saving one's life is more important than romantic ideas like honour is eventually the code by which Gawain acts though he is bitterly ashamed at being found out in it, and the code, by which it is implied, all men in their weakness act. On the other hand, though worldly practicality may put bold heroism in a perspective not usual in romance, it does not seriously undermine the heroic ideal which has too respectable an ancestry to be so easily dismissed. Gawain's 'Of destinés derf and dere/ What may mon do bot fonde?' belongs to the tradition of living finely regardless of death, and this tradition too is supported in other places in *Sir Gawain*, and is eventually the code by which Gawain judges himself. The ending of the poem confirms that it is the irony of juxtaposition the poet is, in part, seeking to create and he therefore neither surrenders unquestioningly to the escapism of romance, nor merges himself completely in the limited world of actual experience.

2. Gawain's adversaries

The most puzzling, and hence the most variously interpreted, element in *Sir Gawain* is the double figure of the Green Knight-cum-Bertilak. He has been seen as Life, Death, God, the Devil, and the force of Nature, as a Wild Man, a primitive hob-goblin, a shape-shifter, as the force of an earthly moral integrity stripping courtly pretension of its class veneer, as a super-human primordial energy mocking the mutabilities of time and human triviality, and more. Most such 'interpretations' are fanciful generalisations based on unanalysed, impressionistic reactions to particular moments in the poem, but the very variety of them is an indication of the multiplicity and the ambivalence which the poet created in the figure of his hero's main tester. The experience which Gawain endures is not clearly sign-posted, as the hero's experience in a medieval allegory or in a poem designed as a moral exemplum would have been. The reader is left to work out for himself whether the poet intended a particular significance in the figure of the Green Knight, and the main problem of the working-out is, to put it crudely, an uncertainty whether he is a Good Thing or a Bad Thing. If his challenge to Camelot was motivated by malice, how can he be accepted as Gawain's instructor in moral conduct? Do we take him as an innocent victim who is obliquely offering apologies at the end? Or has the poet imagined him as so much bigger than the narrative machinery of the poem warrants that we interpret him without reference to internal logic? This last is a desperate remedy, to be resorted to only when the internal logic of the poem can be proved to have failed. Though some readers have suggested that it does fail, few have looked very hard at what the poet really did in order to test the point. I hope that a more accurate sense of the poet's quality as the creator of complex fiction may emerge from an examination of Gawain's opponent and of those associated with him, of how they are presented and of what ideas are developed by the poet through them. Since I am concerned to show the growth of the complexity of impression, I will take the four parts of the poem one at a time.

PART I: THE CHALLENGER

When the Green Knight arrives at Camelot to fulfil the awaited task of challenging the Round Table to an adventure, the narrative is suspended for nearly ninety lines of description, which gives full weight to the startling quality of his appearance, and invites us to consider what he is, as the courtiers are soon pictured doing:

> Ther watz lokyng on lenthe the lude to beholde,
> For uch mon had mervayle quat hit mene myght
> That a hathel and a horse myght such a hwe lach. . .
>
> (232–4)

This statement encourages us to speculate and shows that the poet did not assume any immediately recognisable identity in the figure. The ordinary reaction is astonishment and the surmise of fearful ignorance that he belonged to the world of 'fantoum and fayryye'. He is to be taken on first appearance as a manifestation, startling and puzzling. The only clues to his nature are those

provided in the detailed description, and, as Burrow puts it,
'The most remarkable feature of this description. . . is its richness
and variety of suggestion.'[19] At the human level the figure is
accommodated to a norm of romance description, an animation
of allegorical portraits of Youth, which presents him as of fine
physique and as modishly dressed; by his clothes Camelot would
recognise him as one of themselves, an aristocrat, and have no fear
that they were faced by a wild man of the woods. At the monstrous level he is awesome and grotesque, in colour and size, in
hair and beard possessing wilder qualities which distinguish
him from Camelot. If the green of face and hair suggest a phantom, the green and gold of his clothes belong to the 'merry,
luxurious world of courtly youth'.[20] If the battle-axe in one hand
confirms the threat of his phantom greenness, the green holly-
branch in the other is a re-assurance of seasonal peace, and the
emblems hold out promises of life and death as well as of peace
and war, and of the knight's own power to mete out death and
to survive it. One aspect of the ambivalence is the traditional sense
of Christmas and New Year as a time of endings and beginnings;
the Green Knight has been given suggestions of Janus, 'with
double berd'.[21] The poet also wants us to be reminded of the
indefinable face of Fortune, whose 'hands, right and left, apparently mean good and evil fortune.'[22] The undercurrents give
great power to the figure even before he speaks, in addition to
the impression of his monstrous greenness and imposing size.
The description implies in advance the supernatural moment
when he is both dead and alive, and in its combination of
opposites makes the challenge that follows his appearance more
threatening; in spite of the rules of the game, the mixed nature
of the challenger tells us that the outcome is ultimately uncertain,
and that Gawain, though he has entered into a bargain with
well-defined terms, has nevertheless become a hostage to the unknown, and has, in a sense, offered himself to Fate. As with the
prologue to Shakespeare's *Troilus and Cressida*, the Green Knight's
coming 'sets all on hazard'. The poet has made an extraordinarily
imaginative response to the idea of challenge in his creation of this
enigmatic figure, whose qualities suggest the uncertainties of
which the world of adventure consists. The figure has its seeds
both in romance monsters and in allegorical portraits of mirth

and of mutability, and gatherings together of qualities connected with an abstract idea, such as Chaucer's description of the chapels in *The Knight's Tale*.[23]

When the action begins, our minds have thus been encouraged to think in terms of uncertainty and threat, and we have been given a rich enough range of possibilities in the Green Knight to feel an ambiguous resonance in all his sayings and doings, and a sense of power, with-held and disguised for a purpose, lying beneath his action. If his brusque self-assurance identifies him as a hostile challenger, his proper observance of forms in asking for Arthur and making a formal request, as well as his aristocratic dress and bearing, authenticate his seeking for a sporting duel; his words of scorn, though offensive, are offensive in a traditional heroic manner. The 'merriness' is drawn on in his proposal of a game, his welcoming of Gawain as a worthy undertaker of the challenge, and in his cheery insouciance about the whole affair:

> 'bot slokes!
> Ta now thy grymme tole to the
> And let se how thou cnokez!'   (412–14)

There are several other striking qualities in his speeches. First, there is a jesting, teasing note in his addresses in the first part of the scene. Explaining the reasons for his visit, he says to Arthur, 'for the los of the, lede, is lyft up so hyghe', implying that it has been lifted higher than Camelot deserves, then 'thy burgh and thy burnes best ar holden', implying that though they may be thought best there is some doubt about the matter, and 'here is kydde cortaysye, as I haf herd carp', again implying the doubtful sense, *so they say*.

Secondly his speeches to Gawain before the beheading have a much crisper, business-like quality, and, with the repeated use of legal and formal terms and of the idea of *trawthe*, they make it clear that the bargain is a solemn, binding contract;[24] the effect is disconcerting, as if a party to a gentlemen's agreement had suddenly whipped out three copies of a formal document to be signed. The rules of the game begin to sound like a trap. With the beheading the supernatural force of the earlier description is revived, after lapsing from our attention, and the speech of the severed head adds awe to the solemn insistence on Gawain's promise and the clear declaration that his reputation depends on it:

> 'Therfore com, other recreaunt be calde the behoves.'
> (456)

He disappears as suddenly as he came, with sparks of fire, and goes with a suggestion that he may have no existence once he has gone from view:

> To quat kyth he becom knwe non there,
> Nevermore then thay wyste from quethen he watz wonnen.
> (460–61)

We cannot decide how to view the Green Knight on the basis of Part I because the poet's purpose is to create unsatisfied curiosity and speculation about him, which cannot, in the strategy of the poem, be satisfied until the end, if then. The poet does not wish us to ascribe a personality or identity to him. The 'characterisa‑ tion', if that is the word, combines two devices: the simpler device of characterising according to function in the scene, and the more complex one of creating a multiplicity of suggested possibilities in the figure. Since it is his function not only to challenge but also to create wonder and fear, to disconcert, to tease into rash response, to trap and to get a hold over Camelot, the characterising has a kaleidoscopic quality which feeds on the variety of suggestions in the description, and these suggestions allow the subsequent splitting of the figure into two, metaphori‑ cally as well as literally, and the curious uncertainty with which we view the Green Knight on his re‑appearance in Part IV of the poem. The reader's sense of him shifts also through the identifying words used for him: in the early part of the first scene he is a terrible lord, 'half etayn' and 'mon most'; later he is referred to by neutral words, *gome, schalk* and *freke,* implying, if anything, a social inferior; in conversation with Arthur he rises through *hathel, lude* and *renk,* until, in exchanges with Gawain, he appears on equal terms with the hero as *the knyght in the grene;* when he has gone he is de‑personalised into *that grene.* His refusal to give a name also leaves a threat, and suggests significance in the request for Gawain's name; Gawain's giving a name is another indication that the hero gives himself to Fate, and the Green Knight's anonymity is another facet of his facelessness; he eludes attempts to identify him.

PART II: THE CASTLE

If the impression made by the Green Knight at Camelot is ambiguously sporting and threatening, leaving us on the one hand with a sense that the jest may turn sour and on the other with a sense that the solemn contract must, sworn in such an atmosphere of courtly revelry, be capable of a happy outcome, then the total impression of the Castle where Gawain spends the following Christmas, and of its Lord, its ladies, its courtiers and servants is even more so. The eventual explanation of the plot reveals that for Gawain his stay at the Castle has been a time when he thought he was being welcomed and valued, but when, in reality, he was being tested and found wanting. Are we then to understand that this place and its inhabitants were all a sham, that all were party to the clever game and all laughing at Gawain's unwitting behaviour, that the whole thing was a conspiracy and therefore all the statements about Hautdesert lies? Or even, since it is the malicious fairy, Morgan, who directs affairs there, are we to understand that the whole place was a mirage, filled with plausible life but actually an illusion fabricated for Gawain's benefit? Or perhaps we are simply meant to think that the place is real, the courtiers, guests and servants all what they seem (except for that unexplained guide who rides with Gawain towards the Green Chapel), but the Lord and the two ladies playing a double role? That is what Gawain himself seems to conclude as he struggles with the conflicting feelings of gratitude to the man whose food he has eaten, resentment that he has been tricked, and galling knowledge of his own fault:

> 'Nay, for sothe', quoth the segge, and sesed hys helme,
> And hatz hit of hendely, and the hathel thonkkez,
> 'I haf sojorned sadly: sele yow bytyde,
> And He yelde hit yow yare that yarkkez al menskez.
> And comaundez me to that cortays, your comlych fere,
> Bothe that on and that other, myn honoured ladyez,
> That thus hor knyght wyth hor kest han koyntly bigyled.'
>
> (2407–13)

That is an explanation that we can accept at the mystery-story level of the poem, though it means quelling some niggling questions about the providential arrival of Gawain at Hautdesert and some feeling that the poet has cheated in creating such a favourable impression of the place and its Lord, but it does not seem to provide a satisfactory basis for the moral authority which the poet gives to the Green Knight in his lessons to the hero at the end. Seeking such a basis, some readers have claimed that the moral values of Hautdesert are being presented as a model for Camelot, which needs to be reminded of Christian values; but the ending of the poem hardly supports such an interpretation. There is clearly a problem here, and one which is eventually crucial to our sense of the poem and particularly to our under-standing of its ending. Is Gawain right to be remorseful and Camelot wrong to make light of the matter? Or is Camelot right to be joyous and Gawain too concerned with self in his exaggerated abasement? Was Hautdesert a Castle Perilous, a Bower of Bliss, a place of deceitful and enervating ease and luxury, or a Great Good Place, home of wholesome courtesy and fair welcome?

On first acquaintance it seems surprisingly normal, a luxurious *plaisance* which is also a model of propriety.[25] The picture at Gawain's arrival is one of complete generosity, hospitality and courtesy, and there is no hint from the poet that we are to take the greeting as anything but a display of punctilious good manners and evidence of a well-trained household. For the moment, the poet is on the household's side, as it were, and is presenting an idealised picture of medieval country-house life, without any hint of pretentiousness or self-esteem.

The first ripple of suspicion comes when the courtiers find out that the strange knight is Gawain; the poet's ingenious and imaginative skill here is of a high order:

> Thenne watz spyed and spured upon spare wyse,
> Bi prevé poyntez of that prynce put to hymselven,
> That he beknew cortaysly of the court that he were
> That athel Arthure the hende haldez hym one,
> That is the ryche ryal kyng of the Rounde Table,
> And hit watz Wawen hymself that in that won syttez,
> Comen to that Krystmasse, as case hym then lymp
ed.
> When the lorde hade lerned that he the leude hade,
> Loude laghed he therat, so lef hit hym thoght,

And alle the men in that mote maden much joye
To apere in his presense prestly that tyme,
That alle prys and prowes and pured thewes
Apendes to hys persoun and praysed is ever;
Byfore alle men upon molde his mensk is the most.
Uch segge ful softly sayde to his fere:
'Now schal we semlych se sleghtez of thewez
And the teccheles termes of talkyng noble.
Wich spede is in speche unspurd may we lerne,
Syn we half fonged that fyne fader of nurture.'   (901–19)

A wealth of impressions and nuances are smoothly and profession-
ally fitted together in sequence in this stanza. On the surface the
poet is continuing to display the good breeding of the courtiers
of Hautdesert, and incidentally of Gawain, as they question their
guest with delicacy, and as they show their appreciation of a
model of elegant discourse. The fact that they do this privately
guarantees that they are what they seem and have a genuine, if
possibly superficial, response to Gawain and the chivalry he
represents. But what of their Lord who, according to later
discoveries, must have known who Gawain was? The poet has
neatly got round this by removing the Lord from the scene, so that
his learning 'that he the leude hade' (ominously enough expressed)
cannot be timed; the pluperfect tense preserves the poet from the
accusation of cheating. The reader is put on the alert by the
reminders of Gawain's quest, provided by the reference to Arthur
and his court, and by the allusion to the 'prys and prowes and
pured thewes' symbolised by the pentangle, and by that natural-
sounding line 'Comen to that Krystemasse, as case hym then
lymped'; we know then, with part of our minds, that he is not
there by chance or by the good offices of guardian saints. At the
same time the poet is cleverly preparing the ground for what is
to follow with the imaginative idea of using Gawain's reputation
as a weapon against him; at the moment it seems innocent enough,
but it is significantly presented just before we are given the other
pieces which are needed, in the presentation of the other principal
actors in the drama, the two ladies of Hautdesert. There seems
to me clear evidence in this stanza that the poet is consciously
developing his narrative on more than one level, showing the

reader that there is more than meets the eye and yet endowing what meets the eye with a positive life and virtue. Gawain's experience of Hautdesert is of courtesy and generosity and we are made to share, not always from his point of view, a sense of the castle's positive values. At the same time the poet reserves for himself the possibility of other meanings and gives us hints to that end. We are not encouraged to attempt to resolve the complexity but merely to recognise that it is there; the juxtaposition is the poet's intent and pleasure.

The striking description of the two ladies also works by juxtaposition and contrast and, though much shorter than the description of the Green Knight in Part I, also halts the narrative and provides us with a picture full of suggestion and potentiality. Here at the literal level are two new characters who are to figure in the action, presented in tandem and so making a welcome variation of the medieval romancer's descriptive technique. Beyond that are the moralist's emblems of transience and mutability in the two faces of woman, Youth and Age, the fair and ugly faces of Fortune, as ambiguous as the holly branch and the axe, as reassuring and threatening.[26] Equally the two faces of Hautdesert are displayed, the one belonging to the world of youth, mirth, and complete openness to the eye, the other secretly muffled up, grim and ancient. The poet's most ingenious effect is to weld the two of them together, not only by the antithetical description, but also by presenting the younger as an appendage of the older:

An other lady hir lad bi the lyft honde. . . (947)
and

More lykkerwys on to lyk
Watz that scho hade on lode. (968–9)

The latter statement particularly presents the young lady from the start as one subordinate to and manipulated by another, and even suggests that she, in some sense, is merely a facet of the old woman. I think the poet may well have expected his audience to suspect an allusion to the tale of the Loathly Lady and to have a flashing idea that the two women are really one, present both in her young and old guises. It is a tale several times associated with Gawain, and, though the poet does not develop the suggestion, it is consistent with the poet's other hints that he should make us suspect and wonder about the relationship and about the signifi- cance of the old lady; it is the one place where he does prepare for the revelation of Morgan's role at the end. As with the disconcert- ing effect of the headless knight, however, the poet turns the doubts of his suggestive passage into humorous and social channels, making it the occasion for a display of Gawain's sense of appropri- ateness as he embraces one lady and bows to the other, and is taken off to join the Christmas fun. With this the narrative returns to the favourable presentation of Hautdesert with the Lord's exuberant mirth and the definitive picture of the pleasure, propriety and civility of the Christmas day feast.

The crucial last stanzas of Part II draw on the sense of security and civilisation re-established in our minds and the conversation between the Lord and Gawain is marked by mutual courtesy, as the Lord thanks Gawain for honouring and embellishing his house by his presence, and the hero reciprocates, and by an ap- parently frank and merry intimacy as Gawain reveals his quest and is relieved of his anxiety about finding the Green Chapel. The poem's second bargain is brought about as naturalistically as the first, seeming a natural product of the Lord's liking for sport and of Gawain's relief. The pattern of attack after apparent relief is one we are to meet again in Part III and later it appears part of a consistent psychological campaign to disarm and lull the hero into complacency and consequent rashness, but at the time the scene is simply one of friendly jest. True, the Lord's joy is excessive as he 'let for luf lotez so myry, /As wyy that wolde of his wyt, ne wyst quat he myght', but we, by now, accept him as a maker of mirth, the leader of Hautdesert's *bonhomie* and wholesome courtesy. By the end of Part II the poet has laid out all his materials and now comes to the centre of his work: all is to play for, all in balance and at hazard.

PART III: HUNTSMAN, TEMPTRESS AND HOST

The entertaining ingenuity of Part III of *Sir Gawain* with its two simultaneous actions and patterned structure, marks it as the poem's centre. The poet's primary effect is to create variety and to highlight the qualities of the two actions by the contrast between them. The enclosed intensity of the conversations in Gawain's bed is pointed by the surrounding scenes of action, noise, bustle and crowd, the intricacy of the battle of words relieved by the direct narration of the chase. Part III is not only the most carefully formed passage in Middle English narrative poetry, but also the most wideranging in its poetic effects. The poet engages in a virtuoso display of the flexibility and richness of the alliterative tradition and his own power of modulating his style.

Within the poet's delight in variety of poetic effect lies the structural pleasure itself, both that of making a symbolic pattern of the three days, which prepares for the dénouement of the poem, and that of creating a narrative pattern of repetition with variation, whereby the action of each day is the same in outline but subtly different in detail, proportion and emphasis. The first two days build up to the third where the Lady's movement from wooing to offering gifts and the exchange of winnings between Gawain and the Lord are stressed by their difference from the procedures of the other days. On the first two days the renewal of the contract leads on to the next day's action; the third day also looks forward, but more ominously. The poet's shaping of his matter is made to seem natural, as it follows the passage of the day and the stages appropriate to an ordered household, while simultaneously the parallelism shows it to be unnatural, intended and significant, one of those archetypal threes of folktale and ballad, where the third prince, the third task, the third sister is always the one that matters.

Less frequently pointed out and studied is another aspect of the structuring of Part III, the way in which each day consists of a separation and subsequent bringing together of the different faces of Hautdesert and of courtesy. The division of each day into four parts—hunt, courtly dalliance, hunt, meeting and exchange—continues the alternation of country and court begun in Part II, but with the significant difference that Gawain is absent from the hunts. The poet interweaves scenes of the occupations of the male and female halves of Hautdesert, with Gawain left to a society of ladies, and then brings the two halves together. This neat patterning takes over from the second section's combination of 'favourable' presentation of Hautdesert's courtesy and suggestive hints which arouse suspicion. Now the poet simply divides Hautdesert up, putting all of one type of meaning into the hunting scenes, all of another into the bedroom scenes, and then playing them off against one another in the evening meetings.

The hunting scenes in *Sir Gawain* have often been ill-treated by commentators on the poem, either ignored, or dismissed as mere padding catering to the now obsolete tastes of a medieval upper class. Worse, when they have been discussed, they have been forced to fit into some scheme whereby they symbolically represent the bedroom scenes with detailed parallelism between Gawain and deer, boar and fox;[27] this sort of interpretation survives with difficulty an actual reading of the poem since one is conscious as one reads mainly of the contrast of the two actions and aware of similarity only when it is obvious, as in the semi-humorous relationship between the two kinds of venery, hunting and wooing, or when it is made explicit, as in the parallel between the traditional treachery of the fox and Gawain's behaviour on the third day. Readers seeem reluctant to accept them on their own terms but they seem to me attractive, full of lively pictures of actions and renderings of sounds and sights, and appealing purely because they provide the most direct narrative poetry in the work. The vigorous and precise realisation of exciting scenes, from the panorama of the deer-hunt with its mingling of the noises of dogs, horns and men, to the fiercer and more powerful pursuit and slaughter of the boar and the persistent following of the dodging trail of the fox, provides the sense of physical activity and of masculine prowess in which *Sir Gawain* is, in comparison to most romances, otherwise so conspicuously lacking. The hunting scenes both expose and make up for the essentially passive nature of the hero's own role in the poem. The poem needs these passages of uncomplicated deeds, embedded in a world of things, a mass of animals, men, woods and fields, horns and weapons of slaughter, to set off the play of wits between Gawain and the Lady and also the ingenuity of the structure into which they are fitted.

Into these scenes the poet put all his love for the fictional world he had created in Hautdesert and what it represented, the life of the country and of the well-run manor. Knighthood and the brotherhood of men appear in their realistic forms as the quality of leadership and the sharing of physical activity, conducted with polished expertise. Some of the qualities attributed to Haut-desert earlier only here achieve solidity and convincing presence in the poem. The Lord was described on his first appearance as 'a bolde burne' with 'felle face as the fyre' and 'wel hym semed... To lede a lortschyp in lee of leudez ful gode', but up to now we have seen him mainly capering about the court with hearty laughter for every occasion; in the hunts he becomes a figure to be reckoned with, bold, decisive, nimble, brave and strong, a leader of men and a swift but sporting dealer out of death. The depiction of the men he leads enhances our sense of him as well as ful-filling that impression of Hautdesert as a model of courtly practice and good government which was suggested earlier in the more superficial zones of politeness and the proper serving of meals. Here we turn to men's work, and the cumulative impression of the descriptions of the work of dog-handlers, beaters, riders and the men who cut up the deer and boar and skin the fox is of skill and thorough knowledge of the proper conduct of a gentleman's affairs. And if that nowadays least-loved passage in the poem, the breaking up of the deer (1325ff.) may seem completely out-side the range of modern responses as a point of gentlemanly honour, it surely still works as a brilliantly precise demonstration of the real nature of knightly occupation in the late Middle Ages, a knightly life which has little in common with that romantic picture of knighthood which the Lady keeps urging on Gawain. The display of the good practices of Hautdesert is particularly meaningful to the reader because Gawain is absent and we can-not therefore suspect any element of putting-on a show for his sake. The unavoidable conclusion, unless we decide the poet has no sense of logic, is that whatever else he may be, the Lord is a good master who does things properly, as in observing the close season. Throughout the scenes at Hautdesert this sense of good order and proper custom is drawn to our attention. At the beginning of Part IV the poet twice makes the point, first when Gawain receives his armour and sees that it has been polished and cleansed of rust and more explicitly when Gringolet is brought from the stable in the peak of condition. Gawain's gratitude for hospitality which survives even his irritation at being tricked is thus shown to be earned and supported by the lively presentation of whole-some actions which belong to the sphere of the Lord as leader, as host, and as good master. The hunts are more important in literal terms than has often been implied, because through them at least part of the basis upon which Gawain is finally judged is conveyed as part of the experience of the poem.

If our favourable reactions to a wholesome Hautdesert are channelled into the hunts, then our suspicions all find fulfilment in the bedroom conversations of Gawain and the Lady, though the poet ingeniously complicates our suspicions by developing the scenes as those of a comedy of manners. As with the hunts the primary appeal of the passages is on the level of entertainment: the poet makes us appreciate the comedy of the situation, with Gawain cast in the role of a reluctant Roger the Lodger while the man of the house is out, as well as the more courtly comedy of the verbal fencing and the witty manoeuvres of the two anta-gonists. The whole conception of the Lady's speeches and be-haviour is brilliantly comic, a *tour de force* of clever play-acting as she goes through an extensive repertoire of seductive strategies. The poet's command of tones of speech is subtly displayed in the nebulous amplitude of her syntax, in her mock-serious turning of the courtly metaphor of imprisonment into jesting literal fact, in her arch flattery and her comically indignant reproofs; her speeches come fluting and pouting off the page tailor-made for a Joan Greenwood or a Fenella Fielding. How anyone can suggest that the poet is presenting her as crude and inexpert in some of her speeches passes my comprehension. It seems obvious to me that the poet has imagined her as playing a role and that he conveys to us by touches of exaggeration, hints, and brief allusions to her thoughts, that this is so, and that therefore all her moves are calculated to test out Gawain from different directions and find his weak spot. There is no vulnerability about her but complete assurance from first to last; she, after all, is the one figure in the poem who succeeds and, moreover, the poet manages to suggest that she is enjoying herself. The cool judgement lying behind the fetching performance implies a cynicism refreshingly astringent in comparison to much medieval poetry about love.

The presentation of the Lady is of course a 'dramatic' character-isation, both in that she is presented almost entirely in direct speech, and in that she is almost completely confined to the fulfilling of a particular function in the story, but the poet shows

that he has gone beyond a simple acceptance that role is all there
is to character, by making us aware that this is what she is doing
and suggesting that there is more of the Lady than is seen. So at
the end of each conversation there is a short comment on her
behaviour; on the second day:

> Thus hym frayned that fre, and fondet hym ofte,
> For to haf wonnen hym to woghe, what⁄so scho thoght ellez.
>
> (1549–50)

and on the third:

> Thenne lachchez ho hir leve and levez hym there,
> For more myrthe of that mon moght ho not gete.
>
> (1870–1)

Both of these statements declare her purpose and suggest that
she is capable of judging her own efforts and her degree of suc⁄
cess, 'what⁄so scho thoght ellez', and they confirm the likelihood
that the poet had a similar intention in the disputed corresponding
passage on the first day:

> And ay the lady let lyk as hym loved mych;
> The freke ferde with defence, and feted ful fayre,
> 'Thagh I were burde bryghtest,' the burde in mynde hade,
> 'The lasse luf in his lode for lur that he soght
>   boute hone,
> The dunte that schulde hym deve,
> And nedez hit most be done.'
> The lady thenn spek of leve;
> He granted hir ful sone.
>
> (1281–9)

All attempts to punctuate this so that the Lady is not aware of
the nature of Gawain's quest have been artificial and implausible;[28]
the only way of leaving it open is not to close the direct speech
at all, but to assume that the poet has allowed his character's
voice to merge into the narrator's. I believe, however, that the
poet meant us to realise that the Lady knew more than she
apparently should have done, because he wants us to appreciate
the testing of Gawain and to be aware of the dramatic irony.
The suspense is not destroyed because we are not given enough
information to work it all out and the Lord is carefully left free

of any imputation of guilty knowledge; the dramatic ironies in which he is involved are deliberately ambivalent. Knowledge that the Lady is playing a part and is not a genuinely love-lorn woman is, in any case, implicit in the style the poet developed for her, and this knowledge, together with hints of an ulterior motive, focus attention on the strategy itself, its variety and subtlety, rather than on the Lady's nature and feelings; it is clear that they are a sham put on for the occasion and so we can stop wondering about them, enjoy them for what they are, and pay attention to the reaction of the hero which is what is really under examination.

What the Lady does in her performance is to launch a persistent psychological assault on Gawain, using a clever mixture of attack and defence, as she flatters, lulls and lures on the one hand, and reproves, goads and invites retaliation on the other; it is her aim to disconcert, to catch him out somewhere, to nose out a weakness, find something that Gawain really wants and then to cajole him into accepting it.

We are in no doubt in these scenes that the performance is put on for Gawain's benefit and that he is on trial just as we are in no doubt in the hunting scenes that Hautdesert's following of good practices is on show. The relationship between the two is primarily that of contrast, between outdoor and indoor, between action and passivity, between deeds and words, between a real chivalry of masculine sport and a literary, artificial chivalry of the feminine sport of love, between the solid gains of the one and the insubstantial profits of the other. Lying behind the alternation is the shadow of a debate about the nature of knighthood, with the Lord and the Lady as the spokesmen for the two opposing sides, and Gawain caught in the middle; this impression is aided by the anonymity of Lord and Lady, whose identities are, for this reason, amorphous, pushed at one moment towards allegory, at another towards folk-tale and myth. Because the alternation is part of a continuous narrative, one sees it primarily in terms of the hero's situation and one's judgement of the experience he encounters. So the contrasts also identify the different aspects of Hautdesert, the open, bold masculine society and the secretive, calculating feminine one. The point that emerges from the testing of Gawain at Hautdesert is that it is the demands of the feminine society that Gawain satisfies, not by yielding to its every demand or by accepting its conception of knighthood, but by acting throughout with unblemished courtesy and high moral standards; Gawain's *acceptance* of the belt has nothing wrong with it and, in context, is a courteous act, though, of course, his motive for accepting and his later anti-feminist feeling ironically undermine both aspects of his courtesy. What Gawain betrays is the masculine world of free, generous dealings, of honesty between brothers, of keeping the rules of the game. Because Gawain is to be judged as lacking, that which judges him must itself be worthy, and the Lord is therefore given virtue to which Gawain's may be com- pared and authority by which he may be judged.

The meeting of Gawain and the Lord on the evening of each day is the third element in the pattern of Part III; these meetings are fairly briefly recounted and the passages in which they occur have to act as bridges between one day and the next, but, because they deal with the bargain and sum up the day's action, they have greater weight than their length might seem to imply. As with the Lord's departures and the Lady's arrivals, these passages work to a pattern. First they are fitted into the time-scheme by running on from the Lord's return at dusk from the chase; each thus begins in the atmosphere of homecoming and mirth and is pictured in terms of the Lord entering upon a scene prepared for him. On the first two days he immediately takes the centre of the stage and takes command, summoning the company, displaying his catch, describing the hunt and handing over his winnings. Gawain then decorously repays, with one kiss on the first day and two on the second, the Lord teases and chaffs him and in mirth they sit down at table and swear the bargain again for the next day. The whole thing is very natural and entertaining, but the reader is made conscious of the undercurrents. Here the two faces of Hautdesert meet and the Lord's entry from outdoors to the warm, enclosed world of the hall is a vivid, natural image of this coming together. In the exchanges the venison and boar's head are the solid and admired trophies of the day; in this moment their literal nature is augmented since they represent the Lord's occupations in the outside world of deeds and things. The kisses stand equally for the chivalry of the boudoir, nebulous in comparison, their worth equivocal, an anti-climax unless, as the Lord says, their value is explained by identification of where they come from. So the exchanges lead to teasing, as the Lord suggests that Gawain is on to a good thing, both in getting so much for so little and, presumably, in the winning of the kisses in the first place. The first day sets the pattern. On the second day the poet shows the threads beginning to tangle, as Gawain is seen poised between the two contending forces; it is, of course, through the calculating Lady that the difficulty for Gawain of keeping separate his obligations to Lord and Lady, of satisfying one without offend-ing the other, is revealed:

> Such semblaunt to that segge semly ho made
> Wyth stille stollen countenaunce, that stalworth to plese,
> That al forwondered watz the wyye, and wroth with
> hymselven,
> Bot he nolde not for his nurture nurne hir ayaynez,
> Bot dalt with hir al in daynte, how-se-ever the dede turned
> towrast.   (1658–63)

With characteristic courtesy he restrains the impulse to check the Lady in public and risks offending the husband, and so all remains in balance for the third day, as the terms of the Lord's proposal to renew the bargain emphasise:

> 'For I haf fraysted the twys, and faythful I fynde the.
> Now "thrid tyme throw best" thenk on the morne.'
>   (1679–80)

The crucial third day varies the pattern of the first two in several places, and the significance of the exchange scene, particularly, seems to be stressed by reversal of the expected order of things. The Lord again comes home and finds 'fire upon flet, the freke ther-byside' as expected, but a description of Gawain in blue and ermine, a heraldic picture of loyalty, focuses our eyes on him, not the Lord, as he makes his payment first: thus Gawain's lie is brought into prominence, the Lord's jesting comment given an extra bite, and the handing-over of the fox-skin placed at the end with the Lord's ironic speech.

> 'Mary,' quoth that other mon, 'myn is bihynde,
> For I haf hunted al this day, and noght haf I geten
> Bot this foule fox felle—the fende haf the godez!

And that is ful pore for to pay for suche prys thinges
As ye haf thryght me here thro, suche thre cosses
  so gode.'   (1942-7)

The symbols of betrayal, the fox-skin and the three kisses, fore-
cast the judgement of Gawain's failure to satisfy both of the worlds
he has encountered at Hautdesert, but in dramatic terms it is the
Lord's gift which seems the anti-climax and Gawain, in his
fur-clad elegance, who seems to claim the mastery.

The last two stanzas of Part III return to the manner of Part II,
combining praise of Hautdesert, in Gawain's courteous thanks to
the Lord and his household and the sorrow of the servants at his
departure, with the suspicion of a threat in the Lord's words:

'In god faythe,' quoth the godmon, 'wyth a goud wylle
Al that ever I yow hyght halde schal I redé.' (1969-70)

And so the poet leaves us with those questions about Hautdesert
which I mentioned earlier. By first combining praise of the
house with hints that all might not be as it seems, and then divid-
ing the narrative into two sets of actions, he creates two faces, the
one eliciting our trust and approval, the other arousing our
mistrust, tempered by amused admiration of cleverness and pan-
ache—a combination of reactions similar to that elicited by the
Green Knight at Camelot. The poet has devised a two-faced
household for his Janus-headed knight.

PART IV: THE JUDGE

Since the poet has spent a long time on matters which have,
apparently, little to do with the Green Knight and the challenge
from which the story began, the last section of *Sir Gawain* has
to begin with recapitulation. As the poet moves the story onward with Gawain's early rising, his saying goodbye to Hautdesert and setting out to meet the fearsome foe, he simultaneously
draws the strands together and reminds the reader of what has
gone before. By means of the pictures of the sleepless Gawain
listening to the howling wind, the arming of Gawain and the
wild, bleak landscape through which he rides, and the dialogue
between Gawain and his companion, the poet reminds us of

hazard and death, apprehension and obligation, of the nature
of the Green Knight, of the challenge at Camelot, of Gawain's
earlier arming and setting out, and the lonely journey which
ended at the Castle. The scene with the Guide dramatises
Gawain's keeping of his first promise, recalls to our minds the
fact that this is his major test and that it requires real courage to
reject the temptation to run away and to resolve to ride on alone
to meet death.

The most interesting and ingenious aspect of this is the figure
of the Guide. In him again are combined the two faces of
Hautdesert. His credibility depends on the Castle's good face;
he is a member of the 'meyny' which loves Gawain and which the
hero with extreme courtesy has praised and thanked at his departure; he has the credit of being a good servant of a good master.
His warning to Gawain seems, therefore, an honest impulse of
goodwill. But, with hindsight, one sees that the warning belongs
with the testing, tempting face; it teases Gawain and waits to
see what he will do. The Guide is never explained in logical
terms. What he says has a kind of truth, but it conflicts in factual
detail with the explanation of events given later, and so he remains equivocal. We are not given the information to identify
him either as an agent of the Lord, lying to make Gawain afraid,
or as an honest man, speaking what he believes to be the truth.
This unexplained doubleness creates another 'dramatic' characterisation which leads us on to the scene of climax, and leads us
back to the Janus figure of the Green Knight himself.

The meeting of Gawain and the Green Knight is a powerful
dramatic scene, dramatic both in the sense that it is dominated
by direct speech and in that its ingenious construction provides
a fitting climax of conflict, with suspense, surprise, reversal, and
a complete untying of knots, metaphorical and literal. The
presentation of the Green Knight is initially a striking combination of threatening sounds and gestures, vigorous physical actions
and authoritative speech, alternately courteous and haughty. If
the sound of the whetstone, the unidentified voice from above,
the new axe and the swift, powerful movements of the green man
re-animate the sense of an awesome yet gleeful bogeyman, his
speeches have a business-like certainty; his reproof of Gawain
'with mony prowde wordez' reminds us not only of his scornful

condemnation of Camelot's lack of bravery but, by measuring
Gawain once more against his reputation, also of the scenes at the
Castle.

When the blow is eventually struck the poet shows, with
vivid visual detail, Gawain's flurry of relieved action as he sees
his blood gleaming on the snow and realises that he is still alive
to defend himself against further attack. Our attention is given
to the hero's comically rapid donning of helmet and grabbing of
weapons and the nervously patronising reminder of codes of
gentlemanly conduct which Gawain offers to the Green Knight
by using the word traditionally associated with the halting of
chivalrous duels (ho):[29]

> 'Bot on stroke here me fallez—
> The covenaunt schop ryght so,
> Fermed in Arthurez hallez—
> And therfore, hende, now hoo!'   (2327–30)

This bubble of pretence is soon burst and the reminder becomes
ironic when Gawain himself is given a lesson in chivalry by a
transformed Green Knight, for, by way of the exaggeration of
Gawain's action and the amusement it arouses in the laconic,
observing opponent, the poet makes a brilliant switch from one
characterisation to the other; the Green Knight, with his floating,
undefined suggestions of Hazard, Fortune and Death, is converted into the Lord of Hautdesert, bluff, cheerful commander
and commender. The enemy changes roles and becomes a
friendly adviser, unsparingly honest but indulgent and generous.
He ceases to be identified as the 'gome in the grene' but from now
on is simply 'The hathel', 'that other leude', 'the lorde' until he
departs from the scene with that same effect as at the end of the
first scene at Camelot of total disappearance into limbo. There is
again a subliminal suggestion that with the blow, as in those
folk-tales where a beheading magically restores a transformed
being to his original state of youth and beauty, the magic is
dispelled, though it is the transformed figure who delivers it
rather than receives.

Certainly from the moment of the axe-stroke, the scene is a
slow deflation, a modulation from heroic, supernatural expectation to the level of ordinary human dealings, and the character of

the Green Knight/Lord changes key from moment to moment.
First he speaks in an authoritative voice, echoing the tone used
elsewhere by the poet to represent the spirit of right, justice and
moderation, as in God's final words in *Patience* and some of the
Maiden's reproofs in *Pearl*.

> 'Bolde burne, on this bent be not so gryndel.
> No mon here unmanerly the mysboden habbez,
> Ne kyd bot as covenaunde at kyngez kort schaped.
> I hyght the a strok and thou hit hatz; halde the wel payed.'
>
> (2338–41)

Then he becomes legal and business-like as he explains the rules
of his particular game, and modulates into a matter-of-fact
giver of information, as he tells Gawain how he has been deceived,
and becomes, at the end of his speech, the courteous friendly
host of Hautdesert, addressing Gawain with the polite 'yow':[30]

> 'Now know I wel thy cosses, and thy costes als,
> And the wowyng of my wyf: I wroght hit myselven.
> I sende hir to asay the, and sothly me thynkkez
> On the fautlest freke that ever on fote yede.
> As perle bi the quite pese is of prys more,
> So is Gawayn, in god fayth, bi other gay knyghtez.
> Bot here yow lakked a lyttel, sir, and lewté yow wonted;
> Bot that watz for no wylyde werke, ne wowyng nauther,
> Bot for ye lufed your lyf; the lasse I yow blame.'   (2360–8)

It is Gawain who inflates the terms of the discussion into those
of vice and sin, bringing together, more explicitly than at any
moment since the passage on the pentangle, chivalric standards
and religious ones, and it is, as it seems, in response to Gawain's
own enlargement of the moral importance of the moment, that
the Lord, in his next speech, is given the terminology of confession and penance. The effect of this is, in my view, partly comic;
the Lord with laughter takes up a metaphorical, temporary,
priestly authority to re-assure Gawain and to bring him down from
his exaggerated stance of tragic failure, offers the belt as a token
and returns quickly to ordinary common-sense matters, teasing
Gawain to make light of it all. We are invited to respond to this
primarily in terms of its effect on the hero and as part of the gradual

deflating of heroic exaggeration: the result of the speech is that Gawain speaks with calmer, rueful cynicism, pointing out truthfully that he has been tricked and made use of, but accepting that he has done wrong. The lowering of the level of speech, thought and action culminates in Gawain's speaking at an every/ day, common/sense level and asking his opponent's name.

What more we may read into the Lord's significance at this point is open to some doubt. He speaks as Gawain's judge, but the only bases which, in the reader's eyes, give him the right to judge are, first, the power associated with having, in some sense, won a contest and having worked within the rules; secondly, his earlier fulfilment of the role of host and master; and thirdly, his undefined, shortly to be undermined, supernatural power. For the moment he is able to interpret Gawain's motives and jestingly absolves Gawain, but the poet does not choose to sustain the priestly voice, let alone give any body to the suggestions of divine power, and the standards by which Gawain is judged are primarily contractual and social, the standards of good government, generosity, and fair dealing, which Hautdesert exemplified. The belt is returned as a reminder of the vagaries of fortune; Gawain is offered a lesson in experience. The religious tone of the exchange makes clear the moral basis of the test, but the language is not to be taken literally; it acts rather, on the Lord's lips, as a teasing metaphor for what has been going on, and though Gawain speaks of 'vertue', 'vyse' and 'covetyse', his own judge/ ment of himself is couched in chivalric and social language, which links vice with 'vylany' and defines the nature he has for/ saken as 'larges and lewté that longez to knyghtez'. As in *Pearl* there seems to be more interest in the poet's mind in the hero's actual experiencing of the lesson than in clear didactic exposition and analysis of the lesson itself. It seems to me impossible from this shifting, dramatic succession of plausible reactions and pos/ tures to justify a reading of the poem which places strong emphasis upon moral lessons, or on Christian doctrines.[31]

The identification of the Lord by name disperses any remnants of mystery and his final speech lacks any sense of the majestic and meaningful; at the last the whole affair is deliberately reduced to the level of gentlemanly conduct and the adventure is treated rather as if Gawain had been caught not actually cheating at cards but furtively taking out insurance against loss—not the done thing but nothing really to be disturbed about. The Lord himself, diminished in importance once his mask is off, is further reduced when he reveals that he was merely a puppet dangling from someone else's hands. The most significant feature of this long anti-climax is that the real judge of Gawain is not the awesome grotesque persona of the Green Knight, who belongs to the world of fantasy and exotic mystery, but the 'human' manifestation of the figure. Gawain is judged in the realm of social behaviour, not in one of supernatural challenge, judged for his conduct in a normal situation not in a moment of heroic action. We seem to have been living in a world peopled by looming shadows which disappear beneath the light of simple truth, which leaves us with the inescapable fact that Gawain was afraid and failed to see that all his promises were equally important. Beneath the high-sounding name by which the two-faced challenger is identified, Bertilak de Hautdesert, is the prosaic allegorical identification of Gawain's future burden, 'Bear thy lack of high deserving'. Despite Bertilak's consoling praise, Gawain's remorse seems to show that Morgan's ultimate purpose has been fulfilled, but the poet chooses not to leave it so, restoring our sense of proportion, if not the hero's, by Camelot's laughter and sensible pleasure in Gawain's preservation.

Judged by any naturalistic standards or by the standards of characterisation which one would think inevitable in later fiction, the figures of Gawain's opponents are obviously unsatisfactory in being unexplained and inconsistent. The Guide is a tool unexplained in logical terms; the Lady is characterised merely in terms of her function in the plot, although the poet is subtle enough to suggest that she has unrevealed thoughts and that the rest of her character exists but is not being used for the moment; the importance of Morgan in the plot is not 'justified' by any presentation of her nature and motives, since she exists only as an emblematic picture; the Green Knight/Bertilak is a combination of two natures, which overlap at some places in the poem but which are never fused into one explicable being. Obviously one way of accounting for such figures is to accommodate them to a general principle of medieval dramatic treatment of character, whereby the figures are filled out with plausible, vivid sense of what they must say and do to fulfil their purpose in a particular moment. Geoffrey Shepherd speaks of such treatment of character in *Troilus and Criseyde*:

> The plot is central. But the story, as Chaucer tells it in its wholeness and fullness, generates the characters it needs. If we insist on assessing the individuality and psychology of these characters we do it from outside the poem. They needed not to be psychologically coherent as long as their presentation sustains and gives substance to the *narratio*.[32]

The presentation of the Guide and the Lady are clearly rooted in such animation of the narrative, generated from the plot's need of a tempter and a temptress, and, similarly, the Green Knight at Camelot is basically an inventive filling-out of the role of challenger. But in *Sir Gawain* the way such figures work is unusually complex. Because the plot requires the Lady to act at her husband's bidding, the Guide presumably to act at someone's bidding, though we are not told whose, and the Green Knight at Morgan's bidding, the idea of playing a role, of deliberately acting an assumed part, is made an aspect of the fiction itself. The poet's treatment of behaviour is, in any case, a sophisticated one which knows that action may be an act put on for the benefit of an audience. Arthur's behaviour when he is surprised by the supernatural, but 'let no semblaunt be sene', is a performance of what seems fitting to him as king and husband, and an example of the quelling of private feeling in the interests of decorum and protection of women and social inferiors. The courtiers of Camelot similarly display a sense of appropriate public behaviour as they disguise their grief at the thought of Gawain's doomed quest (539–42). But Gawain's pretence when the Lady first comes to his bedroom is different, embarrassed, self-protective and wary:

> and the burne schamed,
> And layde hym doun lystyly, and let as he slepte. . .
> The lede lay lurked a ful longe quyle,
> Compast in his concience to quat that cace myght
> Meve other amount to.   (1189ff.)

When he does manage to behave in a more fitting way, the 'seemly'

behaviour is presented to us as comic, a pantomime performance
of waking-up in pious innocence:

> Bot yet he sayde in hymself, 'More semly hit were
> To aspye wyth my spelle in space quat ho wolde.'
> Then he wakenede, and wroth, and to hir warde torned.
> And unlouked his yye-lyddez and let as hym wondered,
> And sayned hym, as bi his sawe the saver to worthe,
>   with hande.   (1198–203)

Since the poet indicates to us that the Lady's wooing is a
performance from start to finish as she 'let lyk as hym loved mych',
the ensuing encounters between the two are rich in the delicate
humour of supposed courtly love scenes which are really contests
of false rhetoric. Gawain's sense of seemly public behaviour is
even further tainted by comedy and embarrassment, when it
becomes a matter of manners having to conceal honesty (1658–
1663). Courtesy of speech, which the poet refers to often, is thus
shown to be another romance quality which is two-faced; manners
make good order, but to be civilised may mean to compromise
truth. The particular deed does, of course, turn awry and culminates
in a convincing show of frank honesty from Gawain as he comes
forward to act a lie to the Lord:

> He metez me this godmon inmyddez the flore,
> And al with gomen he hym gret, and goudly he sayde,
> 'I schal fylle upon fyrst oure forwardez nouthe,
> That we spedly had spoken, ther spared watz no drynk.'
> Then acoles he the knyght and kysses hym thryes,
> As saverly and sadly as he hem sette couthe.   (1932–7)

The treatment of this scene shows the poet moving over completely, for the moment, to detached presentation and creating the
irony of a convincing performance of truth which the reader
knows to be false. We are not given such ironic knowledge in
other scenes which we know only at the end of the poem to have
been lies, but retrospectively we recognise that the Lord and the
Guide put up similarly convincing acts. Since the inhabitants
of Hautdesert are presented almost entirely within their roles,
they appear as characters who know their lines, in contrast to
Gawain whom we see in the act of improvisation. We can trust

what we read only when the character's inner thought is revealed; the dialogue itself is constantly suspect. Hence our certainty, if we had any doubts at all, that Gawain is our hero. The figures of the Lord, the Lady, the Guide and the Green Knight are shown to us only as performances, as façades; the poet has significantly not developed their inner life and so they exist as mysterious and threatening talking masks. This effect is augmented both by the fact that, until the end, none of these figures is given a name, and by the poet's use of suggestion in his presentation of them.

Working in conjunction with, and in a similar way to the poet's suggestive, anonymous figures are figures of another kind, the numbers and patterns in the poem. These might seem to imply that the poem's meaning is defined by some symbolic design. The existence of several such patterns, however, prevents one from identifying a single total scheme. The three final days at Hautdesert, with the three hunts, three temptations, three exchanges and the one, two, three kisses, followed by the three blows from the Green Knight's axe form the most obvious pattern; this seems to work mainly as a device of suspense, suggesting to us the familiar folk-tale idea that the third of a series is the one that is significant, and thus throwing into prominence the third exchange scene, and building up the suspense of the delivery of the blow. Another number series is presented in the poet's lengthy explanation of the pentangle, the five-pointed star with its overlapping, endless lines; the identification of the significance of the sign with regard to Gawain is an ingenious piece of arithmetical poetry, explaining in twenty-five alliterative long lines (lines 640–64) five groups of five qualities and emblems. From the stress placed on the symbol and the number, one expects both to play a part later in the story but the pentangle is hardly referred to and, though the number is used later, it is used unobtrusively enough for one to be unsure whether the pattern is accidental or another sign of the poet's teasing ingenuity. Whichever it is, there *is* a pattern of five in the poem. Gawain makes five promises, one to the Green Knight at Camelot, three to the Lord of Hautdesert and one to the Lady (and manages to keep four of them). Gawain is faced by five different figures who, as it appears later, were all tempters and testers, the Green Knight, Bertilak, the Lady, the Guide and Morgan la Fay. But the poet does not point this correspondence, nor, as he easily might have done, explain Gawain's failure in any way which makes us see it as part of this fixed pattern. The pattern fades away as the testers dwindle by the identification of the Green Knight and the Lord, by the reduction of the Lady (and by implication the Guide) and the Green Knight himself to pawns of the one malevolent source, who is in turn deprived of any sense of majesty and power. The pentangle itself is replaced, or rather augmented, by a different, less immutable, kind of knot, a single band of green.

So behind the already piquant combination of a fantastic adventure-story, and a mixed narrative style, the poet has created a further dimension to the poem in the suggestion of larger but nebulous, mythic and allegorical forms, of which the anonymous opponents of the hero are particular but shifting manifestations. The reader is teased into trying to form such shapes into patterns, but the poet skilfully weaves together suggestions without enabling one to make clear identifications. At one moment one perceives Gawain as the centre of a tug-of-war between two allegorical opponents who represent two different conceptions of knighthood, but the Lord and Lady of Hautdesert remain within their social roles and do not solidify into personifications. From another point of view one sees Gawain ringed by a masque of tempters and testers, who present to him façades of normal behaviour, behind which is a sense of mysterious significance, a sense which is never defined but simply dispelled in the closing stages of the poem. Both the Green Knight and Morgan la Fay, for instance, are described in terms which associate them with Death. The Guide says of the Green Knight:

> Ther passes non bi that place so proude in his armes
> That he ne dyngez hym to dethe with dynt of his honde. . .
> (2104–5)

This description of the bringer down of pride regardless of degree is echoed by Bertilak's own words about Morgan:

> Weldez non so hyghe hawtesse
> That ho ne con make ful tame.   (2454–5)

But we are not allowed to make the equation of either with Death itself: the words of the Guide are proved untrue and the words about Morgan are undermined by the reminder, a few lines later, that she is only old Auntie Morgan.

3. The poet's treatment of the hero and his adventure

It was possibly in pursuit of his interest in the 'difficult case' that the poet turned, in *Sir Gawain*, to secular material. God is a tricky subject and the poet has to contend with greater resistance in both material and audience when he deals with scriptural and doctrinal matter. If instead of codes of universal justice and belief, one starts from the earthly code of chivalry, then the values are more ambivalent. It is possible for the poet to set up oppositions between a hero and his challenger without a clear identification of the moral agency which that challenger represents. And so, around the central concept of a traditional hero under-taking a romance quest, the poet creates a shifting, hazardous world, where the ideas which in many other romances are taken for granted are explicitly or implicitly questioned.

The poet's choice of a literary form with a well-defined tradition could be assumed to arouse certain expectations in his audience; it is the poet's ingenious pleasure to attempt to satisfy his reader's interest in adventure while partly frustrating such expectations by eschewing the easy romance path and attempting a more penetrating treatment of the knight, showing him as an individual struggling to accomplish an impossible task. The poet also avoids the hero's easy triumph and colours his 'happy ending' with a sense of partial failure and anticlimax, placing idealism in the light of unheroic reality and deflating comedy. Again, he chose a hero who would already be known to his hearers, and the existence of conflicting traditions of Gawain's nature may well have been something which the poet wished to exploit.[33] The resistance to sexual temptation of a hero who elsewhere in Arthurian tales acts as an impulsive libertine seems a particularly teasing example of moral conduct, intended to surprise the audience as much as the failure of this exemplar of courage completely to pass his more traditional test. The 'dangerous edge of things' is offered for our interest as much as with Jonah, though more lightly, and, like Jonah, Gawain eventually appears as something of an heroic fool who thought wrongly that life played fair and according to the rules, even while he fails to conduct his own life according to them.

Unlike Jonah, however, Gawain is indisputably a hero, though the result of the poet's complex and equivocal treatment of his adventure is that the nature of the heroic role is continually in doubt, and the ending of the poem is designed to make us wonder whether Gawain has fulfilled such a role or not. We are certain, at least, that Gawain is hero in the sense of the central figure of the narrative; once he enters the action in the fifteenth stanza, he is present in every stanza except six scattered verses describing the hunts. Further, once he has left Camelot, the poet shows more and more of his thoughts and feelings, and often, though not always, focuses scenes from Gawain's point of view. He is identified as 'our luflych lede' and the idea of 'our' hero implicitly calls for the reader's sympathetic involvement. It is also clear that he is considered within the world of the poem as a model of noble behaviour, who performs actions fitting to the traditions of chivalry. He is presented in traditional heroic situa∕tions such as being equipped in armour and riding alone into danger. He is given words which ring with echoes of epic stoicism, and he is even accompanied by epic epithets: *Gawayn the gode, Gawayn the hende, gode Gawan*. He is associated throughout with high ideals and standards of behaviour, even if at times ironically; he is praised by the poet and by his opponent. But, of course, the model proves to have a flaw, and the outcome of the story displays the idea of the hero as a model of behaviour in conflict with the idea of the individual who is our emotional concern. This is the poet's major change in the traditional be∕heading tale. Whereas in the analogues the keeping of the promise alone proved the hero's courage and saved his life, the author of *Sir Gawain* portrays a hero who shows courage, keeps his promise, saves his life, and yet does not end with the conventional hero's triumph. Gawain possesses the necessary qualities for the fictional automaton which the hero of romance often seems, but these are played off against ordinary human, even unchivalrous, qualities, particularly fear, to create a figure who eventually seems to possess character and not just characteristics. The change of ending is a turning towards both realism and comedy, for Gawain's failure is no tragic fall, but an anti∕climax. Hence from the start the tone of the poem is intermittently and insidiously comic, and indicates to us that the outcome, though it may be unexpected, is not to be serious. This is of a piece with the poet's other uses of levelling realism and marks *Sir Gawain*, from one point of view, as a romance moving in the direction of *Don Quijote*.[34] But the poet's basic choices, the choice of a testing story and the choice of treatment, indicate not so much a desire to deflate romance as that same interest in the antithesis of opposites, and in the inter-play of ideal behaviour and actual experience, that one can observe, in various ways, in the other three poems. The Beheading Game measures Gawain against the heroic figures of legend, and in following their path, Gawain partakes of their heroic stature. The poet wants us to respond to the elevated, romantic aspects of his tale. At the same time the poet's treatment brings Gawain, like Jonah, to the reader's level of experience.

So, although Gawain fulfils a hero's role, the hero himself is continually being diminished. He is shown repeatedly as sub-ordinate, and therefore being obliged to be deferential, and as passive. At Camelot he appears as liege, nephew and inferior; he is subject to the approval of Arthur and the court, advised and, at the close of the scene, patronised by the King, lectured on his obligations by the Green Knight, and even warned by the narrator, who, by the end of Part I, has left his pretended role of the minstrel repeating a tale, and has turned into the all-seeing, ironic commentator on the action. In Part II Gawain is shown setting out on an adventure in which he is doomed to be the passive recipient of a death-blow, and in which, in the court's eyes, he is the victim of kingly pride and folly. In the arming scene he is presented as a lay-figure being accoutred in equipment whose heroic associations have to contend with a sense of its irrelevance and uselessness in the particular quest he is under-taking. The elaborate explication of Gawain's device accompanies praise of the hero with emphasis on his reliance on forces outside himself and on his possesssion of virtues which are gentle and mild and show deference to the feelings of others, and this is followed by an account of Gawain's journey which gives a brief summary of his acts of valour but enters in detail into his experience of loneliness, cold and anxious uncertainty. The poet thus begins to establish a distinction between the hero's humanity and the heroic pattern of behaviour expected from him; this distinction forms the basis of the complex treatment of the hero, whereby the poet repeatedly reduces Gawain's heroic quality in a variety of related ways, while maintaining in the reader's mind elevated senses of his nature and behaviour.

Much of the time we are asked not to look at him but to perceive through him; as he is faced by unknown places, an unfamiliar society and startling and unnerving experience, so we live through it with him as impressions are presented in the order in which he receives them. This is strikingly so in the last part of the poem, where the poet builds up the suspense preceding the Green Knight's reappearance and the delivery of the blow. The careful focusing through Gawain's perception of the scene in which he first hears and then sees the Green Knight again is characteristic of the way in which the poet creates a bond of sympathy between reader and hero, which is implicitly identifying the hero as an ordinary man, who reacts to the unfamiliar with embarrassment and fear, and whose limitations are inevitably exposed. His 'inadequate' reactions are among the effects in the poem of which the reader can be most sure, because the poet tells us of Gawain's inner thoughts, reminding us from time to time of his fear of the encounter with the Green Knight, and identifying his embarrassment by the Lady of Hautdesert and his sense of the dilemma in which he is placed. On the last day at the Castle, the poet enters into his hero with particular point and emphasis, first identifying his preoccupation during sleep and ominously reminding us of the passive, doomed role which Gawain has yet to fulfil:

> In drey droupyng of dreme draveled that noble,
> As mon that watz in mornyng of mony thro thoghtes,
> How that destiné schulde that day dele hym his wyrde
> At the grene chapel, when he the gome metes,
> And bihoves his buffet abide withoute debate more.
>
> (1750–4)

The hero is shown, that is, at his most vulnerable. Then, as he hastily recovers his wits to deal with the laughing and alluring Lady, bending over him with her fair face, throat and breast enhanced in beauty by jewels and fur, Gawain's instinctive sexual response is indicated both directly and by innuendo:[35]

> He sey hir so glorious and gayly atyred,
> So fautles of hir fetures and of so fyne hewes,
> Wight wallande joye warmed his hert.
> With smothe smyling and smolt thay smeten into merthe,
> That al watz blis and bonchef that breke hem bitwene,
>   and wynne.
>   Thay lanced wordes gode,
>   Much wele then watz therinne.   (1760–7)

Beneath the decorous surface description of conversation runs the current of sexual, physical nuance, identified clearly in 'Wight wallande joye' and obliquely suggested in the physical verbs, *smeten*, *breke* and *lanced*. The threat that the warm courtesies of speech may burst into the hotter pleasures of physical contact is then made explicit by the voice of the all-seeing poet, who states Gawain's moral dilemma, shows his hero suppressing his sexual arousal and at last recognising that he can no longer go on temporising with the Lady without being false to her husband:

> Thay lanced wordes gode,
> Much wele then watz therinne.
> Gret perile bitwene hem stod,
> Nif mare of hir knyght [hym] mynne.
> For that prynce of pris depresed hym so thikke,
> Nurned hym so neghe the thred, that nede hym bihoved
> Other lach ther hir luf, other lodly refuse.
> He cared for his cortaysye, lest crathayn he were,
> And more for his meschef, yif he schulde make synne
> And be traytor to that tolke that that telde aght.
> 'God schylde,' quoth the schalk, 'that schal not befalle!'
>   (1766–76)

This is, of course, a disputed and much discussed passage and one which several critics have seen as central to one's understanding of the moral sense of the tale.[36] It seems to me that the poet is ingeniously combining his reducing and his enhancing of the hero. Gawain's thoughts are on a level of plausible feeling; he wants to maintain a reputation for courtesy to women, but he comes to a moment of self-knowledge in recognising that he cannot, in his situation, both do that and maintain faith to his host. He is a normal male and his physical reactions to the Lady declare (*Nurned*) that he is shamefully near crossing the boundary of another man's territory (*thred*), and so, because faith is more important than courtesy, he forces down, subdues and checks (*depresed*) his urgent sexual desire. The physical undertones of the passage make one view the hero in ordinary terms and enjoy his comic struggle between being a gentleman and avoiding adultery. The morality by which Gawain acts also seems to emphasise common-sense ideas at the expense of romantic notions of knightly conduct; Gawain is no dashing blade, but a cautious man who realises that being polite to a woman stops short of going to bed with her, if one is a guest in her husband's house. The diminishing of the chivalrous hero to bourgeois standards of social behaviour is, however, counter-acted by the sense of a real struggle against temptation and of a decisive act which is ideal in social terms rather than those of either *amour courtois* or Christian celibacy. The decision of a *prynce of pris* to respect the rights of a social inferior, even at the expense of his own reputation for courtliness, is a piece of ideal behaviour which displays Gawain as one of those who have that true 'gentillesse' of which another bourgeois character, the Wife of Bath, so eloquently speaks, through the lady in another intimate bedroom scene, in Chaucer's version of the tale of the Loathly Lady. Again we have a moment in the poem where beneath the surface is a debating point about knighthood, as to which of the two, courtesy to a woman or loyalty to one's host, is the more important. The emphasis on the hero's own overcoming of temptation in lines 1770–91 seems to make the idea of the intervention of the Virgin Mary, which most editors curiously prefer to emendation in line 1769,[37] quite out of keeping with the rest of the section; the poet is thinking more in social than in religious terms.

Gawain's resistance to temptation and his loyalty to his host occur, with an irony which comes to seem typical of the poet, just before the crucial scene in which he yields to the Lady's persuasion and commits himself to an act of disloyalty. The alternation of building-up and letting-down is present throughout the poem and is a second way in which the heroic aspect of Gawain and his enterprise is diminished. The Castle itself, which at first sight seemed full of rich potentiality, is, in romance terms,

an anti-climax. There are no besieged maidens, no predatory
giant; its inhabitants turn out to be, apparently, normal, concerned with sensible matters such as food, warmth and Christmas
entertainment. Gawain is, on his arrival, rapidly disarmed,
domesticated, led to the lulling comfort of fine fresh clothes, fire,
food and drink. What have pentangles and high courage to do in
such a setting? It is no surprise that the Green Chapel turns out to
be just around the corner. The whole business of Gawain's quest
is deflated and made to sound ridiculously easy:

> 'The grene chapayle upon grounde greve yow no more;
> Bot ye schal be in youre bed, burne, at thyn ese,
> Quyle forth dayez, and ferk on the fyrst of the yere,
> And cum to that merk at mydmorn, to make quat yow likez
>   in spenne.
>   Dowellez whyle New Yerez daye,
>   And rys, and raykez thenne.
>   Mon schal yow sette in waye;
>   Hit is not two myle henne.'   (1070–8)

Gawain will not even need to get up early! When he comes to
depict the actual fulfilment of the quest, the poet again builds up
a sense of climax in the account of Gawain's setting forth, his
rejection of the Guide's advice, and the description of the desolate
valley. The Chapel itself is a let-down, but Gawain's imaginings
invest it with eerie force and lead to a further build-up of suspense
with the Green Knight's re-appearance and the preliminaries to
the blow. After the cut all is, for Gawain, bathos. The revelation
of the Lady's deceit, of the meaning of the challenge and of the
identity of the agent leads to the ultimate insulting cosiness of
Bertilak's invitation to Gawain to come back and stay with his
elderly aunt.

   The poet thus seems to take pleasure in putting his hero in
false positions and it is in the scenes at the Castle that he most
ingeniously devised ways of doing it. In this part of the poem
Gawain is imagined as a kind of Wimbledon champion of
chivalry, who has to find again those qualities that made him
champion. Since there is no question that Gawain will, if challenged to direct knightly contest, display superlative powers,
his humbling has to be achieved by guile. Hence the methods at

the Castle are devised to subject him to what is in essence a psychological trial. He is first encouraged by comfort and relief to relax and to consider himself off duty, but, at the same time, is placed beneath a weight of obligation by the overwhelming hospitality which puts him into the role of grateful and deferential guest; the weight grows heavier as he finds himself expected to put on a performance worthy of the reputation accorded to him. Then the Lord deprives Gawain of the opportunity to show his masculine, active qualities of courage and strength in the field. This is typically justified in naturalistic terms: Gawain needs rest and food after his long winter journey. But it reduces him to a passive role and this is highlighted by the constrast of the vigor/ ous, active Lord, fulfilling the role of a leader of men, the 'low/ ande leder of ledez' which Gawain might have been, in a realistic picture of the activities of the rural nobility. So Gawain is held within a pleasant prison, reduced to inactivity. Then he is further placed in a false position and further imprisoned by the Lady, who takes on the lover's role, captures him naked and flat on his back, disarmed in every sense of the word.

This double reversal of roles is made ingeniously comic and subtle by the Lady's use of Gawain's own reputation as a weapon against him. The juxtaposition of the romantic and the real is expressed in their conversations almost in terms of a distinction between literature and life: Gawain appears to have read fewer romances than the Lady and to be ill/versed in the role which is persuasively thrust upon him. This twist of the situation works both to convince the reader of Gawain's reality, since we sympa/ thise with the one who appears the imperfect actor on the stage, struggling to keep up with a plot he is unaware of and to im/ provise appropriate lines, and further to draw a distinction between the limited, actual man and romantic conceptions of a knight as an idealised being. Measured against the example of the hunting Lord and against the Lady's picture of a prototype lover/hero, the real Gawain is continually disconcerted and his standards are questioned by being deliberately confused. On the one hand he is presented with an exaggerated model of fine breeding and courtly expertise by the flattery of the Lady and the courtiers, against which he is forced to demur and to counter over/praise with modest disclaimers; on the other hand, he is forced to defend himself against undervaluation when the Lady accuses him of failing to do what a gentleman ought. The dis/concerting of Gawain takes place in a situation where he is constantly under obligation to express courtly sentiments of service to the Lady, and to defer to his host. He is forced to receive re/peated generosity in the form of the Lord's winnings and to give little in return—a situation repeated in the symbolic moment when Gawain confesses himself bankrupt of courtly gifts and the Lady in reply presses him to accept a valuable ring. He is further put out of countenance by the Lord's teasing and by the Lady's embarrassing hints in her husband's presence. Another element in the concerted attack on him is the attempt to catch him off guard by the exertion of pressure just when the situation might allow him to relax: so the Lord proposes the exchange/bargain just when Gawain has been relieved of anxiety about finding the Green Chapel; the Lady first persuades him to accept a kiss just as she seemed on the point of leaving; the Lady starts the crucial discussion about giving love/tokens only when she appears to have given up her attempt to make Gawain act as lover. Such strategy contributes to an over/all sense of deliberate displacement in the poem, whereby not only is the hero continually caught off/guard, but also the reader is cleverly confused and challenged to read the situation truly.

Trapped at the centre of a web of invidious comparison and subtle teasing attack, Gawain is shown to us from within and without. We are given an intimate, identifying knowledge of him. a knowledge both comic, since we share his experience of embarrassment and uncertainty, and also serious, since we are given private access to his fear, his resistance to temptation and his single/mindedness and determination. But this view of the hero is not consistently maintained and we are shown Gawain's acts at times as they appear to others, the courtiers at Hautdesert, the Lord, the Lady, the Green Knight in the valley, and the Round Table. The outer view of him also has a comic and a serious aspect. His improvised displays of elegant words for the Lady's benefit and his returning of the kisses to her husband are conceived as dramatic scenes offered for the reader's detached, amused enjoyment; the serious aspect is his performance as a keeper of promises, shown mainly in dramatic externalised terms.

The effect of the combination of points of view is to create a division between Gawain's thoughts and his acts, so that the hero's actual conduct is presented as a performance of what is fitting to the moment, whether, in other terms, it is genuine or false. The poet most significantly chooses to withdraw knowledge of Gawain's inner mind in the scenes immediately after his acceptance of the green belt, so that we are shown his going to confession, his mirth, and the last exchange of winnings, from outside. These acts exist in the poem as a performance of virtue, a completely convincing appearance of truth. As we know later, Gawain is here at his most wrong and that he should show at this moment the greatest self-confidence that he displays anywhere in the poem is another of the poet's ironies. The fact that the author makes so little of the matter of Gawain's confession is a sure in-dication that he is more interested in creating an effect of dramatic irony than in making the moral point which so many commenta-tors have tried to elicit from the scene.[38] Gawain is later blamed for lack of loyalty to a fellow man, not for false religious obser-vance, and the sensible conclusion is that the poet wears his religion, as so many other things, lightly and comfortably, re-cognising that this tale is not the place for making points about whether an unconfessed intention to commit sin is to be added to the list of Gawain's failings. The poet remains, interestingly and effectively, vague, leaving us either to assume that 'the more and the mynne' did really include everything and that the priest belongs to the 'good face' of Hautdesert uninvolved in the plot, or that Gawain with sensible practicality went to confession before he had actually done anything wrong and even, if we care to press it that far, before he had finally made up his mind. But the reader is not actually invited to consider such questions: his attention is directed to enjoyment of the performance and the ironic confrontation between a confident, joyful, truthful, open-handed hero and a crest-fallen Lord apologising for his measly fox-pelt.

That Gawain's deeds and words should, in part, be presented to us in terms of putting on an act is the inevitable product of the antitheses basic to the whole poem, between ideal and actual, between the reputation and the real man, between mystery and explanation, between anonymity and identification. Gawain is repeatedly measured against models of behaviour. He is measured against an archetypal sense of the hero's role in a setting with the authority of historical tradition. He is measured in Christian and partly allegorical terms as an Everyman existing in a world of mutability and human weakness. He is measured in terms of a social, courtly, romance ideal of knighthood. Most subtly he is compared to the idea of himself, since the poet offers us definitions of what a Gawain should be, or might be considered to be. Teasingly he is accused of being an impostor, of not really being Gawain at all, first by the Lady:

> 'Bot that ye be Gawan, hit gotz in mynde.'
> 'Querfore?' quoth the freke, and freschly he askez,
> Ferde lest he hade fayled in fourme of his castes.
>
> (1293–5)

The phrase 'in fourme of his castes' places emphasis on the idea of the performance of Gawain which Gawain is managing to put on, and this performance is again questioned by the Lady on the next day (1481–3). It is left to the Green Knight to make the strongest accusation of imposture:

> And thenne repreved he the prynce with mony prowde
>   wordez:
> 'Thou art not Gawayn,' quoth the gome, 'that is so goud
>   halden,
> That never arwed for no here by hylle ne be vale,
> And now thou fles for ferde er thou fele harmez!
> Such cowardise of that knyght cowthe I never here.'
>
> (2269–73)

In the face of these challenges that he is failing to deserve a famous name, Gawain is required to define his own nature, to reply in effect: 'I am Gawain, but Gawain is other than you think.' No other hero of medieval romance is so frequently shown as talking about himself, first with modest, conventional self-depreciation:

> 'I am the wakkest, I wot, and of wyt feblest,
> And lest lur of my lyf, quo laytes the sothe:
> Bot for as much as ye ar myn em I am only to prayse;
> No bounté bot your blod I in my bodé knowe.' (354–7)

This courtly modesty gradually becomes more than conventional as self-depreciation becomes necessary in the face of too great generosity and praise:

> 'In god fayth,' quoth Gawayn, 'gayn hit me thynkkez,
> Thagh I be not now he that ye of speken;
> To reche to such reverence as ye reherce here
> I am wyye unworthy, I wot wel myselven.'   (1241–4)

From this the poet is able to move his hero to a real recognition of limitation, first in response to the Green Knight's scornful words:

> Quoth Gawayn, 'I schunt onez,
> And so wyl I no more;
> Bot thagh my hede falle on the stonez,
> I con not hit restore.'   (2280–3)

This ruefully humorous and true declaration that the comparison between the Green Knight and Gawain is unfair and unreal, rescues Gawain in the reader's eyes from any accusation of cowardice and prepares for the fuller acknowledgement of human frailty which Gawain is later obliged to make:

> 'For care of thy knokke cowardyse me taght
> To acorde me with covetyse, my kynde to forsake,
> That is larges and lewté that longez to knyghtez.
> Now am I fawty and falce, and ferde haf ben ever
> Of trecherye and untrawthe. . .'   (2379–83)

The contest remains an unfair one, and one inducing cynical disillusion with women, if nothing else, but all men must accept the heritage of sons of Eve.

The hero's answer to the question 'What is Gawain?', which the poem implicitly poses, is humble, and his verdict on the quality of the performance of Gawain which he managed to produce, uncharitable, but the poet's combination of inner and outer senses of his hero forces the reader to take a larger view. We have been shown by the end a hero subordinate, deferential, nervous, who is tested, tempted and tricked, and whose difficult path is overhung by reminders of idealistic and romantic conceptions of knighthood. Treading between quicksands, Gawain shows his positive qualities by his *ad hoc* behaviour in the peculiar situations in which he is unexpectedly placed. The poet gives us dramatised instances of his resistance to sexual temptation, his refusal of rich gifts and his rejection of the opportunity to run away. Throughout, the reader is made conscious of the difficulty of fulfilling a heroic role and is asked to respond to a hero who has sufficient imagination to feel fear and to be sensitively aware that at the end of the road waits death. In a difficult place Gawain acts with modesty, courtesy, quick-wittedness and discretion, even to the extent of knowing when to pretend; he has a sympathetic lack of aggressive self-confidence, a capacity for civilised pleasure, a stern sense of duty, and sensible, conventional moral standards. His morality fails him only when basic self-protection is at issue, when he acts, in a way with which the reader is encouraged to sympathise, with sudden irrationality and gullibility.

The picture created by the poet amounts to a characterisation of Gawain, a portrait complex enough to have a kind of realness uncommon in romance literature. The journey in *Sir Gawain* is a journey inward, into the nature of the hero, a journey in which a young, over-serious, inexperienced Gawain, armed with ideal standards of heroic conduct, is gradually transformed through struggling against fear, by resistance to psychological trial, and by discovered weakness into the experienced and self-condemning figure at the close. The comic conception of the poem is based on the idea that such a voyage of discovery is inevitable for all men, leaving us with the sense that Gawain fulfils the role of hero essentially in surviving, particularly since he has survived an unfair trial with honour dented no more than can be accepted as the inevitable price of experience.

The world which the poet has created to embody this experience is a maze through which the bewildered hero has to pick a path. The only way we can account for the figures whose ambiguous faces make up the labyrinth, and can relate to the literal story the nebulous suggestions of allegorical figures, of a masque of testing and temptation, of the fable as a schematised abstraction and so on, is to see the poet's intention as that of creating images and figures who are, in various ways, manifestations of the shifting powers which operate in the sublunary world, the powers of fortune, mutability, hazard, time and mortality. The images of youth and age, of good and bad fortune, of the passing seasons, of the new and old year, fuse together to form a broad, shadowy backcloth to the action. Against this backcloth Gawain's test may be seen as a test not only of knighthood but of humanity, but the poet, having made use of shadows and suggestions as part of the suspense and mystery of his tale, seems to dismiss them as illusions at the end, when the adventure is seen simply. As we read there is no danger of the poet's ingenuity over-reaching itself, because, first, we go through the maze with the hero, and have the shadows and complexities focused for us through his eyes or by having our attention continually directed to him, and, secondly, we are given an over-all, distanced sense of the poem as something belonging to the legendary past, something com-pleted and, therefore, following a course whose conclusion we, in a sense, know in advance; the details may be surprising but, whatever the particular outcome for Gawain, we know that it will be something which we can absorb into our existing know-ledge of Arthurian history.

Though I have referred to the ending of the poem as ambiguous, it is not really so; rather it is humanely ironic. Gawain at the end is powerfully abashed and overcome by his failure, as he sees it. What Gawain feels ashamed of is the *result* of his weakness, that because of fear he was led to act in a way unworthy of his code, and be false to his nature as a knight. His fault is not that of feeling fear but allowing fear to pervert his judgement, allowing human instinct to overcome the acquired ideals of perfect be-haviour. But the poet makes it clear that for this result Gawain has been punished, and therefore left subsequently free of guilt; the green band is a reminder of the punished fault. The actual weak-ness, instinctive love of life, Gawain is not blamed for and Gawain himself, though naturally enough with some rueful bitterness, accepts it. His anti-feminist cynicism is implicitly as much an acceptance of his share in the Fall as the explicit state-ment a few lines later of human frailty, and the poet's choice of this way of recognising one's limitations clearly identifies wry and worldly humour as his conception of a mature attitude to life. Gawain's sorrow and shame convey the bitter sadness of recognis-ing limitation and uphold the value of the romantic ideals with which literary knighthood is identified. What else can men do but build civilisations, establish standards of fair dealing, affront destiny, and attempt to surpass the boundaries of man by creating ideals, orders and structures? The beauty of an ideal life, such as it can be in the world, remains. But the poet persuades us that the joyous assembly at the end is right, even if in all human dealings there is an element of folly, to laugh and to honour Gawain and the belt. By the standards of common sense what matters is that Gawain 'the grace hade geten of his lyve'. The cause of Gawain's failure is itself the reason for going on, absorbing experience and joyfully continuing to pursue ideals which will inevitably have to combat the mutations of time and human nature. The view the poem represents is an essentially generous and comic sense of life, a sympathetic, mature view, containing a dash of cynicism as to whether honour can set to a leg, which accepts the weakness of men but shows the pain of living with intelligence and sympathy. Gawain's progress through the courtly maze of experience to a kind of bitter-sweet maturity seems, eventually, to be a fair enough fictional image of one part of life.

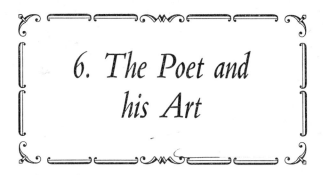

6. The Poet and his Art

1. The poet's view of things

The most striking common feature to emerge from a consecutive reading of *Pearl*, *Purity*, *Patience* and *Sir Gawain and the Green Knight* is the poet's combination, or his attempt at combination, of different levels of meaning. In all four poems the reader is led to perceive an internal and an external sense of the narrative. The internal sense works in literal terms and invites one to share the experience of the main figures. It envisages, in both a serious and a comic mood, individual men living through difficulty. The external sense sets experience in the perspective of the universal. It tends, in places, towards allegory, and sees man in terms of the continuity of his mutable history and of repeated instances of his inevitable folly and limitation. Of course, such a combination is not peculiar to these poems, and in itself is not enough even to support an argument that the four poems are by a common author, though it is enough to confirm the idea that it is with the most intelligent and ambitious of medieval poems that they must be classed. If one seeks comparable instances in the period, only Langland and Chaucer seem to view their material with a degree of complexity sufficient to create a similar multiplicity in the reader's mind. The obvious comparisons are between the *Gawain*-poet's work and *Troilus and Criseyde* and *Piers Plowman*. In *Troilus and Criseyde*, Chaucer makes the reader experience developing emotions and scenes at close hand, but he also asks one to see the story from a long way off, as an historical instance fading into triviality when viewed as part of changing time and in the perspective of the changeless values of heavenly love. Langland's brilliant cartoon pictures of English society and of instances of moral confusion have a literal, moment-by-moment liveliness, behind which lies the allegorical sense of general forces at work in the nature of man and in this earthly life.

Some version of such combinations of the particular and the general was almost bound to be present in the mind of educated and sophisticated writers, at a time when intellectual activity was so concerned with hierarchies of various kinds, when education and culture were so closely identified with a religion based on authority, when books and art, and, following their example, life itself, were seen so much in terms of emblems and allegories. To these influences one may add the facts that writers and the educated part of their audiences were likely to have been trained in debate, and that the patrons of and audiences for literature, at any decent level of sophistication and intelligence, might well feel that the pleasure of poetry and narrative had to be justified in terms of moral improvement, the confirmation of accepted beliefs, and constant reminders that the pleasures and sufferings of life should be regarded in the context of sanctity, sin and death. The double view is not in itself remarkable or unexpected, although only a few writers had enough insight and skill successfully to give it articulate expression in subtle art, as opposed to the crude connections made by exemplum-writers.

What is most interesting and individual in the major poets of the late fourteenth century is not the presence in their works of two aspects of their subjects, but the particular relationship between the aspects which each poet developed for himself. For the impression given by Chaucer is, obviously, not the same as that given by the Gawain-poet, though in both we may find elements that suggest that some of the old hierarchies were, in the latter part of the fourteenth century, less stable than they had been. There are good reasons for expecting at this time some signs of disturbance of old orders. The authority of king and pope had seldom seemed more vulnerable; conflicts about the rights of nobility and peasantry, about the relationship between church and state, about the relationships among religious orders, about money and education, were all controversies which poets of different kinds might well reflect in their verse, even if they avoided intellectual debates about the nature of God and the nature of reality. The increase in works in the English language was also likely to lead to a growth in sophistication and adventurousness among its users. Such sophistication and such reflection of con-temporary controversies and uncertainties seem most character-istically to be expressed, however, not by rejection of old forms and ideas, but by modification of them through irony. So in the works of Chaucer, Langland and the *Gawain*-poet one is re-peatedly presented with pictures of what is, considered in the light of what ought to be. In all three the 'what is' is presented in terms of the multiplicity, absurdity, sinfulness and suffering of human nature, and viewed as inevitable; for good or ill it is simply there. The 'what ought to be' appears, also in all three, as beautiful, good, right, but impossible and unrealistic, an idea which by its nature can never be fulfilled but is there to be aimed at and used as a measure. Within the works of the three poets there is a consider-able range of variation in the ways in which these ideas are used and, since it would take too long to explore the ironic juxta-positions of Langland, let alone the more varied and more subtle ones of Chaucer, I must leave the reader to make his own com-parisons with the forms of irony and double perspective which the *Gawain*-poet developed in his work.

What seems individual to the *Gawain*-poet in his joining together of two levels of thought is an interest in the points at which they conflict with and even contradict one another. Hence the reader is, at many points in his work, conscious of being asked to perceive two things at once. Most obviously in *Purity* and *Patience*, but also, in my opinion, in the other two poems, the poet elicits from the reader a set of reactions which have the effect of running counter to the framework of thought which the poets puts forward as a 'right' view. The reader's sympathy often has an uncomfortable and ironic relationship to the direction of the moral teaching, such as it is, in the four poems. In comparison to Langland and Chaucer (and other contemporary writers) the *Gawain*-poet composed works which have greater brevity and intensity than was usual in fourteenth-century verse, and these qualities stem from the poet's conception of narrative art as the creation and exploitation of conflict and tension. The evidence for this is of several different kinds.

First, the *Gawain*-poet's choice of subjects indicates an interest in difficult cases. In his secular romance he chooses a hero with a dubious literary reputation, chooses to incorporate a sense of failure into his portrayal of the chivalrous knight, and ingeniously plays about with his figures so that the knight's enemy turns into a friendly moral instructor and the dubious Gawain proves to be a staunch resister of sexual temptation. The reader's view of the hero's failure is complicated by the sympathy for him which the poet elicits and by the fact that his failure paradoxically enhances the ideal aims of knighthood which he, like all men, cannot hope utterly to fulfil. In his vision-poem the poet explores a man's reactions to the aspect of life most difficult to bear, and the difficult test of mortality is presented to him in the most extremely distressing and most testing form, the death of an innocent child. In *Purity* and *Patience* the virtues praised by the narrator are tested by negative examples, rather than proved by positive ones, so that the idea of virtue has to exist in a context where the poet makes the reader experience the drama and the suffering involved in the punishment of vice. All four seem to show a seeking out of themes and stories which could be devel-oped in terms of conflict, disagreement, disconcerting reproofs and pained defences, and which could be presented partly by means of dramatic confrontations and disputes. All four contain those elements of the equivocal which difficult cases are designed to produce. They are all tragi-comic, though in different ways. All four finally offer a resolution which one can view either as inadequate to account for the range of reactions which the poet's varied and vivid imagining of his narratives has elicited, or as, at least, leaving the sense that the only way open to man is to make the best of a bad job. The poet's interest in hard cases is also indicated by his use of New Testament parable. The parable of the Wedding Garment and the parable of the Workers in the Vineyard are both enigmatic, to an extent. Both present ideas of the Kingdom of Heaven in terms of stories in which the rules of normal human society, though offered as a parallel to divine order, prove to be contradicted by the behaviour of the God-figure. The poet seems deliberately to complicate the reader's

understanding by making the literal level of the narrative more
vivid and persuasive, as if he wanted the tension between literal
and allegorical meanings to be extreme. The poet's use of symbols and of suggestions (together with the absence, in some places,
of clear identifications) argues a liking for enigmas, which the
reader has to seek to define.

A second kind of evidence, though, as I have said, dependent
on the first, is the dramatic element in the poems. The poet con-
ceives his narratives as a series of scenes. He devotes his consider-
able skill in visualisation to creating a sense of place and setting
for his actions and gives emphatic weight to set scenes dominated
by direct speech. All four poems provide examples of the poet's
focusing of the tale in crucial encounters, whether in ceremonious,
public scenes or in more intimate, face-to-face meetings of two
leading figures. Powerful, varied dialogues of conflict are presented between Jonah and God, Abraham and God, the Pearl-
Maiden and the Dreamer (especially the earlier part), Gawain
and the Lady, Gawain and the Green Knight, Lot and the men
of Sodom. The poet's exploration of enmity, flattery, persuasion,
exasperation, embarrassment, stubbornness, just anger and calm
reasonableness in these dialogues creates for the reader a wide
range of vividly present experiences of conflicting feelings, of
interchange, and of acceptance and rejection. The large amount of
direct speech in the poems means that one reads for much of the
time in the present tense and is thereby invited to live through the
experiences presented and to be jerked to and fro by the tensions
between the speakers. Dramatically effective in a different way
are the public scenes, the New Year's assembly at Camelot and
Belshazzar's Feast, and the moments of cataclysm and revelation.
Here too is a sense of focusing on the crucial, heightened aspects
of the tale, but the focusing is done by means of a massing together of descriptive detail which builds up to and expressively
envisages the moment of wonder, supernatural horror, destructive
fury or ecstatic vision. No other medieval English poet created
so much in terms of impressive moments, of scenes of melodrama,
of the unnatural, of violence and destruction, of actions which
astonish, of human beings faced with and changed by the
extraordinary. Though some of these moments may be seen
as the poet's way of showing the limitation of the human world

in the perspective of the awesome power of God and of the forces beyond men's comprehension, it is not the didactic distinction which seems common to all such scenes, but rather the poet's desire for sheer dramatic impact.

The actual thematic or notional force of dramatic, cataclysmic and supernatural events varies from one place to another, accord/ ing to the poet's conception of the individual tale. At some mom/ ents the poet emphasises the vengeful anger of and the relentless pursuit by the divine agent of 'unnatural' acts, as with the Flood and the storm in *Patience*. At others he is interested in the astonish/ ing effect on the witnesses, and does not specify the agency but presents simply a manifestation, as with the first appearance of the Pearl/Maiden, the magic survival of the Green Knight and the appearance of the hand at Belshazzar's Feast. The relationship, that is, of the human world and of the supernatural is not always the same, and it is an over/simple view which reduces the poems simply to illustrations of the weakness of man and the strength of God. This is another aspect of the works where conflict is evident in the *Gawain*/poet's particular interpretations of a concept common to all writers of the age. He is not content simply to assert accepted belief, but sees fiction as the place where accepted belief is put to the test. So, without denying the weak/ ness and sinfulness and comic inadequacy of man, he portrays men at their most pitiably vulnerable, at their most understand/ ably confused, in their most earnest and courageous attempts to make sense of the tangle of experience. And without denying the power, justice and mercy of God, he portrays divine authority as it can seem to men, at its nearest to tyranny and arbitrariness, and shows supernatural forces in terms of the difficulty and be/ wilderment they create for the world of nature. Within the frame/ work of conventional belief, the poet tends to push elements to their extremes. This argues again a conception of art in terms of antithesis and conflict, piquancy and dramatic reversal.

One gets a similar impression if one looks at the poet's central figures. *Pearl*, *Patience* and *Sir Gawain* have in common central figures who make a journey which exposes them to new and strange experience through which they are offered moral lessons; all three are vulnerable, and in varying degrees, wrong. But, in making such a generalisation one makes the poems sound more

similar than they are, since the three figures differ and the kinds
of experience they undergo are even more at variance. One also
implies that the feature is something individual to the *Gawain*-
poet, whereas the idea of the vulnerable hero undergoing a process
of moral education is found in all ages of fiction, is inherent in the
medieval vision-poem, and is shared by other medieval poems.
It is rooted in medieval Christian images of the pilgrimage of life
and in conventional views of the flawed nature of man and his
inevitable exposure when brought face to face with ideal judgement. What is peculiar to the poet is the particular variety of
guises in which the vulnerable hero appears. The poet is especially
concerned to bring out the difficulty of the educative experience,
giving to it both a comic sense of embarrassment and exposure
and a tragic sense of mental and physical suffering. All three
find themselves put at risk, though in different ways. Jonah puts
himself there, through rebellious fear:

> Thagh he wolde suffre no sore, his seele is on anter.
>
> *(Patience* 242)

Gawain has to accept hazard and the world of 'anter' as part of
the rules of the game:

> 'Of destinés derf and dere,
> What may mon do bot fonde?'
>
> *(Sir Gawain* 564-5)

But the Dreamer is put into the hazardous, uncertain world of
the unknown by grace, because his state of mind can only be
resolved by a removal from the known self into the world of the
spirit:

> My goste is gon in Godez grace
> In aventure ther mervaylez meven.
>
> *(Pearl* 63-4)

In terms of the external narratives the three journeys also differ,
but the inner sense which the poet gives to his tales shows them
as more akin, insofar as they all imply journeys inward, into the
nature of the 'hero'. The three are disconcerted, rebuked and
chastised by experience and all end uneasy in their acquired
knowledge. The Dreamer is reconciled to fate, but sadly conscious

of life as a diminished thing; Jonah is forced to receive a deserved moral lesson, but protests to the last; Gawain is ashamed, remorseful, and, in his own eyes, diminished by having to accept the disillusion of failure and limitation. Beneath the individual qualities which the poet developed for each out of a common pattern, there are threads which seem to indicate recurrent ideas on the poet's part. One of these is the idea of hazardous adventure. Another is its corollary, the idea of resentful protest. All three figures find experience at times strange and deceiving, hostile and making a mockery of them, and the poet gives to each a striking expression of bitter protest against the way prosperity and happiness are given with one hand and taken away with the other. The distinction between worldly and otherworldly standards of judgement is nowhere more forcefully expressed than in the Dreamer's angry question to the Maiden:

> 'What servez tresor bot garez men grete
> When he hit schal efte wyth tenez tyne?'
>
> (*Pearl* 331–2)

When 'treasure' is a metaphor for beloved flesh and blood, the question expresses pain which the doctrinal answer cannot assuage but can only dismiss. Gawain's protest (2414–28) is, in context, more comic, but underlying his recognition of kinship in frailty with Adam and his successors in male gullibility, is justified resentment and convincing selfjustification. For Gawain, as for even the noblest men of old, earthly prosperity, ostensibly the sign of the generosity of God, has been a snare, and it is through woman, the most personal of God's gift to man, that the deception has been accomplished. The only appropriate way of coping with the deceitful nature of man's lot seems to be for men themselves to practice duplicity, to love women well but not believe a word they say. To Jonah is given the strongest protest of all, a protest which again is, in terms of the drama the poet has created, justified, and for which the poet has imagined the most memorable lines in *Patience*:

> 'A, thou maker of man, what maystery the thynkez
> Thus thy freke to forfare forbi alle other?
> With alle meschef that thou may, never thou me sparez.'
>
> (482–4)

The mood varies, since the Dreamer is sorrowful, Gawain rueful and Jonah despairingly furious, but the burden of all three is that life is unfair. Each speaks in a souring moment of realisation that he has been used and played with.

The idea of fairness and justice provides another of the poet's recurrent threads, found particularly in the repetition of the theme of payment and reward and in the idea that human weakness expresses itself in a need for fixed rules, limits and amounts. Gawain, the Dreamer and Jonah all face a figure who possesses not only greater power but also greater generosity than themselves, and in the face of generosity the three are characterised as men wanting to see things in measured terms and yet having no true sense of Measure. All three are concerned with principles and rules and can be seen as varied representatives of the attempt to cope with a life too complex and contradictory to be defined in the simple terms that rules imply. So they are reproved both for lack and for excess, and the crime that they share is lack of judgement and a sense of proportion. In order to bring this out they are exposed to experience which disconcerts and reverses expectation. The Dreamer's joy at the sight of his pearl is rudely destroyed as she turns out be other than he had expected. Jonah's newfound humility and obedience are not strong enough to withstand the shock of God's forgiveness of the Ninevites. Gawain finds himself not triumphing over an enemy but apologising to his host. They are all pathetically and comically bewildered. Another thread which links them is the sense of life as a trap and the recurrent images of enclosure and imprisonment. The enclosing 'erber' in which the Dreamer mourns and dreams has become enlarged by the end of the poem but only to become a symbol for a larger prison, the 'doeldoungoun' of the world. Jonah's refuges, the ship, the whale and the bower, are all places of illusory safety, all traps and places of bitter humiliation. Between the high banks of the threatening valley Gawain is as much caught and put on the spot as within the curtains of his bed and the warm, welllit walls of Hautdesert.

Because *Purity* does not have a single central figure, the effect in that poem is different and I would accuse myself of forcing it to fit into a mould devised from the other three if I tried to make it sound similar, but some of these ideas obviously occur. In the scriptural tales of crime and punishment the ideas of payment and justice are necessarily present; in Noah and Lot the poet dealt with figures who were required by God's ordinance to put their 'seele on anter'; Belshazzar is faced by disconcerting experience which is sent to humble pride and to teach reverence and acceptance. The closest connection with the other poems, however, is found in the cumulative effect of the series of punishments, in that the repeated instances of generosity and ingratitude, of invitings in and castings out, present another version of the poet's fascination with the contrary faces of fortune. The poem is full of places of apparent safety and generous welcome which turn out to be places of judgement, and of examples of God's giving and taking away. The use of meals as symbolic events, through which the ideas of decorum and courtesy may be examined, is a thread connecting *Purity* with *Sir Gawain*.[1]

The poet's interest in creating narratives whose effect depends on the juxtaposition of and tension between opposing senses and conflicting forces is, then, indicated in several different ways: in his choice of difficult cases, in his dramatic shaping and colouring of the tales, in his pushing to extremes aspects of accepted thought, in his imagining for his central figures a sense of complex and bewildering experience, and in his use of recurrent images and themes. In these features one finds the individuality in the *Gawain*-poet's combination of two levels of meaning, of which I spoke earlier.

It is inevitable that, of the two levels at which the poems work, one should give greater weight to the literal level of human experience because in *Pearl*, *Sir Gawain* and *Patience* the reader is given a central figure through whom the experience of the poem is shown in terms of plausible reactions, and in terms of feeling and inner conflict; though in *Purity* the poet shifts his ground from tale to tale, there too he is concerned to realise his narratives in literal terms and asks the reader to live through the various types of action. The forces which challenge the limited human beings are less consistently presented and have a coherent identity only in the most broadly generalised sense. The 'nonhuman' figures have a variety of faces.

Purity, *Patience* and *Pearl* use the summit of existence as the setting for and contrast to the immediate level of human exper ience. The sinners in *Purity* are faced by a vengefully righteous, all-powerful God. Jonah is confronted by a scale of life which is beyond him. The Dreamer in learning to acknowledge the truth of mortality is led from the human level of apprehension towards the divine one which he cannot hope to attain. But the divine authority is presented obliquely in *Pearl*, at second or third hand, through the voice of the Maiden, who has to function at both literal and allegorical levels and who, as a result, has a nebulous anonymity; this voice is, in turn, filtered through the sensibility of the narrator who is describing his dream, so that it is the effect, the actual experiencing of images of immutability which is most clearly characterised. In *Patience* the energetic realisation of the tale presents God in human terms, developing from an impatient overlord to an example of tolerant forgiveness and care for his people; God is imagined as a better man than Jonah and his divinity is present as a sense simply of his being able to do things that human beings cannot do; his more than human power creates a world which is seen, through the central figure, as arbitrary and unstable. In *Purity* the sense of authority is even more uncertainly present because God is depicted in a variety of ways; at one moment he is a two-faced giver and depriver, a setter-up and bringer-down of human authority and pride, at another a sympathetic, anthropomorphic divinity who responds to human pleas for mercy and who sorrows at the need to punish mankind. Only if we overlook these variations and uncertainties and absorb the various figures into a general sense of medieval Christian faith in the absolute power of God and the inevitable frailty and transience of the human world, can we describe the poet's intention in the three poems as that of placing human activity in the context of the absolute.

In *Sir Gawain* the voice of authority is completely equivocal, since in the Green Knight the poet created an ambiguous, shifting figure who is never allowed to simplify into an abstraction. Though, by avoiding the cosmic scale of the other three, *Sir Gawain* could be seen as a less ambitious work of art, the poem is more effective in its handling of the idea of the other world which challenges, precisely because it allows more freedom to the imagination. It seems clear to me, from looking at the authoritative aspects of the four poems, that the poet was always more interested in the effect on human beings of an ideal scale of values than he was in exploring the ideal itself. By creating a world which is absolutely one of ambiguity and flux, the poet in *Sir Gawain* gives himself more rich and varied opportunities. It is a work of mellow maturity which presents a more open view of life and a more real and subtle view of the complexities of living than the closed scheme of *Pearl*, however universal its central theme. If, for critical purposes, one does temporarily reduce *Pearl*, *Patience* and *Purity* to poems which define living in terms of real human experience divided by a gulf from the authority of God, then it is obvious that *Sir Gawain* has gone beyond that point to a realisation that experience itself may be real and unreal. Codes of behaviour, whether chivalric or Christian or both, themselves over-simplify a world which is difficult to interpret and understand. What may to the distanced observer appear as a pattern is a maze to the man who has to live through it. By choos-ing a more limited sphere of action, the poet has been able to create a more comfortable relationship between the simultaneous perception of the hero's point of view and that of the detached shaper of and commentator on the narrative.

It will be obvious from these remarks that I find A. C. Spearing's characterisation of the *Gawain*-poet both too simple and too urbane, despite his many wise insights and just comments.[2]

His most interesting description of the central figure in the *Gawain*-poet's works is as follows:

> He struggles to defeat the power with which he is confronted, to evade or outwit it, but his struggle is necessarily vain, and therefore absurd. Thus the hero . . . becomes a hero manqué, a would-be hero. His aspirations to heroic or even tragic action are thwarted and the heroic image of man is undercut and presented ironically.[3]

This view, accepted and echoed by Burrow, who further develops the idea of the comic insignificance and weakness of man as characteristic of English poetry of the period,[4] is, as far as it goes, sane and just enough, but it does not tell the whole story. The presentation of the central figure varies from poem to poem; within each poem the experience facing the figure is complex and confusing; authority has a number of faces, not all of them working to deflate heroic aspiration. As a result it is not true to one's experience of reading the poems to characterise the 'would-be hero' in a simple way. He is absurd but he is not only absurd. The 'sympathetic insight'[5] with which the main human figures are presented may be a knowledge ultimately of weakness, but weakness itself may be viewed in a variety of ways, and the distinctive quality of the Gawain-poet's view of life is its sensitive and flexible awareness of varied ways of seeing. The weakness of Jonah and the Dreamer is given its tragic as well as its comic moments. The power which confronts Gawain is characterised as deceptive, ambiguous and unfair. There is a greater expression of pain and loneliness in the poems than can be encompassed in a view of life which is no more than 'at once religious and comic'.[6] The dramatic focusing of the narratives and the poet's choice of testing instances give the body of the Gawain-poet's work a quality which is both more sharply delineated and more challenging than is indicated by a view of him as an ironic tracer of the absurdity of man's pretensions in a world controlled by absolute, if merciful, divine power. The poet creates ambiguous and shifting narratives in the course of which the imagination is delighted by the poetic evocation of a wide range of images, feelings and insights. There are many moments of particular truth about appearances, behaviour and feeling. But the poet knows that the perception of larger truths varies according to where one is standing when one looks at them.

2. The poet's artistic aims

The Gawain-poet was then, in my view, a man of more complex mind and literary intentions than he appears to some commentators on the poems. Certainly he was no purveyor of conventional moral lessons who happened to have a lively verbal talent with which to ginger up a homiletic purpose. He treats his subjects in ways calculated to arouse mixed reactions in the reader. The appeal of his poetry consists in his enlargement of our sense of different areas of life; his vivid instances and his ironies challenge a too simplified view of things. In the four poems the poet works within a framework, which is provided by the genre, the plot or theme, and the narrator's voice. Inside the frame the poet invites us to experience a variety of specific pictures, and dramatised moments which combine to embellish and to fill the framework with animation—sometimes to fill it so full that the frame is strained and threatens to burst asunder.

The presence of frame and content is a feature naturally result-ing from medieval assumptions that narratives were a re-treating of known matter, in which the function of the poet's imagination is to give body to the incidents, figures and themes and to realise the potentialities for delight and profit within the material. Yet, as with other 'conventional' aspects of his writing, the Gawain-poet does not merely accept the pattern. Rather he highlights it and makes the reader more conscious of the two elements than any of his contemporaries. His realising is more literal, more energetically projected and visualised, and more diverse; but equally his framing draws more attention to itself. This pushing to extremes of the two elements faces the reader, in several places in the poems, with a conflict between the creative impulses which the two embody: the impulse to shape, classify, simplify, illustrate and generalise, as opposed to the impulse to envisage, individualise, complicate, decorate and specify. These two im-pulses are the most clearly identifiable artistic aims in the Gawain-poet's work and the relationship between them seems to me at the core of his creativity, and the source of his poetic power over the reader.

It is easiest to separate out these aims when they are least satis-factorily controlled. The intention of giving vivid realisation to the narrative and the intention of creating a form or pattern out of the material can both seem obtrusive. At its worst, the impulse to realise leads to an irrelevant literalness, which confuses rather than enriches the outlines of the story. This is possibly what has happened in the poet's curious handling of the parable of the Man without a Wedding Garment in Purity, although its effect is too ambiguous for one to be sure. It is certainly what has happen-ed in the early part of the Belshazzar's Feast episode; the desire to fill out the bare outlines of the narrative has led to invention of details of bloodshed and pillage which arouse a sympathy which eventually seems random. The impulse to make patterns, at its worst, leads the poet into ingenuity which is not made a necessary part of the total shaping of the matter, and which, therefore,

seems ingenuity for its own sake. I find the pentangle passage in
Sir Gawain obtrusive in this way, though many readers will not
agree with me, and the use of number patterning in *Pearl* and
Purity is ingenious rather than organic. (On the other hand, the
obtrusive creation of a pattern out of the Beatitudes in *Patience*
seems part of a deliberate characterisation and distancing of the
voice of the narrator.) The awkwardnesses in the poems draw one's
attention and invite speculation about the intentions, unsatisfactor-
ily carried out, lying behind them. If I have diagnosed them
correctly, they seem to show exaggerated forms of creative aims
which we can recognise, in more controlled and moderate guises,
as the basis of all four poems.

If asked to name one quality in the *Gawain*-poet's work which
distinguishes him from his contemporaries and which makes him
an outstanding writer, I think that most readers would plump
for the 'real' quality of his fictions. As Spearing puts it: 'For
him, every event within his fictions is as fully realized, as fully
present to all the senses, as if it were part of everyday reality—more
realized, indeed, than reality itself as most of us experience it for
most of the time.'[7] The world of the narrative parts of the poems
has a precision and solidity which makes scenes, figures, objects
and actions dominate, over-shadowing concepts and significa-
tions. The poet has a superb ability to imagine his narratives in
space and time and is thus able to project the reader into the world
of adventure and wonder to which such imagining inherently
belongs. The poet's sense of concreteness works to give a texture of
real experience even to unreal things, to supernatural happenings,
to worlds which are essentially fantasy worlds. The stinking high-
roads along which Jonah stumbles within the whale's belly
take the reader beyond any symbolic picture of the horror within
hell-mouth into a grotesque particularisation of the world of
nightmare. The hard brilliance of stones gleaming like stars on
a cold night in the water of the dream landscape of *Pearl* converts
the idea of the Kingdom of Heaven into something perfected
to the senses; the effect is aesthetic, not metaphysical. The physical,
real quality of the poems invites one always to explore and discover
as one reads, to be surprised, moved, amused, rather than to
accept what is known, rather than to be instructed or assured.
The particular imagination of the poet created fictions which

live in the individuality of the moment, of the scene, or of the figure; each tale becomes peculiar to itself.

That this quality may be seen as an artistic aim on the poet's part emerges most clearly from a comparison between *Purity* and *Patience* and their Vulgate sources. His expansions and modifica, tions, though varying from place to place, seem consistently designed to bring the moments of the narrative to a particular life rather than to underline the tale's supposed illustrative point. The creation of dramatic scenes, bewildering experiences and ambiguous figures in *Sir Gawain*, and the focusing of the matter of *Pearl* through the reality of the narrator's feelings, seem to be designed to work similarly. They turn attention to the specific uncertainties of the passing moment and the world of the senses more than to the securities of faith and moral judgement.

On the other hand, it is equally obvious that the *Gawain*, poet had a more highly developed sense of form than most medieval writers. Each of his works shows a sense of unified design. Within the period only *The Knight's Tale* and *Troilus and Criseyde* show a similar interest in patterned, symmetrical structure. The creator of such works is not using poetry merely as a convenient or acceptable way of conveying a message or passing an audience's time; nor is he working in terms only of plot and theme, but is consciously shaping his material into a unique thing. The variation of metre among the four poems shows, similarly, adjustment of the poetic unit and its rhythm and pattern to the individual case and the needs of varying genres. The com, bination of several narrative strands in *Sir Gawain*, the fusing of the different roles of the narrator/dreamer in *Pearl*, the linking together of disparate tales in *Purity* and the juxtaposition of nar, rative and narrator's comment in *Patience*, all indicate a desire to create a sense of unity out of diversity, to put different things together and yet to make them seem one, even when the matter is actually composed of elements of doubtful compatibility. The narrative roles which the different genres required the poet to assume are all used to control and combine the varied matter, even while these roles are themselves being explored and extended. The use of numbers, repetitions and echoes, and the structural technique of enclosing, even, in *Sir Gawain* and *Pearl*, to the extent of making each into a sort of palindrome, are all devices employed in the service of turning fable into pattern. Although if compared to some later masters of literary form, the *Gawain*-poet might not emerge as an outstanding designer of fiction, nevertheless, considered within his period, he created works which are the most concentrated, controlled and defined by structural patterns and formal designs. That the four poems are distinguished by the disciplined intelligence and intelligibility of their shaping is very obvious if we set their qualities against the essential randomness of the working of Langland's imagination, which responds to stimuli within the imagined world, regardless of subordination to the over-all effect of a particular section of *Piers Plowman*, let alone of the poem as a whole.

Yet, when this has been said, it is necessary to make some qualification, for it is finally not in formal shaping that the *Gawain*-poet's greatness lies. He was certainly interested in design and he places reliance on form; I would suggest that he sought a certainty and stability in the use of pattern. However, because of his treatment of narrative, the patterns eventually come to seem mere forms, which define only the externals of his adventures; they work in a more simple way than that of the complex exper-iences which the poet has imagined. There is a reassurance in the continuity and enclosure of the poem's framing, but the narratives do not confirm the sense of security, for the impulse to realise is, by its nature, an impulse to complicate and diversify, to qualify judgements, to perceive ironies, to modify moral lessons through experience.

Geoffrey Shepherd has said of medieval use of detailed verbal pictures, specifically in *Piers Plowman*:

> In Langland the detail is chosen, rejected and replaced not with a view to its striking force on the sensuous imagination, but, according to its estimated usefulness, that, when fixed in the memory, it can generate concepts in the mind. The detail is not a penetrating point, but the barb which holds the *imago agens* in position. Invention operates to make abstraction memorable.[8]

That the *Gawain*-poet is less of a philosopher and moralist than Langland is clear if we try to apply this wise comment to *Sir Gawain*, *Purity*, *Patience* and *Pearl*, for the detail in these poems does not, to my mind, contribute to a similar effect. The *Gawain*-poet may have learnt to use detail from examples of the making of *picturae*, but he has pushed it so far in the direction of the literal that in his work invention operates to make abstraction fail to work as abstraction. There is a continual tension in the four poems between the poet's realising and his structuring. When the two are most effectively combined, the formal shaping functions essentially as a check to the imaginative impulse to range widely and to multiply images and instances. The frame and its content then seem to be profitably at odds and the combination creates that sense of double perspective and of complexity of outlook and meaning of which I spoke in the preceding section.

Study of the four poems in terms of the relationship of the two creative aims of giving life and a sense of real experience to borrow-ed matter, and of containing and generalising from experience by formalising it in patterns and symbols, is one of the ways in which we can come to judge the relative effectiveness of the four poems, and to suggest possible lines of development in the poet.

Pearl is obviously the most highly patterned of the four. It is more elaborate than the rest, in its use of both alliteration and a completely rhymed stanza, in its stanza-linking and its stanza-grouping by refrains, and it is, inevitably, more rigid in effect; the return at the close to the words and ideas of the opening stanza gives a much more fixed, enclosed stamp to the whole poem than the use of a similar device in *Patience* and *Sir Gawain*, because the opening line is made into part of the circular pattern of concatenation. In *Pearl*, symbolism, too, is most in evidence and most central to the matter and meaning of the work. The realisation in *Pearl* is, on the other hand, not as vivid, energetic and dramatic as that in the scriptural narratives and the romance, as far as the depiction of actual events and scenes goes, because it does not develop a tale but an analysis of feelings, attitudes and reactions. However, the realisation is, in effect, more intense here because the matter is presented as the personal experience of the narrator, and is not distanced by the use of a detached voice; the reader is confronted directly by feelings and images and is drawn into a powerful poetic expression of pain, confusion and revela-tion. It is in *Pearl* that there is the greatest tension between the truth of real feeling and the creator's imposition of a pattern upon the material. The conflict between the rigid certainty, implied by the structure and the allegorical cast of the work, and the exploratory, developing complexity, associated with the Dreamer's painful acquisition of insight, gives to *Pearl* a more taut and concentrated quality than is found in any other medieval poem of similar length. But, as a result, it is difficult to maintain one total view of the poem.

In *Purity* the metrical form and the framing are of a looser kind, but the framework is still a binding one which seems to restrict the meaning of the poem to a smaller area than its main material, the narratives, actually occupies. The restrictive force is the authoritative function which the poet has given to his narrator, against whose instructive voice the reader feels resistance. The realisation in *Purity* is at its most vivid and whole-hearted; by imagining the events of the tales and expanding and dramatising them, the poet pushes each separate narrative further into its own individual particularity and further away from its illustrative function. Because they are too insistent, the poet's attempts to create unity, by linking and repetition, make one conscious of the essential separateness of the parts from which the whole is compiled.

It is significant that it is in *Pearl* and *Purity* that the poet speaks most forcefully and unequivocally about feeling and belief, and where he composes poetry of greatest sublimity. But, in both, he falls between stools; he neither manages a complete harmony of disparate elements, nor creates a consistent irony from them. There are, however, signs that the poet was moving towards an ironic view of things, but that he has failed fully to articulate it.

In *Patience* the framing is of the same simple type as in *Purity*, but the narrator's voice is given a personality which modifies the authoritative voice of the homilist and allows some freedom of reaction to the reader. The realising of the tale is vivid and disturbing, but the narrator's ironic comments intermittently undercut and distance the dramatic rendering of Jonah's tormented foolishness. The two elements are thus fused and cross over into one another, creating a total irony and equivocal effect.

In *Sir Gawain and the Green Knight*, although numbers and symbols create patterns within the narrative, the structuring of the poem is least emphasised of the four. The framing of the tale is a relaxed and casual one, through which the poet places the story in a context of traditional history, rather than enclosing it within a definition of moral purpose. The patterning of the poem highlights the journey and return shape, endemic to romance quests, and seems, therefore, to grow naturally from the material rather than to be imposed upon it. The realising is vivid and varied, and consistently both amusing and puzzling to the reader, who is involved in mystery and suspense and yet presented with real-seeming pictures of action and feeling, of dramatic encounters and of civilisation. The shaping of the poem is part of this mystery. The inter-play of pattern and reality itself seems a dramatisation of the hero's struggle to cope successfully with a bewildering test whose nature he does not perceive until too late. The poet creates a complicated masque in which ideals and roles are juxtaposed with a sense of a human being trying to identify them and act them out. The irony of the double view of the hero and the detached observer is finally modulated into a mature, wordly-wise, sense of the mutable continuity of history and of man's weak and yet heroic attempts to pursue high standards in both morality and civilisation. The harmony between the opposing aims produces a combination of the particular and universal, ironic and yet humane.

In their fusion of opposite but complementary creative aims and in their creation of a richly satisfying narrative tension and complexity, *Patience* and *Sir Gawain* are more perfect works of art than the other two. The poet has made a harmonious tension from the different elements in his imagination and produced subtle and ironic works, with shifting perspective. What they lose by this greater control is some degree of passionate and whole-hearted expression of convictions and sensations. In this they are akin to other great works of the late fourteenth century. Chaucer too paid for the subtlety of pervasive irony with its inevitable limitations. As J. A. Burrow says of late fourteenth-century poets:

> because the poet so rarely 'speaks out' in direct, unguarded utterance, passages of full-throated grandeur or pathos are uncommon in Ricardian verse... To this extent, Matthew Arnold was right when he said that Chaucer lacked 'high

poetic seriousness' . . . [which] implies speaking straight, not obliquely, to some great matter. Neither Chaucer nor his great contemporaries are often in this sense 'serious'.⁹

This comment is less true of *Pearl* and *Purity* where one does find more than the isolated passage which is concerned with direct treatment of great issues. The passion of God's speech to Abraham about human love and the epic nobility of the treatment of the Flood in *Purity*, and the intensity and sublimity of response to images of immutability in the revelatory passages in *Pearl* show the poet as capable of grandeur and seriousness as poets in any age of English poetry, but the works in which they occur are not perfectly shaped and controlled as a whole.

Whether the intense and sublime poetic expression of noble themes within a not completely successful work represents a greater achievement than a harmonised relationship of complex intentions, which produces irony and obliqueness, is a matter of individual judgement, and, in a sense, it does not matter. In my view, *Patience* and *Sir Gawain* show the poet at his most mature and detached and they mark the successful end of a search for ironic expression, which one can see more clumsily at work in the composition of *Purity*. In the sequence in the manu-script, *Pearl*, *Purity*, *Patience*, *Sir Gawain*, one can see a growth of open-mindedness and an extending range of subject-matter. These are accompanied by an increasing detachment and humour, a gradually more exploratory and uncertain sense of the nature of reality, and a more casual, urbane handling of narrative and structure, though, there is, in contrast, a decrease in intensity and commitment. But, whatever one's view of the order of composi-tion, it must surely be true that *Pearl* and *Sir Gawain* are, despite the things they have in common, the two furthest apart in mood, shaping and purpose.

3. The man behind the masks

The *Gawain*-poet remains, as yet, anonymous, both in that we do not know his name, and in that his poems tell us even less about their creator than do the works of his great contemporaries. He seems to hide himself almost completely behind the conventional narrative roles appropriate to the genres he used. Even with the seemingly personal *Pearl* one cannot be sure that the poet com-memorates a particular death, let alone that he speaks of his own loss. Some day, and perhaps soon, someone will establish a convincing case for a particular identification. I have wanted to write about the poet before this happens, and thus to be able to think again about what the poems alone say to the reader. If one tries to discover anything about the writer from the works, one finds no easy information, and nowadays we have learned to be more cautious about the relationship between literature and life than commentators fifty or a hundred years ago. We do not need to suggest that the *Gawain*-poet must have been a sailor because he knows technical terms connected with boats, nor even that he was poor because his narrator in *Patience* claims poverty as his lot. It has become clear that fourteenth-century narratives are often sophisticated pretences and we can take little on trust.[10] Perhaps the only aspect of the *Gawain*-poet's personality of which we can make even tentative identification is in the matter of what his works show him to respond to, what some of his tastes were.

One element in his make-up, whether it came from tempera-ment or training, was a liking for 'university wit'. He was not, in my opinion, particularly intellectual and seems at his most limited when dealing with ideas, arguments and beliefs, tending to write stiffly in passages explicitly concerned with morality and the conceptualisation of behaviour. But he does seem to have had a taste for intellectual ingenuity in the form of word-play, pattern-making, emblems and enigmas. The metrical intricacy of *Pearl* and the consequent verbal echoes, puns and ambiguities, and the puns, patterns, finicking distinctions and urbane pleasantries of the prologue to *Patience* show a delight in cleverness and the creation of complex verbal knots. The over-insistent antitheses and the use of flashy rhetoric in the Belshazzar's Feast section of *Purity* show a similar taste betraying the poet into glib super-ficiality; the modulation from one sense of the word 'clene' to another in the the link passage which introduces the tale shows a more successful use of ingenuity with words. Even more evident is the poet's pleasure in finding five sets of five and of fitting them into twenty-five lines and his fascinated delight in the mathematical, inter-laced quality of Sir Gawain's five-pointed star and its endlessly interlocking lines. His love of numbers and patterns goes beyond the needs of his narratives, and even the numbers in *Pearl*, though they have reference to the actual scriptural use of numbers in Revelations, whence he took them, seem more decora- tive than meaningful, because the poet sports with numbers without being fully committed to them as carriers of meaning. The hundred and one stanzas of *Pearl* and *Sir Gawain* and the superficial, linking threes of *Purity* do have some structural usefulness, but only the threes of *Sir Gawain* really work to con- vincing literary effect in the total structure of the work. Other evidence of a taste for academic cleverness includes scattered puns and occasional flashes of etymological and semantic analysis. The love of ingenuity betrays itself as a matter of the poet's per- sonal taste because it sometimes obtrudes. It is at the heart of the poet's creation of irony, his dramatic contrasts, his ambiguities, his repeated references to knots of different kinds in *Sir Gawain*, his desire to bind together and 'fettle in one form' the different aspects of his tales, and, employed with great skill, of the labyrin- thine experience which he created for his hero and his readers in *Sir Gawain*.

This ingenious lover of word-play and pattern-making was, fortunately, also a man of unusually wide sympathies. His capacity for seeing from the point of view of his figures endows each of his works with a pleasing sense of what it feels like to be in the situations he has imagined. The narrative point of view is, as a result, always satisfyingly complex. Though the poet takes up the stance of a teacher in *Patience* and *Purity* and of an entertainer in *Sir Gawain*, and so seems to accept the role which the genre establishes for him, he shifts his ground when the narrative gets going and becomes a universal observer, able to give us glimpses of the story from the angle of the main character, of by-standers, of a knowing confidant of the audience, as well as to make observa- tions in his assumed public role. In *Pearl* the combination of a past and a present self and his splitting into human and divine halves of his perception of mortality creates a different kind of complex perspective. His sympathy also expresses itself in the sense in his works of a living world of nature. The animals which 'wyth a loud rurd rored for drede' at the coming of the Flood, the birds which 'pitosly ther piped for pyne of the colde', the whale which was made, by the discomfort of an ingested prophet, 'to wamel at his hert', Reynard who went away to the wood 'With alle the wo on lyve', and even the plants which send out their healing scents over the pearl's grave, are all, even when the poet's reference to them is rhetorical or symbolic, touched with an imaginative sympathy which places the action of the poems against a background of sentient nature, and which argues in the poet an awareness of the world around him and a response to its multiplicity. Hence comes his capacity for visualising and giving apprehensible forms to the abnormal and the supernatural. Though the descriptions of the Flood, of the destruction of the Cities of the Plain, of the inside of Jonah's whale, of the heavenly kingdom, of the bewildering paths along which Gawain rides are all, in a sense, symbolic, rather than literal descriptions, their power over the reader comes from a projection of the poet's imagination into unknown places; the symbolic import becomes complicated and enriched by a sense of what the literal experience must have been like. Such entering in gives to his major figures, the Dreamer, Jonah and Gawain, memorable dramatic seriousness and credibility; the experience of uncertainty, suffering, loss and anger gives to the poems a painful intensity, even within a comic situation, which extends the range of feeling beyond that conveyed by even Chaucer.

The quality which links together his love of verbal and structtural ingenuity and his sympathy is the poet's sensitive ear, and the sheer love of words which one can detect in his versemaking. Although attention to sound is basic to the alliterative technique, his expression goes beyond the mere demands of the metre for soundrelated synonyms and other forms of variation. The *Gawain*poet was fascinated by words themselves and there is a higher degree of purely verbal pleasure in his verse than in that of his contemporaries. The verbal texture in the majority of Middle English poems is thin; the sense is so often spread out among redundant phrases and other features of dilution, endemic to urbane, oral verse. This is so even in Chaucer's work, although he had enough skill to create effects of intimacy and informality from repetitions and from punctuating phrases, and even to make artistic capital of them in extended dramatic monologues, particu larly in *The Wife of Bath's Prologue*. Yet it remains true that Chaucer works in long leisurely units, and that his poetic effect-iveness is seldom something which can be conveyed in brief extracts, and that one of the reasons for this is a lack of verbal concentration. This is less true of alliterative poetry in general and the excesses of alliterative poets tend in the other direction: if Chaucer's longueurs are examples of polished emptiness, those of alliterative poets result from over-insistence and verbal clutter, though they are prone to their own forms of redundancy and repetitiveness. The *Gawain*-poet is distinguished from fellow alliterative poets as much as from writers of other forms of Middle English verse, by his richness of vocabulary and the precision with which, on the whole, he makes use of it. Inevitably in his work one can find padding, clichés and tags, looseness of ex-pression, inflation and mannerism, but one has only to compare his writing with most other alliterative poetry to appreciate the greater discrimination, delicacy and flair with which he handled the common currency of alliterative language, and to perceive the greater variety of tone and the richness of expression with which he managed to enlarge its range. An even more revealing comparison is between the *Gawain*-poet and Gower; Gower has greater purity of style and a wholesome plainness of expression which can be refreshing to a reader sated with the *tours de force* of, to choose an extreme instance, the *Alliterative Morte Arthur*, but the *Gawain*-poet's work makes one very conscious of the verbal poverty of *Confessio Amantis*.

The *Gawain*-poet's love of words shows itself in his use of clusters of exotic expressions (in *Purity* particularly), his realisation of actions through the technical and specialist vocabulary of, for example, hunting, ship-tackle, jewels and materials, and the wide range of his vocabulary from foreign sources, as well as in many individual instances of sensitivity to the shape and sound of words, such as his combination of and distinction between *maskeles* and *makeles* in *Pearl*. Even more striking is the evidence of his ear for the different colours and textures of language, which enables him to create variation of tone, to move from formal, ceremonial speech to plain expression, to load his alliterative lines with descriptive detail in some places, in others to leave them spare and simple, to let a succession of active verbs take the lines racing along or to retard them with a crowding of adjectives and participles.

Such aspects of the professional character of the poet are the nearest we can safely get to a biographical sketch. All else is, in some degree, guesswork. We may infer that he was reasonably well-read in the literature of his age and that he had university training. I would guess that he knew some of Chaucer's work and that he had some acquaintance with Franciscan teaching and the views of Wyclif. Clearly he was aware of theological ideas and debates about morality and salvation, though, in my view, he did not have a profound interest in either, except insofar as they could provide a framework for the imaginative exploration of situations and feelings. We might, fairly safely, suppose that in life he was an orthodox Christian, a man of orderly habits, with a liking for security, but also a humorous, teasing desire to disturb conventional expectations and adventurously to explore people's reactions to living; but such supposing moves very easily into self-indulgent and self-deluding fantasy; we might just as well guess that he was a man liable to excesses of emotion.

The truth is that, as with Shakespeare, it seems likely that we can only ever know him as an artist, not as a man, even if his identity is discovered. In contrast to Shakespeare, even as an artist he will only ever be fully known to a handful of readers. It is the greatest tragedy of the linguistic development of English, that the work of a writer with such a lively and subtle mind, capable of such sensitive and memorable expression, may be accurately enjoyed only by the persistent, linguistically gifted student and by the professional scholar. It is my hope that this book may, in some ways, help to make the *Gawain*-poet's work available to a few more.

Notes

CHAPTER ONE: INTRODUCTION

1. The principle of Ockham's razor is applied to the case by Everett, p. 68, and Spearing, p. 37, among others.

2. Spearing, p. 40.

3. The case for common authorship (and arguments against it) may be studied in: Menner, p. xi ff.; J. P. Oakden, *Alliterative Poetry in Middle English* (Manchester, Vol. I 1930, Vol. II 1935), I, pp. 247–57, II, pp. 89–94 and 179–81; questioning essays by J.W. Clark in *PQ* 28 (1949), *JEGP* 49 (1950), *MLN* 65 (1950), and *MLQ* 12 (1951); J. D. Ebbs, 'Stylistic Mannerisms of the *Gawain*-Poet', *JEGP* 57, 1958, 522–5; Everett, ch.3; Brewer 'The Gawain Poet'; TG/Davis pp. xxiixxv; Spearing, pp. 32–40; W. Vantuono, '*Patience, Cleanness, Pearl* and *Gawain*: The Case for Common Authorship', *Annuale Mediaevale* 12, 1971, 37–69.

4 Ten Brink, *Early English Literature* (New York, 1883), Vol. I, pp. 337–51.

5. See Menner, pp. xxviixxxviii.

CHAPTER TWO: *PEARL*

1. See, for example, Edward Wilson, 'WordPlay and the Interpretation of *Pearl*', *Medium Ævum* 48, 1971, 116–34.

2 E.g. as in 'Annot and John' in *The Harley Lyrics,* ed. G. L. Brook (Manchester, 1948) p. 31 and 'A Lover's Farewell to his Mistress' in *Secular Lyrics of the XIV & XVth Centuries* ed. R. H. Robbins (Oxford, 1955), poem 205, l. 93.

3. See W. A. Davenport, 'Desolation, not Consolation: *Pearl* 19–22', *ESts* 55, 1974, 421–3, where I have argued for this interpretation more fully; it seems quite inappropriate to see any indication of consolation here.

4. I agree with P. M. Kean's punctuation, but not with her interpretation of the passage; see Kean, p. 22.

5. Spearing, p. 141.

6. Ibid. p. 140.

7. See Edward Wilson, '"Gromlyoun" (Gromwell) in *Pearl*', *N&Q* n.s. 18, 1971, 42–4.

8. I differ from Gordon's punctuation; he begins a new sentence with 'I slode', but line 59 seems to me to give the consequence of line 58.

9. Psalm xxi in the Vulgate numbering, 22 in AV; this psalm is also referred to in line 363 and line 382 and is very relevant to the Dreamer's thought and feeling especially 'thou didst make me hope when I was upon my mother's breasts' and 'thou hast brought me into the dust of death'.

10. See Spearing, pp. 158–9.

11. See Spearing, pp. 127–37 for a discussion of this question which makes further comment here unnecessary.

12. See Brewer, 'Courtesy', p. 65, note 1.

13. The manuscript has 'Flor and fryte may not be fede'; Gordon (p. 47) interprets *fede* as a rare adjective meaning 'faded'. It seems more appropriate to the context to take it as the verb 'feed' and to emend *be* to *bot*: 'flower and fruit cannot but feed'; *schynez* in line 28 must be taken as a future tense. E. Vasta, 'Immortal Flowers and the Pearl's Decay', *JEGP* 66, 1967, 519–31, takes *fede* as the past participle 'fed' and understands the line as expressing the hope that the pearl shall be free from corruption and that spices may *not* be nourished by its decay.

14. See Gordon, pp. xi–xix for discussion of the debate, and p. lv for a brief summary of some allegorical interpretations published in the first third of this century. See also R. Wellek, *The Pearl: An Interpretation of the Middle English Poem,* Studies in English IV, Charles University (Prague, 1933), reprinted in Blanch, with other interpretations. Also Spearing, pp. 128–9.

15. See particularly, on *consolatio*, Bishop, p. 16ff. Kean also studies the poem in relationship to medieval Latin literary sources, among other things.

16. See Spearing, pp. 107–27 for a discussion of the relationship of *Pearl* to the traditions of religious visions and dream-poems.

17. See Kean, p. 92. Some romance elements in *Pearl* are pointed out by John Stevens, *Medieval Romance* (London, 1973), pp. 233–5.

18. In this there is some resemblance to the spiritual progress of the mystic, more than is implied by Spearing, pp. 112–17.

19. Spearing, p. 120.

20. See Spearing, pp. 125–7 and George Kane, *Piers Plowman: the Evidence for Authorship* (London, 1965), pp. 53–7.

21. See Spearing, pp. 107–17.

22. Everett, p. 95, suggests that the 'poet has split himself in two'.

23. *The Kingis Quair,* lines 75–82.

24. The punctuation is mine, since I differ from Gordon's view of the meaning. The two *So* clauses are mutually dependent; it is well with the Dreamer insofar as the Maiden's words were precious to him, but lines 1185–6 express the doubt as to whether he has really experienced revelation of truth.

25. See Everett, p. 87 and comments thereon in Bishop, p. 32ff.

26. Gradon, p. 200; see also Bishop, pp. 66–8 on *aenigma*.

27. For other discussions of this aspect of the poem see the essay by E. Wilson cited in note 1 above; O. D. Macrae-Gibson, '*Pearl*: the Link-Words and the Thematic Structure', *Neophilologus* 52, 1968, 54–64 (reprinted in Conley), John C. McGalliard, 'Links, Language and Style in *The Pearl*' in *Studies in Language, Literature and Culture of the Middle Ages and Later*, Studies in honour of Rudolph Willard, ed. E. B. Atwood and A. A. Hill (Austin, Texas, 1969), pp. 279–99; James Milroy, '*Pearl*: The Verbal Texture and the Linguistic Theme', *Neophilologus* 55, 1971, 195–208.

28. See Brewer, 'Courtesy' and Brewer, 'The Gawain-Poet'.

29. See Kean, p. 178.

30. By coincidence (?) the one stanza which has eleven instead of twelve lines (469ff.) is also probing the question of quantity.

31. Gollancz, Osgood.

32. Gordon, pp. 71–2, note on line 733.

33. Gordon, p. 71, note on line 721.

34. See P. M. Kean, 'Numerical Structure in *Pearl*', *N & Q* n.s. 12, 1965, 49–51 and Burrow *RP*, p. 60.

35. The symbolism of the pearl is an important aspect of the poem well discussed in published work and therefore I have dealt briefly with it; see especially Spearing, pp. 137–52 and 159–70.

36. The idea that the elegy was for a child called Margery was suggested by Gollancz in his edition of *Pearl* (London, 1891), p. xliii.

37. See, for example, Barbara Nolan and David Farley-Hills, 'The Authorship of *Pearl*: Two Notes', *RES* n.s. 22, 1971, 295–302. See also essays by C. J. Peterson in *RES* n.s. 25, 1974.

CHAPTER THREE: *PURITY*

1. The basic discussions are: Menner, pp. xliii-liii; Everett, pp. 68–74; Moorman, pp. 78–87; Spearing, pp. 41–73; Gradon, pp. 119–23. See also M. Foley, 'A Bibliography of *Purity* (*Cleanness*), 1864–1972', *The Chaucer Review* 8, 1973–4, 324–34.

2. My punctuation differs from Menner's; I take the clause 'that amounted the mase' to mean 'The one who built up the confusion', i.e. God, and the beginning of a new sentence.

3. Spearing, p. 70.

4. Ibid., p. 70.

5. Ibid., p. 64.

6. When the poet writes a somewhat similar passage of imagined instance as an introduction to the story of Jonah in *Patience*, he puts *himself* into the situation of

the supposed wrong-doer, which creates a very different impression, and shows a
more advanced sense of how to create ironic effects.

7. Gradon, p. 122.

8. Menner, p. lii.

9. Everett, p. 70.

10. Spearing, p. 62.

11. I do not think it necessary to discuss this aspect of the poem in further
detail because it has been well analysed by others; see Menner, Spearing, Gradon.

12. Menner, p. xlvii.

13. Moorman, p. 81.

14. Gradon, pp. 122–3.

15. Charlotte C. Morse, 'The Image of the Vessel in Cleanness', *University of
Toronto Quarterly* 40, 1970–1, 202–16.

16. Moorman; the quotations are from various passages from p. 78 to p. 85.

17. Spearing, pp. 41–2.

18. Ibid., p. 62.

19. Burrow, *RP*, p. 86.

20. Gradon, p. 123.

CHAPTER FOUR: *PATIENCE*

1. As with *Purity* it has been suggested that this poem should be read in quatrains,
though, since there is an odd number of lines, the system does not fit exactly;
following Gollancz, Anderson discards lines 513–15 as the poet's uncancelled
first thoughts. See Anderson, p. 68; also W. Vantuono, 'The Question of
Quatrains in *Patience*', *Manuscripta* 16, 1972, 24–30.

2. Other writers have, naturally, studied this aspect of the poem. See Spearing,
pp. 74–95, and Anderson, p. 5ff. and Notes, *passim*. A particularly good discussion
of *Patience* in general, to which I am, at various points, indebted, is David J.
Williams, 'The Point of *Patience*', *MP* 68, 1970–1, 127–36.

3. 'For as Jonas was three days and three nights in the whale's belly; so shall
the Son of man be three days and three nights in the heart of the earth.'

4. See Anderson, p. 18 and Moorman, pp. 68–9.

5. See O. F. Emerson, 'A Parallel between the Middle English Poem *Patience*
and an early Latin Poem attributed to Tertullian', *PMLA* 10, 1895, 242–8;
Patience ed. Bateson, pp. xi–xlv; O. G. Hill, 'The Late Latin *De Jona* as a Source
for *Patience*', *JEGP* 66, 1967, 21–5.

6. For further comment on the traditions involving Jonah, see Paul E. Szarmach,
'Two Notes on *Patience*', *N&Q* n.s. 18, 1971, 125–7; R. H. Bowers, *The Legend
of Jonah* (The Hague, 1971); W. Vantuono, 'The Structure and Sources of
Patience', *MS* 34, 1972, 401–21; F. N. M. Diekstra, 'Jonah and *Patience*: The
Psychology of a Prophet', *ESts* 55, 1974, 205–17.

7. Like *Purity*, *Patience* has often been described as a 'verse homily' (Anderson, p. 7), though readers have again felt that it is as narrative that the poem impresses (Everett, p. 70), and some have gone so far as to suggest that the vividness unbalances the homiletic purpose; this has usually emerged in the curious but persistent idea that the poet has elaborated the Vulgate in order to make 'a striking appeal to a popular circle', as Bateson puts it (*Patience* ed. Bateson, p. xxxix); see also *Patience* ed. I. Gollancz (London, 1913) and N. Berlin, '*Patience*: A Study in Poetic Elaboration', *Studia Neophilologica* 33, 1961, 80–5.

8. See *The Canterbury Tales*, III, 1195–200.

9. This was probably a standard witticism; compare *Piers Plowman* (B) Passus VI, 23.

10. J. Schleusener, '*Patience*, lines 35–40', *MP* 67, 1969–70, 64–6.

11. A. C. Cawley suggested the idea of a fool's paradise; see Anderson, p. 14, note 4.

12. Spearing, p. 88.

13. Gordon Leff, *Medieval Thought* (Harmondsworth, 1958), p. 280.

14. Anderson, p. 9.

15. D. J. Williams, 'The Point of *Patience*', *loc. cit.*, pp. 135–6.

CHAPTER FIVE: *SIR GAWAIN*

1. Basic discussions are those in TG/Davis, M. W. Bloomfield, 'Sir Gawain and the Green Knight: An Appraisal', *PMLA* 76, 1961, 7–19, reprinted in Howard and Zacher and in Bloomfield's *Essays and Explorations* (Cambridge, Mass. and London, 1970), Benson, Burrow, *Reading*, Waldron and Spearing.

2. For discussion of *Sir Gawain* in the context of romance see Dieter Mehl, *The Middle English Romances of the Thirteenth and Fourteenth Centuries* (London, 1969, translated from the original German [Heidelburg, 1967]), pp. 193–206; John Stevens, *Medieval Romance* (London, 1973), pp. 170–4, 188–91 and *passim*.

3. See Donald R. Howard, 'Structure and Symmetry in *Sir Gawain*', *Speculum* 39, 1964, 425–33, reprinted in Howard and Zacher.

4. See, for discussion of other aspects of technique, Marie Borroff, *Sir Gawain and the Green Knight: A Stylisitic and Metrical Study* (New Haven and London, 1962).

5. For discussion of the sources of *Sir Gawain* see G. L. Kittredge, *A Study of Sir Gawain and the Green Knight* (Cambridge, Mass., 1916); Laura H. Loomis, Chapter 39 of *Arthurian Literature in the Middle Ages*, ed. R. S. Loomis (Oxford, 1959); Benson, esp. pp. 16–37; TG/Davis, pp. xiv–xxi; *Two Old French Gauvain Romances* ed. R. C. Johnston and D. D. R. Owen (Edinburgh and London, 1972), Part II.

6. See Burrow, *Reading*, pp. 74–7.

7. Two classic books which explore some of the distinctive features of romance

are W. P. Ker, *Epic and Romance* (London, 1897) and E. Vinaver, *The Rise of Romance* (Oxford, 1971).

8. J. Speirs, *Medieval English Poetry: The Non-Chaucerian Tradition* (London, 1957), p. 218.

9. As George Kane argues: 'the success comes principally from the poet's remarkable visualisation of the action and setting of his story, and only to a lesser extent from the conceptions of conduct upon which the characters act' *Middle English Literature* (London, 1951), p. 76.

10. The vast number of essays published about the poem is testimony to the freedom of response (and the abuse); it is impracticable to give a list, since it would have to be lengthy. Some range of opinion may be seen in Howard and Zacher, Blanch, and D. Fox (ed.), *Twentieth Century Interpretations of Sir Gawain and the Green Knight* (Englewood Cliffs, N.J., 1968), and the summaries in the annual volumes of *The Year's Work in English Studies*.

11. Burrow, *Reading*, p. 179.

12. It was not good enough for Chaucer either, as his treatment of magic in *The Squire's Tale* and *The Franklin's Tale* makes clear. See comments in Burrow, *Reading*, pp. 60–1 and p. 171ff.

13. An attitude found, in various guises, in several recent critics, e.g. Benson, pp. 214–18, Moorman, pp.109–10.

14. *Sir Orfeo* ed. A. J. Bliss, 2nd edn. (Oxford, 1966), the Auchinleck text, lines 49–50.

15. Burrow, *Reading*, p. 177.

16. See D. A. Pearsall, 'Rhetorical "Descriptio" in *Sir Gawain and the Green Knight*', *MLR* 50, 1955, 129–34.

17. See Robert W. Ackerman, 'Castle Hautdesert in *Sir Gawain and the Green Knight*' in *Mélanges de langue et de littérature du Moyen Âge et de la Renaissance offerts à Jean Frappier . . .*, ed. J. C. Payen and C. Regnier (Geneva, 1970).

18. See Waldron, pp. 23–4.

19. Burrow, *Reading*, p. 13.

20. Ibid., p. 15.

21. Chaucer, *The Franklin's Tale*, a passage which Burrow cites as a comparison to the opening of Part II of *Sir Gawain* (Burrow, *Reading*, p. 35).

22. H. R. Patch, *The Goddess Fortuna in Medieval Literature* (1927, reprinted London 1967), p. 44.

23. The arrival of a different sort of messenger at the court of Cambuskan, in *The Squire's Tale*, affords an interesting comparison.

24. See Burrow, *Reading*, pp. 22–3.

25. See Benson, pp. 199–201.

26. See Waldron, pp. 23–4.

27. Notably by H. L. Savage, 'The Significance of the Hunting Scenes in *Sir Gawain and the Green Knight*', *JEGP* 27, 1928, 1–15, repeated in *The Gawain-*

Poet (Chapel Hill, N.C., 1956); for a more moralistic version see, for example, Gerald Gallant, 'The Three Beasts: Symbols of Temptation in *Sir Gawain and the Green Knight*', *Annuale Mediaevale* 11, 1970, 35–50.

28. See the unconvincing note on lines 1283–5 in TG/Davis, p. 110.

29. See W. A. Davenport, 'Sir Gawain's Courteous "Whoa!"', *English Language Notes* 11, 1973–4, 88–9.

30. See Allen A. Metcalf, '*Sir Gawain* and *You*', *Chaucer Review* 5, 1970–1, 165–78, for a full analysis of the poet's careful distinctions of usage in the poem as a whole.

31. For a very different view of this section of the poem see Burrow, *Reading*, pp. 127–33.

32. Geoffrey Shepherd, '*Troilus and Criseyde*' in *Chaucer and Chaucerians* ed. D. S. Brewer (London. 1966), p. 78.

33. See B. J. Whiting, 'Gawain: His Reputation, His Courtesy and His Appearance in Chaucer's *Squire's Tale*', *MS* 9, 1947, 189–234, Gordon M. Shedd, 'Knight in Tarnished Armour: The Meaning of *Sir Gawain and the Green Knight*', *MLR* 62, 1967, 3–13 and comments in *Two Old French Gauvain Romances* (see Note 5 above).

34. See D. D. R. Owen, 'Burlesque Tradition and *Sir Gawain and the Green Knight*', *FMLS* 4, 1968, 125–45.

35. I have argued the point more fully and commented on this passage as a whole in 'The Word *norne* and the Temptation of Sir Gawain', *Neuphilologische Mitteilungen* 78, 1977, (in press).

36. See Burrow, *Reading*, pp. 99–101 and Spearing's detailed discussion of the question of Gawain's chastity (p. 194ff.), with specific comments on Burrow's view of the passage at pp. 204–6. Also Ian Robinson, *Chaucer and the English Tradition* (Cambridge, 1972), p. 231.

37. See the note on lines 1768–9 in TG/Davis, p. 121.

38. Especially Burrow, *Reading*, pp. 104–10. See also G. J. Engelhardt, 'The Predicament of Gawain', *MLQ* 16, 1955, 218–25.

CHAPTER SIX: THE POET AND HIS ART

1. For further exploration of this theme see Brewer, 'Courtesy'.

2. Spearing, Chapter 1, *passim,* particularly pp. 29–32.

3. Ibid., p. 30.

4. Burrow, *RP*, p. 102ff.

5. Spearing, p. 31.

6. Ibid.

7. Ibid., p. 37.

8. Geoffrey Shepherd, *The Nature of Alliterative Poetry in Late Medieval England,*

Sir Israel Gollancz Memorial Lecture, British Academy (London 1970), p. 19.

9. Burrow, *RP*, pp. 44–5.

10. The classic demonstration of fourteenth-century sophistication in the handling of illusion is *The Nun's Priest's Tale*, where an unreliable 'Chaucer' reports an unreliable priest telling of an unreliable Chantecleer's summarising of questionable authorities.

Index